新经典 ENGLISH MAJOR

高等学校英语专业系列教材

U0488069

HISTORY AND
ANTHOLOGY OF
AMERICAN
LITERATURE

吴伟仁 （编）

美国文学史及选读

重排版 ②

外语教学与研究出版社
FOREIGN LANGUAGE TEACHING AND RESEARCH PRESS
北京 BEIJING

图书在版编目 (CIP) 数据

美国文学史及选读：重排版．2 ／ 吴伟仁编．— 北京：外语教学与研究出版社，2013.6（2018.4 重印）
高等学校英语专业系列教材
ISBN 978-7-5135-3169-6

Ⅰ. ①美… Ⅱ. ①吴… Ⅲ. ①英语－阅读教学－高等学校－教材 ②文学史－美国－高等学校－教材 Ⅳ. ①H319.4: I

中国版本图书馆 CIP 数据核字 (2013) 第 111840 号

出 版 人	蔡剑峰
责任编辑	祝文杰　邢贺兰
封面设计	外研社设计部
版式设计	吴德胜
出版发行	外语教学与研究出版社
社　　址	北京市西三环北路 19 号（100089）
网　　址	http://www.fltrp.com
印　　刷	三河市北燕印装有限公司
开　　本	650×980　1/16
印　　张	15.5
版　　次	2013 年 7 月第 1 版　2018 年 4 月第 8 次印刷
书　　号	ISBN 978-7-5135-3169-6
定　　价	29.90 元

购书咨询：（010）88819926　电子邮箱：club@fltrp.com
外研书店：https://waiyants.tmall.com
凡印刷、装订质量问题，请联系我社印制部
联系电话：（010）61207896　电子邮箱：zhijian@fltrp.com
凡侵权、盗版书籍线索，请联系我社法律事务部
举报电话：（010）88817519　电子邮箱：banquan@fltrp.com
法律顾问：立方律师事务所　刘旭东律师
　　　　　中咨律师事务所　殷　斌律师
物料号：231690001

出版说明 >>

《英国文学史及选读》和《美国文学史及选读》是吴伟仁教授编写的一套经典英美文学教材,自出版以来,迄今已重印四十余次,受到广大读者的一致称赞。本套教材根据英语专业英美文学教学的实际需求,通过"史"、"选"结合的方式对英美文学的核心内容进行了全面梳理和系统讲解,在全国高校英语专业师生中有着广泛而深远的影响。

因出版年代久远,编者资料有限,该套教材在文学史介绍及选篇部分存在个别舛错,并且有少量印刷错误,我们在此次重排版中均进行了认真核实、修改。同时,我们调整了部分内容的顺序、体例,使全书结构更加清晰明了。此外,还对教材封面和内文版式进行了全新设计,使之更加美观易读。

英美文学界在对某些文学史的讲述、作品版本的选择、个别作家生卒年代及作品写作与出版年代等方面,经常存在争议。在重排版中,我们充分尊重编者的研究视角、方法和成果,除对明显的错误进行更正外,对涉及争议的以上内容,除与权威版本(如 *The Norton Anthology of English Literature*,*The Norton Anthology of American Literature*,*Encyclopedia Britannica* 等)存在重大出入处我们进行了修改外,尽量尊重原文而未擅作改动。特此说明。

前言

　　我国高等院校英语专业在高年级课程中，开设有"英美文学史"和"英美文学作品选读"两门课程。讲授"文学史"以伴随"文学作品选读"为宜。因为文学史是根据历史的顺序以系统讲授为主，由于课时的限制，往往重头轻尾，完不成全面教学的任务。文学作品的讲授，由于课时限制，只能选一部分重要作家和重要作品进行讲授，略古详今。这样，"史"和"选读"分作两门课程讲授，往往不能相辅而行，容易形成脱节和重复；从时间上说，也有课时不经济的情况。因此，这两门课程最好结合起来，"史"的部分在书中简明扼要地概述，"选读"部分尽可能遴选文学史上的重要作家和重要作品进行讲授。教师根据班级的具体情况，可多选，也可少选，灵活掌握，自由调整。

　　本套教材编写的体例，除"史"的部分有简明扼要的叙述以外，作家作品部分有：(1) 作家生平与创作介绍；(2) 作品内容提要（如选文为作品节录时）；(3) 选文；(4) 注释。在教学中每周以四学时计，共两个学期（有的院校是四个学期），课堂以讲授作品为主，"史"的部分由教师掌握，供学生参考，"史"与"选读"结合，进行教学，可事半功倍，收到良好的教学效果，这是编写《英国文学史及选读》和《美国文学史及选读》的目的。

　　《美国文学史及选读》分为两册：第一册是殖民地时期至浪漫主义时期美国文学，第二册是现实主义时期至20世纪美国文学。

　　本套教材可供高等院校英语专业作为英美文学史和文学作品选读的教学用书或参考书，也可供广大中学英语教师及具有一定程度的英语自学者和英美文学爱好者作为进修读物。

　　教材定稿前，曾由原国家教委高校外语教材编审委员会召开审稿会。参加审稿会的有主审人山东大学的张健教授、审稿人北京师范大学的孟广龄教授、南开大学的常耀信教授和山东大学的李乃坤教授。会议期间，审稿人提出了许多有关作家、选文和注释方面的宝贵意见。编者根据这些意见作了必要的修改。在此，对参加审稿的同志表示衷心的感谢。

　　由于编者水平有限，书中错误、缺点和考虑不周之处在所难免，恳切希望读者批评指正。

编者

CONTENTS >>

Part IV The Literature of Realism 1

    Chapter 18 **Walt Whitman** 8
        Song of Myself 9
        I Sit and Look Out 11
        Beat! Beat! Drums! 12

    Chapter 19 **Emily Dickinson** 13
        I Taste a Liquor Never Brewed 15
        I Felt a Funeral, in My Brain 16
        A Bird Came down the Walk— 16
        I Died for Beauty—But Was Scarce ... 17
        I Heard a Fly Buzz—When I Died— .. 18
        Because I Could Not Stop for Death— 18

    Chapter 20 **Harriet Beecher Stowe** 20
        Uncle Tom's Cabin 21

    Chapter 21 **Mark Twain** 40
        The Adventures of Tom Sawyer 42

    Chapter 22 **O. Henry** 52
        The Cop and the Anthem 54

    Chapter 23 **Henry James** 61
        The Portrait of a Lady 63

History and Anthology of American Literature

Chapter 24	Jack London	85
	The Sea Wolf	87
	Martin Eden	95

Chapter 25	Theodore Dreiser	108
	Sister Carrie	110

Part V Twentieth-Century Literature 123

Chapter 26	Ezra Pound	128
	A Virginal	130
	Salutation the Second	131
	A Pact	131
	In a Station of the Metro	132
	The River-Merchant's Wife: A Letter	132

Chapter 27	Edwin Arlington Robinson	134
	The House on the Hill	135
	Richard Cory	136
	Miniver Cheevy	137

Chapter 28	Robert Frost	139
	After Apple-Picking	140
	The Road Not Taken	141
	Stopping by Woods on a Snowy Evening	142
	Departmental	143
	Design	144
	The Most of It	145

Chapter 29	Carl Sandburg	147
	Chicago	148
	The Harbor	150
	Fog	150

IV

CONTENTS

     Cool Tombs 150
     Flash Crimson 151
     The People, Yes 152

Chapter 30 **Wallace Stevens** **156**
     Peter Quince at the Clavier 158
     Anecdote of the Jar 161
     The Emperor of Ice-Cream 161

Chapter 31 **T. S. Eliot** **163**
     The Love Song of J. Alfred Prufrock 166
     Preludes 172
     Journey of the Magi 174
     The Hollow Men 176

Chapter 32 **F. Scott Fitzgerald** **181**
     The Great Gatsby 182

Chapter 33 **Ernest Hemingway** **194**
     A Farewell to Arms 196

Chapter 34 **John Steinbeck** **217**
     The Grapes of Wrath 218

Chapter 35 **William Faulkner** **227**
     A Rose for Emily 229

References **239**

Part IV
The Literature of Realism

Political Background

By the end of the Civil War (1861–1865) most of the forces that would typify twentieth-century America had begun to emerge. Northern industrialism had triumphed over Southern agrarianism, and from that victory came a society based on mass labor and mass consumption. Mechanization spread rapidly as steam engines, linked to machines, displaced hand work on farms and in factories. The conditions of labor changed, for the new machines, with their great cost and efficiency, seemed far more valuable and more useful than the workers who tended them. Yet increasing numbers of Americans left the farms to seek jobs in urban factories.

In the cities, swollen with growing numbers of the poor and the unskilled, angry forces were stirring that would profoundly alter the nation's politics and its social ideals. Traditional political alliances had begun to shift as the lower classes sought greater power at the polls. The great age of big-city bossism began, and the art of political patronage and graft rose to new heights throughout the land. During the Civil War the powers of the federal government rapidly expanded. The first conscription laws were passed, the first federal income taxes were levied, and a national currency, controlled by the federal government, was issued. In 1865 the first step toward racial equality was made when the Thirteenth Amendment to the Constitution was adopted, abolishing slavery within the United States. Business growth and exploitation of natural resources created new wealth, concentrating vast riches and economic power in the hands of a few. It was the beginning of what Mark Twain called "The Gilded Age," an age of excess and extremes, of decline and progress, of poverty and dazzling wealth, of gloom and buoyant hope.

In the first decades after the Civil War, Americans ceased to be isolated from the world and from each other. Telegraph lines spanned the nation, and in 1866 a trans-Atlantic cable joined America and Europe. The first transcontinental railroad was completed in 1869, linking the Atlantic and the Pacific. Soon the United States had the most extensive railroad system in the world, which in turn generated enormous commercial expansion. The cost of transporting raw materials and finished goods dropped. Products once made locally by costly handwork were replaced by inexpensive goods.

Part IV The Literature of Realism

The tempo of life accelerated as Americans became increasingly mobile. Journeys of weeks or months were reduced to a few days. In the last surge of westward expansion, Americans, lured by the promise of free land, settled the last of the first forty-eight states. By 1890 the frontier, the westward-moving line of settlement begun three hundred years before on the Atlantic Coast, ceased to exist. Yet its influence would long remain, shaping the life of the nation and inspiring the legends, novels, and western movies by which the world would come to know America.

The period between the end of the Civil War and the beginning of World War I was a time of steel and steam, electricity and oil. Steel production in the United States increased more than six hundred times, and steelmaking became the nation's dominant industry. Alternating electrical current was introduced in 1886. Incandescent lamps illuminated the cities with electricity provided by giant, steam-driven dynamos. The tallow candles and whale-oil lamps of rural America were replaced by lanterns filled with kerosene made from crude oil. The American petroleum industry began, and with it came the age of the automobile.

From 1870 to 1890 the total population of the United States doubled. Villages became towns, towns became cities, and cities grew to a size and with a speed that would have astonished the Founding Fathers. From 1860 to 1910 the population of Philadelphia tripled, that of New York City more than quadrupled, while the population of Chicago increased twenty times to two million, making it the nation's second largest city.

As the population doubled, the national income quadrupled, and by the mid-1890s the United States could boast 4,000 millionaires. The rich prospered mightily, and immense power came to such industrial and banking magnates as John D. Rockefeller, Andrew Carnegie, and J. Pierpont Morgan. Yet the growth of business and industry also widened the gulf between the rich and the poor, giving rise to reform movements and labor unions that voiced the grievances of debt-ridden farmers and of immigrant workers living in city slums and laboring in giant, impersonal factories. It was a time of radiant prospects, when ministers preached (and congregations believed) a gospel of wealth, suggesting that riches were at last in league with virtue and the age of unlimited progress had finally dawned.

Increased wealth, and the desire for its conspicuous display, gave rise to a gingerbread era of American design whose prime function was to attract attention. American millionaires built Gothic and Romanesque mansions and decorated them with towers, domes, columns, stained-glass windows, and ornamental gimcracks of wood and iron. Their rooms were filled with art imported from Europe, as were most symbols of culture. Well-to-do Americans adopted European dress styles and manners, sent their sons to Europe for an education, and eagerly married off their daughters to European noblemen.

Literary Characteristics of the Age

In the latter half of the nineteenth century, women became the nation's dominant cultural force, a position they have never relinquished. Ladies' journalism began to flourish. In 1891, *The Ladies Home Journal* (founded in 1883) became the first American magazine to exceed a circulation of half a million; by 1905 it had reached a million. A new generation of women authors appeared whose poetry and fiction enlivened the pages of popular ten-cent monthly and weekly magazines. The greatest woman writer of the age, Emily Dickinson, was almost completely unknown; her first collection of poetry was not published until 1890, four years after her death. But Harriet Beecher Stowe, the author of *Uncle Tom's Cabin* (1852), had become an American institution and the most famous literary woman in the world. The American reading public's appetite for sentiment and sensation was constantly fed by such writers as Mrs. E. D. E. N. Southworth, who filled uncountable numbers of novels with romantic extravagance: ancestral curses, sudden passions, villains blasted, and heroes triumphant. Sales of such "molasses fiction" far exceeded the sales of works by such highly regarded writers as William Dean Howells, Edith Wharton, Henry James, and even Mark Twain.

Although Americans continued to read the works of Irving, Cooper, Hawthorne, and Poe, the great age of American romanticism had ended. By the 1870s the New England Renaissance had waned. Hawthorne and Thoreau were dead; Emerson, Lowell, Longfellow, Holmes, and Whittier had passed their literary zenith. Melville, living in obscurity, had ceased to publish his fiction. Only Whitman continued to offer a new literary vision to the world, issuing a fifth edition of *Leaves of Grass* in 1870 and publishing *Democratic Vistas* in 1871. As New England's cultural dominance declined, New York replaced Boston as the nation's literary center, drawing writers from New England, the South, and the West to the publishing houses and periodicals of the nation's largest city. From 1865 to 1905 the total number of periodicals published in the United States increased from about seven hundred to more than six thousand to satisfy the demands of a vast new reading audience that was hungry for articles, essays, fictions, and poems.

A host of new writers appeared, among them Bret Harte, William Dean Howells, Hamlin Garland, and Mark Twain, whose background and training, unlike those of the older generation they displaced, were middle-class and journalistic rather than genteel or academic. Influenced by such Europeans as Zola, Flaubert, Balzac, Dostoyevsky, and Tolstoy, America's most noteworthy new authors established a literature of realism. They sought to portray American life as it really was, insisting that the ordinary and the local were as suitable for artistic portrayal as the magnificent and the remote.

As in most literary rebellions, the new literature rose out of a desire to renovate the literary theories of a previous age. Realists had grown scornful of artistic ideals that had been trivialized, worn thin by derivative writers eager to supply the "great popular want" for sentiment, adventure, and "tingling excitement." In contrast, the realists had what Henry James called "a powerful impulse to mirror the unmitigated realities of life." Earlier in the nineteenth century, James Fenimore Cooper had insisted on the author's right to present an idealized and poetic portrait of life, to avoid representations of "squalid misery." But by the end of the nineteenth century the realists, and the literary naturalists who followed them, rejected the portrayal of idealized characters and events. Instead, they sought to describe the wide range of American experience and to present the subtleties of human personality, to portray characters who were not simply all good or all bad.

Realism had originated in France as *réalisme*, a literary doctrine that called for "reality and truth" in the depiction of ordinary life. Realism first appeared in the United States in the literature of local color, and an amalgam of romantic plots and realistic descriptions of things was immediately observable: the dialects, customs, sights, and sounds of regional America. Bret Harte in the 1860s was the first American writer of local color to achieve wide popularity, presenting stories of western mining towns with colorful gamblers, outlaws, and scandalous women. Thereafter editors, ever sensitive to public taste, demanded, and such writers as Harte, Harriet Beecher Stowe, Kate Chopin, Joel Chandler Harris, and Mark Twain provided, regional stories and tales of the life of America's Westerners, Southerners, and Easterners. Local-color fiction reached its peak of popularity in the 1880s, but by the turn of the century it had begun to decline as its limited resources were exhausted and as its most popular writers grew tediously repetitious or turned to other literary modes.

The arbiter of nineteenth-century literary realism in America was William Dean Howells. He defined realism as "nothing more and nothing less than the truthful treatment of material," and he best exemplified his theories in such novels as *A Modern Instance* (1882), *The Rise of Silas Lapham* (1885), and *A Hazard of New Fortunes* (1890). Howells spoke for a generation of writers who attempted to sustain an objective point of view and who found their subject matter in the experiences of the American middle class, describing their houses, families, and jobs, their social customs, achievements, and failures. The bulk of America's literary realism was limited to optimistic treatment of the surface of life. Yet the greatest of America's realists, Henry James and Mark Twain, moved well beyond a superficial portrayal of nineteenth-century America. James probed deeply into the individual psychology of his characters, writing in a rich and intricate style that supported his intense scrutiny of complex human experience. Mark Twain, breaking out of the narrow limits of local color fiction, described the breadth of American experience as no one had ever done before, or since, and he created, in *Adventures of Huckleberry Finn* (1884), a masterpiece of American realism that is one of the great books of world literature.

In the 1880s, Howells spoke out against the writing of a bleak fiction of failure and despair. He called for the treatment of the "smiling aspects of life" as being the more "American," insisting that America was truly a land of hope and of possibility that should be reflected in its literature. But at the end of the century, a generation of writers arose whose ideas of the workings of the universe and whose perception of society's disorders led them to naturalism, a new and harsher realism. America's literary naturalists dismissed the validity of comforting moral truths. They attempted to achieve extreme objectivity and frankness, presenting characters of low social and economic classes who were dominated by their environment and heredity. In presenting the extremes of life, the naturalists sometimes displayed an affinity to the sensationalism of early romanticism, but unlike their romantic predecessors, the naturalists emphasized that the world was amoral, that men and women had no free will, that their lives were controlled by heredity and the environment, that religious "truths" were illusory, that the destiny of humanity was misery in life and oblivion in death.

Naturalism, like realism, had come from Europe. In America it had been shaped by the war, by the social upheavals that undermined the comforting faith of an earlier age, and by the disturbing teachings of Charles Darwin. Darwinism seemed to stress the animality of man, to suggest that he was dominated by the irresistible forces of evolution. The pessimism and deterministic ideas of naturalism pervaded the works of such writers as Stephen Crane, Frank Norris, Jack London, Henry Adams, and Theodore Dreiser. Their detailed descriptions of the lives of the downtrodden and the abnormal, their frank treatment of human passion and sexuality, and their portrayal of men and women overwhelmed by the blind forces of nature still exert a powerful influence on modern writers.

Although realism and naturalism were products of the nineteenth century, their final triumph came in the twentieth century, with the popular and critical successes of such writers as Edwin Arlington Robinson, Willa Cather, Sherwood Anderson, Robert Frost, and William Faulkner. But the triumph of realism, even in the twentieth century did not bring an end to the extremes of romanticism, for they still abound in the popular television heroes and heroines of unspotted virtue and dazzling accomplishments.

Chapter 18

Walt Whitman (1819–1892)

Whitman was one of the great innovators in American literature. In the cluster of poems he called *Leaves of Grass* he gave America its first genuine epic poem. The poetic style he devised is now called free verse—that is, poetry without a fixed beat or regular rhyme scheme. Whitman thought that the voice of democracy should not be haltered by traditional forms of verse. His influence on the poetic technique of other writers was small during the time he was writing *Leaves of Grass*, but today elements of his style are apparent in the works of many poets. During the twentieth century, poets as different as Carl Sandburg and the "Beat" bard, Allen Ginsberg, have owed something to him.

Whitman grew up in Brooklyn, New York, and worked there as a schoolteacher, as an apprentice to a printer, and as the editor of various newspapers. He had very little schooling but read a great deal on his own. He was especially intrigued by the works of Shakespeare and Milton. Strangely enough, his only contact with the Eastern religions or with German Transcendentalists, whose ideas he frequently used in his poetry, was what he had read of them in the writings of Emerson.

In the 1840s Whitman supported Jackson's Democratic Party; he also favored the exclusion of slavery from new states in his newspaper writings and because of this, in 1848, he was dismissed from his job. He then worked sporadically at carpentry and odd jobs, and had some of his writing—which was conventional and undistinguished—printed in newspapers.

In 1848 he visited New Orleans, Chicago, and the Western frontier; the latter impressed him greatly. There is speculation that some of his experiences on this trip marked a turning point in his career, though it is more likely that he was gradually developing as an artist. At any rate, soon after this he became famous. He published the first edition of *Leaves of Grass* in 1855, setting the type for the book himself, and writing favorable reviews of it in the papers, anonymously. He continued to add new poems to the collection, and to rearrange and revise them, until his death in 1892. His best work is usually considered to have been done before 1871.

Most of the poems in *Leaves of Grass* are about man and nature. However, a small number of very good poems deal with New York, the city that fascinated Whitman, and with the Civil War, in which he served as a volunteer male nurse. In his poetry, Whitman combined the ideal of the democratic common man and that of the rugged individual. He envisioned the poet as a hero, a savior and a prophet, one who led the community by his expressions of the truth.

With the publication of *Leaves of Grass*, Whitman was praised by Ralph Waldo Emerson and a few other literati but was attacked by the majority of critics because of his unconventional style. He wanted his poetry to be for the common people but, ironically, it was ignored by the general public.

Song of Myself (excerpt)

1

I celebrate myself, and sing myself,
And what I assume you shall assume,
For every atom belonging to me as good belongs to you.

I loafe and invite my soul,
I lean and loafe at my ease observing a spear of summer grass.   5

My tongue, every atom of my blood, form'd from this soil, this air,
Born here of parents born here from parents the same, and their parents
    the same,
I, now thirty-seven years old in perfect health begin,
Hoping to cease not till death.   10

Creeds and schools in abeyance,
Retiring back a while sufficed at what they are, but never forgotten,
I harbor for good or bad, I permit to speak at every hazard,
Nature without check with original energy.

10

Alone far in the wilds and mountains I hunt,
Wandering amazed at my own lightness and glee,
In the late afternoon choosing a safe spot to pass the night,
Kindling a fire and broiling the fresh-kill'd game,
Falling asleep on the gather'd leaves with my dog and gun by my side.

The Yankee clipper is under her sky-sails, she cuts the sparkle and scud,
My eyes settle the land, I bend at her prow or shout joyously from the deck.

The boatmen and clam-diggers arose early and stopt for me,
I tuck'd my trowser-ends in my boots and went and had a good time;
You should have been with us that day round the chowder-kettle.

I saw the marriage of the trapper in the open air in the far west, the bride was a red girl,
Her father and his friends sat near cross-legged and dumbly smoking, they had moccasins to their feet and large thick blankets hanging from their shoulders,
On a bank lounged the trapper, he was drest mostly in skins, his luxuriant beard and curls protected his neck, he held his bride by the hand,
She had long eyelashes, her head was bare, her coarse straight locks descended upon her voluptuous limbs and reach'd to her feet.

The runaway slave came to my house and stopt outside,
I heard his motions crackling the twigs of the woodpile,
Through the swung half-door of the kitchen I saw him limpsy[1] and weak,
And went where he sat on a log and led him in and assured him,
And brought water and fill'd a tub for his sweated body and bruis'd feet,

And gave him a room that enter'd from my own, and gave him some
    coarse clean clothes,   40
And remember perfectly well his revolving eyes and his awkwardness,
And remember putting plasters on the galls of his neck and ankles;
He staid with me a week before he was recuperated and pass'd north,
I had him sit next me at table, my fire-lock lean'd in the corner.

Note

1. limpsy: limping or swaying

I Sit and Look Out

I sit and look out upon all the sorrows of the world, and upon all oppression
    and shame;
I hear secret convulsive sobs from young men, at anguish with themselves,
    remorseful after deeds done;
I see in low life the mother misused by her children, dying, neglected, gaunt,   5
    desperate;
I see the wife misused by her husband—I see the treacherous seducer of
    young women;
I mark the ranklings of jealousy and unrequited love attempted to be hid—
    I see these sights on the earth;   10
I see the workings of battle, pestilence, tyranny—I see martyrs and prisoners;
I observe a famine at sea—I observe the sailors casting lots who shall be kill'd
    to preserve the lives of the rest;
I observe the slights and degradations cast by arrogant persons upon laborers,
    the poor, and upon negroes, and the like;   15
All these—all the meanness and agony without end, I sitting, look out upon,
See, hear, and am silent.

🌿 Beat! Beat! Drums!

Beat! beat! drums!—blow! bugles! blow!
Through the windows—through doors—burst like a ruthless force,
Into the solemn church, and scatter the congregation,
Into the school where the scholar is studying;
Leave not the bridegroom quiet—no happiness must he have now with his   5
   bride,
Nor the peaceful farmer any peace, ploughing his field or gathering his grain,
So fierce you whirr and pound you drums—so shrill you bugles blow.

Beat! beat! drums!—blow! bugles! blow!
Over the traffic of cities—over the rumble of wheels in the streets;   10
Are beds prepared for sleepers at night in the houses? no sleepers must sleep
   in those beds,
No bargainers' bargains by day—no brokers or speculators—would they
   continue?
Would the talkers be talking? would the singer attempt to sing?   15
Would the lawyer rise in the court to state his case before the judge?
Then rattle quicker, heavier drums—you bugles wilder blow.

Beat! beat! drums!—blow! bugles! blow!
Make no parley—stop for no expostulation,
Mind not the timid—mind not the weeper or prayer,   20
Mind not the old man beseeching the young man,
Let not the child's voice be heard, nor the mother's entreaties,
Make even the trestles to shake the dead where they lie awaiting the
   hearses,
So strong you thump O terrible drums—so loud you bugles blow.   25

Chapter 19

Emily Dickinson (1830–1886)

Emily Dickinson wrote her whimsical, darting verse with sublime indifference to any notion of being a democratic or popular poet. Her work, far different from that of either Whitman or Longfellow, illustrated the fact that one could take a single household and an inactive life, and make enchanting poetry out of it.

Miss Dickinson was born in Amherst, Massachusetts, where her father was a prominent lawyer and politician and where her grandfather had established an academy and college. Emily's family was very closely knit and she and her sister remained at home and did not marry. Emily seldom left Amherst; she attended college in a nearby town for one year, and later made one trip as far as Washington and two or three trips to Boston. After 1862 she became a total recluse, not leaving her house nor seeing even close friends. Her early letters and descriptions of herself in her youth reveal an attractive girl with a lively wit. Her later retirement from the world, though perhaps affected by an unhappy love affair, seems mainly to have resulted from her own personality, from a desire to separate herself from the world. The range of her poetry suggests not her limited experiences but the power of her creativity and imagination.

When she began writing poetry, Emily had relatively little formal education. She did know Shakespeare and classical mythology and was especially interested in women authors such as Elizabeth Browning and the Brontë sisters. She was also acquainted with the works of Emerson, Thoreau and Hawthorne. Though she did not believe in the conventional religion of her family, she had studied the Bible, and many of her poems resemble hymns in form.

There were several men who, at different times in her life, acted as teacher or master to Emily. The first was Benjamin Newton, a young lawyer in her father's law office who improved her literary and cultural tastes and influenced her ideas on religion. She refers to him as "a friend, who taught me Immortality."

Emily's next teacher was Charles Wadsworth, a married, middle-aged minister who provided her with intellectual challenge and contact with the outside world. It appears that she felt an affection for him that he could not return, and when he moved to San Francisco in 1862, she removed herself from society even more than she had before. Wadsworth may have been the model for the lover in her poems, though it is just as likely that the literary figure is purely imaginary.

Miss Dickinson's greatest outpouring of poems occurred in the early 1860s, and because she was so isolated, the Civil War affected her thinking very little. At this time she sent some of her works to Thomas Higginson, a prominent critic and author. He was impressed by her poetry, but suggested that she use a more conventional grammar. Emily, however, refused to revise her poems to fit the standards of others and took no interest in having them published; in fact she had only seven poems published during her lifetime. In Higginson she did, nevertheless, gain an intelligent and sympathetic critic with whom to discuss her work.

In the last years of her life Emily seldom saw visitors, but kept in touch with her friends through letters, short poems and small gifts. After her death in 1886, her sister found nearly 1,800 poems that she had written. Many of the poems were finally published in 1890s, and Emily Dickinson, like Melville, was rediscovered by the literary world in the 1920s.

Emily Dickinson's poetry comes out in bursts. The poems are short, many of them being based on a single image or symbol. But within her little lyrics Miss Dickinson writes about some of the most important things in life. She writes about love and a lover, whom she either never really found or else gave up. She writes about nature. She writes about mortality and immortality. She writes about success, which she thought she never achieved, and about failure, which she considered her constant companion. She writes of these things so brilliantly that she is now ranked as one of America's great poets.

Chapter 19 Emily Dickinson

Her poetry is read today throughout much of the world and yet its exact wording has not been completely determined, nor have its arrangement and punctuation. Since Emily never prepared her poems for publication, one of the bitterest battles in American literary history has been fought over who should publish and edit what she wrote. However, regardless of details or conflicts, there is no doubt that the solitary Miss Dickinson of Amherst, Massachusetts, is a writer of great power and beauty.

I Taste a Liquor Never Brewed

I taste a liquor never brewed—
From Tankards scooped in Pearl—
Not all the Frankfort Berries
Yield such an Alcohol!

Inebriate of Air—am I—   5
And Debauchee of Dew—
Reeling—thro endless summer days—
From inns of Molten Blue—

When "Landlords" turn the drunken Bee
Out of the Foxglove's door—   10
When Butterflies—renounce their "drams"—
I shall but drink the more!

Till Seraphs[1] swing their snowy Hats—
And Saints—to windows run—
To see the little Tippler   15
From Manzanilla[2] come!

Notes

1. Seraphs: six winged angels believed to guard God's throne
2. Manzanilla: a busy port in Cuba

I Felt a Funeral, in My Brain

    I felt a Funeral, in my Brain,
    And Mourners to and fro
    Kept treading—treading—till it seemed
    That Sense was breaking through—

    And when they all were seated,   5
    A Service, like a Drum—
    Kept beating—beating—till I thought
    My Mind was going numb—

    And then I heard them lift a Box
    And creak across my Soul   10
    With those same Boots of Lead, again,
    Then Space—began to toll,

    As all the Heavens were a Bell,
    And Being, but an Ear,
    And I, and Silence, some strange Race   15
    Wrecked, solitary, here—

    And then a Plank in Reason, broke,
    And I dropped down, and down—
    And hit a World, at every plunge,
    And Finished knowing—then—   20

A Bird Came down the Walk—

    A Bird came down the Walk—
    He did not know I saw—
    He bit an Angleworm in halves
    And ate the fellow, raw,

And then he drank a Dew   5
From a convenient Grass—
And then hopped sidewise to the Wall
To let a Beetle pass—

He glanced with rapid eyes
That hurried all around—   10
They looked like frightened Beads, I thought—
He stirred his Velvet Head

Like one in danger, Cautious,
I offered him a Crumb
And he unrolled his feathers   15
And rowed him softer home—

Than Oars divide the Ocean,
Too silver for a seam—
Or Butterflies, off Banks of Noon
Leap, plashless[1] as they swim.   20

Note
1. plashless: splashless

🕊 I Died for Beauty—But Was Scarce

I died for Beauty—but was scarce
Adjusted in the Tomb
When One who died for Truth, was lain
In an adjoining Room—

He questioned softly "Why I failed"?   5
"For Beauty," I replied—

"And I—for Truth—Themself are One—
We Brethren, are," He said—

And so, as Kinsmen, met a Night—
We talked between the Rooms— 10
Until the Moss had reached our lips—
And covered up—our names—

🌿 I Heard a Fly Buzz—When I Died—

I heard a Fly buzz—when I died—
The Stillness in the Room
Was like the Stillness in the Air—
Between the Heaves of Storm—

The Eyes around—had wrung them dry— 5
And Breaths were gathering firm
For that last Onset—when the King
Be witnessed—in the Room—

I willed my Keepsakes—Signed away
What portion of me be 10
Assignable—and then it was
There interposed a Fly—

With Blue—uncertain stumbling Buzz—
Between the light—and me—
And then the Windows failed—and then 15
I could not see to see—

🌿 Because I Could Not Stop for Death—

Because I could not stop for Death—
He kindly stopped for me—

Chapter 19 Emily Dickinson

The Carriage held but just Ourselves—
And Immortality.

We slowly drove—He knew no haste   5
And I had put away
My labor and my leisure too,
For His Civility—

We passed the School, where Children strove
At Recess—in the Ring—   10
We passed the Fields of Gazing Grain—
We passed the Setting Sun—

Or rather—He passed Us—
The Dews drew quivering and chill—
For only Gossamer, my Gown—   15
My Tippet[1]—only Tulle—

We paused before a House that seemed
A Swelling of the Ground—
The Roof was scarcely visible—
The Cornice—in the Ground—   20

Since then—'tis Centuries—and yet
Feels shorter than the Day
I first surmised the Horses Heads
Were toward Eternity—

Note

1. Tippet: shoulder cape

Chapter 20

Harriet Beecher Stowe (1811–1896)

Harriet Beecher Stowe was born into a respectable family that was to become famous: Her father Lyman was a renowned clergyman; two of her brothers, Henry Ward and Edward, were celebrated preachers; and her older sister, Catherine, pioneered in women's education. The family was dominated by the father who ruled with the kind of wrathful severity that he imagined were the chief characteristics of the God he worshiped and feared. The boys were expected to become preachers, the girls to marry preachers.

Harriet began school in 1816 in Litchfield, Connecticut, and when Catherine established the Hartford Female Seminary in 1824, she joined her sister there. Their father became president of Lane Theological Seminary in Cincinnati in 1832, and the sisters reluctantly rejoined the family in this "London of the West," as he described what was still a small, raw frontier town. Harriet continued to work for her domineering older sister at the Western Female Institute she initiated, and seemed to head for a lifetime as an unknown housebound spinster. Harriet escaped this fate in part by converting her lifelong interest in writing into magazine stories which in the 1830s and 1840s earned her a few welcomed dollars. In 1836 she married Calvin Ellis Stowe, one of the leading professors at Lane, and bore the first four of their seven children within four years. The fees from her writing were useful in keeping the family on the respectable side of genteel poverty.

After eighteen years living across the Ohio River from slave-holding communities—and absorbing from fugitive slaves and visits to the South a personal knowledge of the institution of slavery—Harriet returned to New England in 1850 when her husband took a professorship at Bowdoin College in Brunswick, Maine. Partly inspired by the moral outrage she greeted the Fugitive Slave Act of 1850 (that allowed owners to pursue and recover their "property" in free states), partly liberated by her return to her New England roots, *Uncle Tom's Cabin; or, The Man That Was a Thing* (as it was originally entitled) was conceived early in February, 1851.

The novel began serially in the *National Era* on June 5, 1851, and the last installment appeared on April 1, 1852. The *National Era* was essentially, but not exclusively, devoted to promoting abolitionist principles, but it did so with less evangelical indignation than William Lloyd Garrison's *The Liberator*. Even so, Stowe did not find a book publisher easily. When the novel did appear, however, it was an overnight success. It sold 350,000 copies during the first year, and since then has been published in some forty languages and has been read by millions of people around the world. The power of the novel unquestionably comes from the investment of the author's sense of her own suffering and oppression (as well as her determination to be free) in the characters of Tom and his fellow slave Eliza, the protagonists of the book's two main plots.

Stowe probably was never fully aware of this source of the novel's strength or of its effect on readers, and certainly she did not anticipate the sensation it created. To cope with southern opposition and challenges to the accuracy of the novel, she wrote the nonfiction *A Key to Uncle Tom's Cabin*, with documented case histories to support what she had portrayed fictionally. *Dred: A Tale of the Great Dismal Swamp* (1856) was another antislavery novel, which may best be understood as an unsuccessful attempt to repeat the theme and extend the argument of her masterpiece: that a society resting on slavery could not long survive.

Uncle Tom's Cabin[1]

The Story

Because his Kentucky plantation was encumbered by debt, Mr. Shelby made plans to sell one of his slaves to his chief creditor, a New Orleans slave dealer named Haley. The dealer shrewdly selected Uncle Tom as part payment on Mr. Shelby's debt. While they were discussing the transaction, Eliza's child, Harry, came into the room. Haley wanted to buy Harry too, but at first Shelby was unwilling to part with the child. Eliza listened to enough of the conversation to be frightened. She confided her fears to George Harris, her husband, a slave on an adjoining plantation. George, who was already bitter because his master had put him to work in the fields when he was capable of doing better work, promised that some day he would have his revenge upon his hard masters. Eliza had been brought up more indulgently by the Shelbys and she begged him not to try anything rash.

After supper in the cabin of Uncle Tom and Aunt Chloe, his wife, the Shelby slaves gathered for a meeting. They sang songs, and young George Shelby, who had eaten his supper there, read from the Bible. In the big house Mr. Shelby signed the papers making Uncle Tom and little Harry the property of Haley. Eliza, learning her child's fate from some remarks of Mr. Shelby to his wife, fled with her child, hoping to reach Canada and safety. Uncle Tom, hearing of the sale, resigned himself to the wisdom of Providence.

The next day, after Haley had discovered his loss, he set out to capture Eliza. However, she had a good start. Moreover, Mrs. Shelby purposely delayed the pursuit by serving a late breakfast. When her pursuers came in sight, Eliza escaped across the Ohio River by jumping from one floating ice cake to another, young Harry in her arms.

Haley hired two slave-catchers, Marks and Loker, to track Eliza through Ohio. For their trouble, she was to be given to them. They set off that night.

Eliza found shelter in the home of Senator and Mrs. Bird. The senator took her to the house of a man known to aid fugitive slaves. Uncle Tom, however, was not so lucky. Haley made sure Tom would not escape by shackling his ankles before taking him to the boat bound for New Orleans. When young George Shelby heard Tom had been sold, he followed Haley on his horse. George gave Tom a dollar as a token of his sympathy and told him that he would buy him back one day.

At the same time George Harris began his escape. White enough to pass as a Spaniard, he appeared at a tavern as a gentleman and took a room there, hoping to find before long a station on the Underground Railroad.

Chapter 20   Harriet Beecher Stowe

Eliza was resting at the home of Rachel and Simeon Halliday when George Harris arrived in the same Quaker settlement.

On board the boat bound for New Orleans, Uncle Tom saved the life of young Eva St. Clare, and in gratitude Eva's father purchased the slave. Eva told Tom he would now have a happy life, for her father was kind to everyone. Augustine St. Clare was married to a woman who imagined herself sick and therefore took no interest in her daughter Eva. He had gone north to bring back his cousin, Miss Ophelia, to provide care for the neglected and delicate Eva. When they arrived at the St. Clare plantation, Tom was made head coachman.

Meanwhile Loker and Marks were on the trail of Eliza and George. They caught up with the fugitives and there was a fight in which George wounded Loker. Marks fled, and so the Quakers who were protecting the runaways took Loker along with them and gave him medical treatment.

Unused to lavish Southern customs Miss Ophelia tried to understand the South. Shocked at the extravagance of St. Clare's household, she attempted to bring order out of the chaos, but she received no encouragement because the slaves had been humored and petted too long. Indulgent in all things, St. Clare was indifferent to the affairs of his family and his property. Uncle Tom lived an easy life in the loft over the stable. He and little Eva became close friends with St. Clare's approval. Sometimes St. Clare had doubts regarding the institution of slavery, and in one of these moods he bought an odd pixie-like child, Topsy, for his prim New England cousin to educate.

Eva grew more frail. Knowing that she was about to die, she asked her father to free his slaves, as he had so often promised. After Eva's death St. Clare began to read the Bible and to make plans to free all his slaves. He gave Topsy to Miss Ophelia legally, so that the spinster might rear the child as she wished. Then one evening he tried to separate two quarreling men. He received a knife wound in the side and died shortly afterward. Mrs. Clare had no intention of freeing the slaves, and she ordered Tom sent to the slave market.

At a public auction he was sold to a brutal plantation owner named Simon Legree. Legree drank heavily, and his plantation house had fallen to ruin. He kept dogs for the purpose of tracking runaway slaves. At the slave quarters Tom was given his sack of corn for the week, told to grind it himself and bake the meal into cakes for his supper. At the mill he aided two women. In return they baked his cakes for him. He read selections from the Bible to them.

For a few weeks Tom quietly tried to please his harsh master. One day he helped a sick woman by putting cotton into her basket. For this act Legree ordered him to flog the woman. When Tom refused, his master had him flogged until he fainted. A slave named Cassy came to Tom's aid. She told Tom the story of her life with Legree and of a young daughter who had been sold years before.

Then she went to Legree's apartment and tormented him. She hated her master and she had power over him. Legree was superstitious. When she talked, letting her eyes flash over him, he felt as though she were casting an evil spell. Haunted by the secrets of his guilty past, he drank until he fell asleep. But he had forgotten his fears by the next morning, and he knocked Tom to the ground with his fist.

Meanwhile, far to the north, George and Eliza and young Harry were making their way slowly through the stations on the Underground Railroad toward Canada.

Cassy and Emmeline, another slave, determined to make their escape. Knowing the consequences if they should be caught, they tricked Legree into thinking they were hiding in the swamp. When Legree sent dogs and men after them, they sneaked back into the house and hid in the garret. Legree suspected that Tom knew where the women had gone and decided to beat the truth out of his slave. He had Tom beaten until the old man could neither speak nor stand.

Two days later George Shelby arrived to buy Tom back, but he came too late. Tom was dying. When George threatened to have Legree tried for murder, Legree mocked him. George struck Legree in the face and knocked him down.

Still hiding in the attic, Cassy and Emmeline pretended they were ghosts. Frightened, Legree drank harder than ever. George Shelby helped them to escape. Later, on a river boat headed north, the two women discovered a Madame de Thoux, who said she was George Harris' sister. With this disclosure, Cassy learned also that Eliza, her daughter, was the Eliza who had married George and with him and her child had escaped safely to Canada.

These relatives were reunited in Canada after many years. In Kentucky George Shelby freed all his slaves when his father died. He said he freed them in the name of Uncle Tom.

CHAPTER VII
The Mother's Struggle

It is impossible to conceive of a human creature more wholly desolate and forlorn than Eliza, when she turned her footsteps from Uncle Tom's cabin.

Her husband's suffering and dangers, and the danger of her child, all blended in her mind, with a confused and stunning sense of the risk she was running, in leaving the only home she had ever known, and cutting loose from the protection of a friend whom she loved and revered. Then there was the parting from every familiar object,—the place where she had grown up, the trees under which she had played, the groves where she had walked many an evening in happier days, by the side of her young husband,—everything, as it lay in the clear, frosty starlight, seemed to speak reproachfully to her, and ask her whither could she go from a home like that?

But stronger than all was maternal love, wrought into a paroxysm of frenzy by the near approach of a fearful danger. Her boy was old enough to have walked by her side, and, in an indifferent case, she would only have led him by the hand; but now the bare thought of putting him out of her arms made her shudder, and she strained him to her bosom with a convulsive grasp, as she went rapidly forward.

The frosty ground creaked beneath her feet, and she trembled at the sound; every quaking leaf and fluttering shadow sent the blood backward to her heart, and quickened her footsteps. She wondered within herself at the strength that seemed to be come upon her; for she felt the weight of her boy as if it had been a feather, and every flutter of fear seemed to increase the supernatural power that bore her on, while from her pale lips burst forth, in frequent ejaculations, the prayer to a Friend above—"Lord, help! Lord, save me!"

If it were *your* Harry, mother, or your Willie, that were going to be torn from you by a brutal trader, to-morrow morning,—if you had seen the man, and heard that the papers were signed and delivered, and you had only from twelve o'clock till morning to make good your escape,—how fast could *you* walk? How many miles could you make in those few brief hours, with the darling at your bosom,—the little sleepy head on your shoulder,—the small, soft arms trustingly holding on to your neck?

For the child slept. At first, the novelty and alarm kept him waking; but his mother so hurriedly repressed every breath or sound, and so assured him that if he were only still she would certainly save him, that he clung quietly round her neck, only asking, as he found himself sinking to sleep,

"Mother, I don't need to keep awake, do I?"

"No, my darling; sleep, if you want to."

"But, mother, if I do get asleep, you won't let him get me?"

"No! so may God help me!" said his mother, with a paler cheek, and a brighter light in her large dark eyes.

"You're *sure*, an't you, mother?"

"Yes, *sure*!" said the mother, in a voice that startled herself; for it seemed to her to come from a spirit within, that was no part of her; and the boy dropped his little weary head on her shoulder, and was soon asleep. How the touch of those warm arms, the gentle breathings that came in her neck, seemed to add fire and spirit to her movements! It seemed to her as if strength poured into her in electric streams, from every gentle touch and movement of the sleeping, confiding child. Sublime is the dominion of the mind over the body, that, for a time, can make flesh and nerve impregnable, and string the sinews like steel, so that the weak become so mighty.

The boundaries of the farm, the grove, the wood-lot, passed by her dizzily, as she walked on; and still she went, leaving one familiar object after another, slacking not, pausing not, till reddening daylight found her many a long mile from all traces of any familiar objects upon the open highway.

Chapter 20 Harriet Beecher Stowe

She had often been, with her mistress, to visit some connections, in the little village of T——, not far from the Ohio river, and knew the road well. To go thither, to escape across the Ohio river, were the first hurried outlines of her plan of escape; beyond that, she could only hope in God.

When horses and vehicles began to move along the highway, with that alert perception peculiar to a state of excitement, and which seems to be a sort of inspiration, she became aware that her headlong pace and distracted air might bring on her remark and suspicion. She therefore put the boy on the ground, and, adjusting her dress and bonnet, she walked on at as rapid a pace as she thought consistent with the preservation of appearances. In her little bundle she had provided a store of cakes and apples, which she used as expedients for quickening the speed of the child, rolling the apple some yards before them, when the boy would run with all his might after it; and this ruse, often repeated, carried them over many a half-mile.

After a while, they came to a thick patch of woodland, through which murmured a clear brook. As the child complained of hunger and thirst, she climbed over the fence with him; and, sitting down behind a large rock which concealed them from the road, she gave him a breakfast out of her little package. The boy wondered and grieved that she could not eat; and when, putting his arms round her neck, he tried to wedge some of his cake into her mouth, it seemed to her that the rising in her throat would choke her.

"No, no, Harry darling! mother can't eat till you are safe! We must go on—on—till we come to the river!" And she hurried again into the road, and again constrained herself to walk regularly and composedly forward.

She was many miles past any neighborhood where she was personally known. If she should chance to meet any who knew her, she reflected that the well-known kindness of the family would be of itself a blind to suspicion, as making it an unlikely supposition that she could be a fugitive. As she was also so white as not to be known as of colored lineage, without a critical survey, and her child was white also, it was much easier for her to pass on unsuspected.

On this presumption, she stopped at noon at a neat farmhouse, to rest herself, and buy some dinner for her child and self; for, as the danger decreased with the distance, the supernatural tension of the nervous system lessened, and she found herself both weary and hungry.

The good woman, kindly and gossipping, seemed rather pleased than otherwise with having somebody come in to talk with; and accepted, without examination, Eliza's statement, that she "was going on a little piece, to spend a week with her friends,"—all which she hoped in her heart might prove strictly true.

An hour before sunset, she entered the village of T——, by the Ohio river, weary and foot-sore, but still strong in heart. Her first glance was at the river, which lay, like Jordan[2], between her and the Canaan of liberty on the other side.

It was now early spring, and the river was swollen and turbulent; great cakes of floating ice were swinging heavily to and fro in the turbid waters. Owing to the peculiar form of the shore on the Kentucky side, the land bending far out into the water, the ice had been lodged and detained in great quantities, and the narrow channel which swept round the bend was full of ice, piled one cake over another, thus forming a temporary barrier to the descending ice, which lodged, and formed a great, undulating raft, filling up the whole river, and extending almost to the Kentucky shore.

Eliza stood, for a moment, contemplating this unfavorable aspect of things, which she saw at once must prevent the usual ferry-boat from running, and then turned into a small public house on the bank, to make a few inquiries.

The hostess, who was busy in various fizzing and stewing operations over the fire, preparatory to the evening meal, stopped, with a fork in her hand, as Eliza's sweet and plaintive voice arrested her.

"What is it?" she said.

"Isn't there any ferry or boat, that takes people over to B——, now?" she said.

"No, indeed!" said the woman; "the boats has stopped running."

Eliza's look of dismay and disappointment struck the woman, and she said, inquiringly,

"May be you're wanting to get over?—anybody sick? Ye seem mighty anxious?"

Chapter 20   Harriet Beecher Stowe

"I've got a child that's very dangerous," said Eliza. "I never heard of it till last night, and I've walked quite a piece to-day, in hopes to get to the ferry."

"Well, now, that's onlucky," said the woman, whose motherly sympathies were much aroused; "I'm re'lly consarned for ye. Solomon!" she called, from the window, towards a small back building. A man, in leather apron and very dirty hands, appeared at the door.

"I say, Sol," said the woman, "is that ar man going to tote them bar'ls over to-night?"

"He said he should try, if 't was any way prudent," said the man.

"There's a man a piece down here, that's going over with some truck this evening, if he durs' to; he'll be in here to supper to-night, so you'd better set down and wait. That's a sweet little fellow," added the woman, offering him a cake.

But the child, wholly exhausted, cried with weariness.

"Poor fellow! he isn't used to walking, and I've hurried him on so," said Eliza.

"Well, take him into this room," said the woman, opening into a small bed-room, where stood a comfortable bed. Eliza laid the weary boy upon it, and held his hands in hers till he was fast asleep. For her there was no rest. As a fire in her bones, the thought of the pursuer urged her on; and she gazed with longing eyes on the sullen, surging waters that lay between her and liberty.

Here we must take our leave of her for the present, to follow the course of her pursuers.

Though Mrs. Shelby had promised that the dinner should be hurried on table, yet it was soon seen, as the thing has often been seen before, that it required more than one to make a bargain. So, although the order was fairly given out in Haley's hearing, and carried to Aunt Chloe[3] by at least half a dozen juvenile messengers, that dignitary only gave certain very gruff snorts, and tosses of her head, and went on with every operation in an unusually leisurely and circumstantial manner.

For some singular reason, an impression seemed to reign among the servants generally that Missis would not be particularly disobliged by delay; and it was wonderful what a number of counter accidents occurred constantly, to retard the course of things. One luckless wight contrived to upset the gravy; and then gravy had to be got up *de novo*[4], with due care and formality, Aunt Chloe watching and stirring with dogged precision, answering shortly, to all suggestions of haste, that she "warn't a going to have raw gravy on the table, to help nobody's catchings[5]." One tumbled down with the water, and had to go to the spring for more; and another precipitated the butter into the path of events; and there was from time to time giggling news brought into the kitchen that "Mas'r Haley was mighty oneasy, and that he couldn't sit in his cheer no ways, but was a walkin' and stalkin' to the winders and through the porch."

"Sarves him right!" said Aunt Chloe, indignantly. "He'll get wus nor oneasy, one of these days, if he don't mend his ways. *His* master'll be sending for him, and then see how he'll look!"

"He'll go to torment, and no mistake," said little Jake.

"He desarves it!" said Aunt Chloe, grimly; "he's broke a many, many, many hearts,—I tell ye all!" she said, stopping, with a fork uplifted in her hands; "it's like what Mas'r George reads in Ravelations,—souls a callin' under the altar! and a callin' on the Lord for vengeance on sich!—and by and by the Lord he'll hear 'em—so he will!"[6]

Aunt Chloe, who was much revered in the kitchen, was listened to with open mouth; and, the dinner being now fairly sent in, the whole kitchen was at leisure to gossip with her, and to listen to her remarks.

"Sich'll be burnt up forever, and no mistake; won't ther?" said Andy.

"I'd be glad to see it, I'll be boun'," said little Jake.

"Chil'en!" said a voice, that made them all start. It was Uncle Tom, who had come in, and stood listening to the conversation at the door.

"Chil'en!" he said, "I'm afeard you don't know what ye're sayin'. Forever is a *dre'ful* word, chil'en; it's awful to think on 't. You oughtenter wish that ar to any human crittur."

"We wouldn't to anybody but the soul-drivers[7]," said Andy; "nobody can help wishing it to them, they's so awful wicked."

"Don't natur herself kinder cry out on 'em?" said Aunt Chloe. "Don't dey tear der suckin' baby right off his mother's breast, and sell him, and der little children as is crying and holding on by her clothes,—don't dey pull 'em off and sells 'em? Don't dey tear wife and husband apart?" said Aunt Chloe, beginning to cry, "when it's jest takin' the very life on 'em?—and all the while does they feel one bit,—don't dey drink and smoke, and take it oncommon easy? Lor, if the devil don't get them, what's he good for?" And Aunt Chloe covered her face with her checked apron, and began to sob in good earnest.

"Pray for them that 'spitefully use you, the good book says,"[8] says Tom.

"Pray for 'em!" said Aunt Chloe; "Lor, it's too tough! I can't pray for 'em."

"It's natur, Chloe, and natur's strong," said Tom, "but the Lord's grace is stronger; besides, you oughter think what an awful state a poor crittur's soul's in that'll do them ar things,—you oughter thank God that you an't *like* him, Chloe. I'm sure I'd rather be sold, ten thousand times over, than to have all that ar poor crittur's got to answer for."

"So'd I, a heap," said Jake. "Lor, *shouldn't* we cotch it, Andy?"

Andy shrugged his shoulders, and gave an acquiescent whistle.

"I'm glad Mas'r didn't go off this morning, as he looked to," said Tom; "that ar hurt me more than sellin', it did. Mebbe it might have been natural for him, but 't would have come desp't hard on me, as has known him from a baby; but I've seen Mas'r, and I begin ter feel sort o' reconciled to the Lord's will now. Mas'r couldn't help hisself; he did right, but I'm feared things will be kinder goin' to rack, when I'm gone. Mas'r can't be spected to be a pryin' round everywhar, as I've done, a keepin' up all the ends. The boys all means well, but they's powerful car'less. That ar troubles me."

The bell here rang, and Tom was summoned to the parlor.

"Tom," said his master, kindly, "I want you to notice that I give this gentleman bonds to forfeit a thousand dollars if you are not on the spot when he wants you; he's going to-day to look after his other business, and you can have the day to yourself. Go anywhere you like, boy."

"Thank you, Mas'r," said Tom.

"And mind yourself," said the trader, "and don't come it over your master with any o' yer nigger tricks; for I'll take every cent out of him, if you an't thar. If he'd hear to me, he wouldn't trust any on ye—slippery as eels!"

"Mas'r," said Tom,—and he stood very straight,—"I was jist eight years old when ole Missis put you into my arms, and you wasn't a year old. 'Thar,' says she, 'Tom, that's to be *your* young Mas'r; take good care on him,' says she. And now I jist ask you, Mas'r, have I ever broke word to you, or gone contrary to you, 'specially since I was a Christian?"

Mr. Shelby was fairly overcome, and the tears rose to his eyes.

"My good boy," said he, "the Lord knows you say but the truth; and if I was able to help it, all the world shouldn't buy you."

"And sure as I am a Christian woman," said Mrs. Shelby, "you shall be redeemed as soon as I can any way bring together means. Sir," she said to Haley, "take good account of who you sell him to, and let me know."

"Lor, yes, for that matter," said the trader, "I may bring him up in a year, not much the wuss for wear, and trade him back."

"I'll trade with you then, and make it for your advantage," said Mrs. Shelby.

"Of course," said the trader, "all's equal with me; li'ves trade 'em up as down, so I does a good business. All I want is a livin', you know, ma'am; that's all any on us wants, I s'pose."

Mr. and Mrs. Shelby both felt annoyed and degraded by the familiar impudence of the trader, and yet both saw the absolute necessity of putting a constraint on their feelings. The more hopelessly sordid and insensible he appeared, the greater became Mrs. Shelby's dread of his succeeding in recapturing Eliza and her child, and of course the greater her motive for detaining him by every female artifice. She therefore graciously smiled, assented, chatted familiarly, and did all she could to make time pass imperceptibly.

At two o'clock Sam and Andy brought the horses up to the posts, apparently greatly refreshed and invigorated by the scamper of the morning.

Sam was there new oiled from dinner, with an abundance of zealous and ready officiousness. As Haley approached, he was boasting, in flourishing style, to Andy, of the evident and eminent success of the operation, now that he had "farly come to it."

"Your master, I s'pose, don't keep no dogs," said Haley, thoughtfully, as he prepared to mount.

"Heaps on 'em," said Sam, triumphantly; "thar's Bruno—he's a roarer! and, besides that, 'bout every nigger of us keeps a pup of some natur or uther."

"Poh!" said Haley,—and he said something else, too, with regard to the said dogs, at which Sam muttered,

"I don't see no use cussin' on 'em, no way."

"But your master don't keep no dogs (I pretty much know he don't) for trackin' out niggers."

Sam knew exactly what he meant, but he kept on a look of earnest and desperate simplicity.

"Our dogs all smells round considerable sharp. I spect they's the kind, though they han't never had no practice. They's *far* dogs, though, at most anything, if you'd get 'em started. Here, Bruno," he called, whistling to the lumbering Newfoundland, who came pitching tumultuously towards them.

"You go hang!" said Haley, getting up. "Come, tumble up now."

Sam tumbled up accordingly, dexterously contriving to tickle Andy as he did so, which occasioned Andy to split out into a laugh, greatly to Haley's indignation, who made a cut at him with his riding-whip.

"I's 'stonished at yer, Andy," said Sam, with awful gravity. "This yer's a seris bisness, Andy. Yer mustn't be a makin' game. This yer an't no way to help Mas'r."

"I shall take the straight road to the river," said Haley, decidedly, after they had come to the boundaries of the estate. "I know the way of all of 'em,—they makes tracks for the underground."[9]

"Sartin," said Sam, "dat's de idee. Mas'r Haley hits de thing right in de middle. Now, der's two roads to de river,—de dirt road and der pike,—which Mas'r mean to take?"

Andy looked up innocently at Sam, surprised at hearing this new geographical fact, but instantly confirmed what he said, by a vehement reiteration.

"Cause," said Sam, "I'd rather be 'clined to 'magine that Lizy'd take de dirt road, bein' it's the least travelled."

Haley, notwithstanding that he was a very old bird, and naturally inclined to be suspicious of chaff, was rather brought up by this view of the case.

"If yer warn't both on yer such cussed liars, now!" he said, contemplatively, as he pondered a moment.

The pensive, reflective tone in which this was spoken appeared to amuse Andy prodigiously, and he drew a little behind, and shook so as apparently to run a great risk of falling off his horse, while Sam's face was immovably composed into the most doleful gravity.

"Course," said Sam, "Mas'r can do as he'd ruther; go de straight road, if Mas'r thinks best,—it's all one to us. Now, when I study 'pon it, I think de straight road do best, *deridedly*."

"She would naturally go a lonesome way," said Haley, thinking aloud, and not minding Sam's remark.

"Dar an't no sayin'," said Sam; "gals is pecular; they never does nothin' ye thinks they will; mose gen'lly the contrary. Gals is nat'lly made contrary; and so, if you thinks they've gone one road, it is sartin you'd better go t' other, and then you'll be sure to find 'em. Now, my private 'pinion is, Lizy took der dirt road; so I think we'd better take de straight one."

This profound generic view of the female sex did not seem to dispose Haley particularly to the straight road; and he announced decidedly that he should go the other, and asked Sam when they should come to it.

"A little piece ahead," said Sam, giving a wink to Andy with the eye which was on Andy's side of the head; and he added, gravely, "but I've studded on de matter, and I'm quite clar we ought not to go dat ar way. I nebber been over it no way. It's despit lonesome, and we might lose our way,—whar we'd come to, de Lord only knows."

"Nevertheless," said Haley, "I shall go that way."

"Now I think on 't, I think I hearn 'em tell that dat ar road was all fenced up and down by der creek, and thar, an't it, Andy?"

Andy wasn't certain; he'd only "hearn tell" about that road, but never been over it. In short, he was strictly noncommittal.

Chapter 20 Harriet Beecher Stowe

Haley, accustomed to strike the balance of probabilities between lies of greater or lesser magnitude, thought that it lay in favor of the dirt road aforesaid. The mention of the thing he thought he perceived was involuntary on Sam's part at first, and his confused attempts to dissuade him he set down to a desperate lying on second thoughts, as being unwilling to implicate Eliza.

When, therefore, Sam indicated the road, Haley plunged briskly into it, followed by Sam and Andy.

Now, the road, in fact, was an old one, that had formerly been a thoroughfare to the river, but abandoned for many years after the laying of the new pike. It was open for about an hour's ride, and after that it was cut across by various farms and fences. Sam knew this fact perfectly well,—indeed, the road had been so long closed up, that Andy had never heard of it. He therefore rode along with an air of dutiful submission, only groaning and vociferating occasionally that 't was "desp't rough, and bad for Jerry's foot."

"Now, I jest give yer warning," said Haley, "I know yer; yer won't get me to turn off this yer road, with all yer fussin'—so you shet up!"

"Mas'r will go his own way!" said Sam, with rueful submission, at the same time winking most portentously to Andy, whose delight was now very near the explosive point.

Sam was in wonderful spirits,—professed to keep a very brisk lookout,—at one time exclaiming that he saw "a gal's bonnet" on the top of some distant eminence, or calling to Andy "if that thar wasn't 'Lizy' down in the hollow"; always making these exclamations in some rough or craggy part of the road, where the sudden quickening of speed was a special inconvenience to all parties concerned, and thus keeping Haley in a state of constant commotion.

After riding about an hour in this way, the whole party made a precipitate and tumultuous descent into a barn-yard belonging to a large farming establishment. Not a soul was in sight, all the hands being employed in the fields; but, as the barn stood conspicuously and plainly square across the road, it was evident that their journey in that direction had reached a decided finale.

"Wan't dat ar what I telled Mas'r?" said Sam, with an air of injured innocence. "How does strange gentleman spect to know more about a country dan de natives born and raised?"

"You rascal!" said Haley, "you knew all about this."

"Didn't I tell yer I *know'd*, and yer wouldn't believe me? I telled Mas'r 't was all shet up, and fenced up, and I didn't spect we could get through,—Andy heard me."

It was all too true to be disputed, and the unlucky man had to pocket his wrath with the best grace he was able, and all three faced to the right about, and took up their line of march for the highway.

In consequence of all the various delays, it was about three-quarters of an hour after Eliza had laid her child to sleep in the village tavern that the party came riding into the same place. Eliza was standing by the window, looking out in another direction, when Sam's quick eye caught a glimpse of her. Haley and Andy were two yards behind. At this crisis, Sam contrived to have his hat blown off, and uttered a loud and characteristic ejaculation, which startled her at once; she drew suddenly back; the whole train swept by the window, round to the front door.

A thousand lives seemed to be concentrated in that one moment to Eliza. Her room opened by a side door to the river. She caught her child, and sprang down the steps towards it. The trader caught a full glimpse of her, just as she was disappearing down the bank; and throwing himself from his horse, and calling loudly on Sam and Andy, he was after her like a hound after a deer. In that dizzy moment her feet to her scarce seemed to touch the ground, and a moment brought her to the water's edge. Right on behind they came; and, nerved with strength such as God gives only to the desperate, with one wild cry and flying leap, she vaulted sheer over the turbid current by the shore, on to the raft of ice beyond. It was a desperate leap—impossible to anything but madness and despair; and Haley, Sam, and Andy, instinctively cried out, and lifted up their hands, as she did it.

The huge green fragment of ice on which she alighted pitched and creaked as her weight came on it, but she staid there not a moment. With wild cries and desperate energy she leaped to another and still another cake;—stumbling—leaping—slipping—springing upwards again! Her shoes are gone—her stockings cut from her feet—while blood marked every step; but

Chapter 20   Harriet Beecher Stowe

she saw nothing, felt nothing, till dimly, as in a dream, she saw the Ohio side, and a man helping her up the bank.

"Yer a brave gal, now, whoever ye ar!" said the man, with an oath.

Eliza recognized the voice and face of a man who owned a farm not far from her old home.

"O, Mr. Symmes!—save me—do save me—do hide me!" said Eliza.

"Why, what's this?" said the man. "Why, if 'tan't Shelby's gal!"

"My child!—this boy!—he'd sold him! There is his Mas'r," said she, pointing to the Kentucky shore. "O, Mr. Symmes, you've got a little boy!"

"So I have," said the man, as he roughly, but kindly, drew her up the steep bank. "Besides, you're a right brave gal. I like grit, wherever I see it."

When they had gained the top of the bank, the man paused.

"I'd be glad to do something for ye," said he; "but then there's nowhar I could take ye. The best I can do is to tell ye to go *thar*," said he, pointing to a large white house which stood by itself, off the main street of the village. "Go thar; they're kind folks. Thar's no kind o' danger but they'll help you,—they're up to all that sort o' thing."

"The Lord bless you!" said Eliza, earnestly.

"No 'casion, no 'casion in the world," said the man. "What I've done's of no 'count."

"And, oh, surely, sir, you won't tell any one!"

"Go to thunder, gal! What do you take a feller for? In course not," said the man. "Come, now, go along like a likely, sensible gal, as you are. You've arnt your liberty, and you shall have it, for all me."

The woman folded her child to her bosom, and walked firmly and swiftly away. The man stood and looked after her.

"Shelby, now, mebbe won't think this yer the most neighborly thing in the world; but what's a feller to do? If he catches one of my gals in the same fix, he's welcome to pay back. Somehow I never could see no kind o' critter a strivin' and pantin', and trying to clar theirselves, with the dogs arter 'em, and go agin 'em. Besides, I don't see no kind of 'casion for me to be hunter and catcher for other folks, neither."

So spoke this poor, heathenish Kentuckian, who had not been instructed in his constitutional relations, and consequently was betrayed into acting in a sort of Christianized manner, which, if he had been better situated and more enlightened, he would not have been left to do.

Haley had stood a perfectly amazed spectator of the scene, till Eliza had disappeared up the bank, when he turned a blank, inquiring look on Sam and Andy.

"That ar was a tolable fair stroke of business," said Sam.

"The gal's got seven devils in her, I believe!" said Haley. "How like a wildcat she jumped!"

"Wal, now," said Sam, scratching his head, "I hope Mas'r'll 'scuse us tryin' dat ar road. Don't think I feel spry enough for dat ar, no way!" and Sam gave a hoarse chuckle.

"*You* laugh!" said the trader, with a growl.

"Lord bless you, Mas'r, I couldn't help it, now," said Sam, giving way to the long pent-up delight of his soul. "She looked so curi's, a leapin' and springin'—ice a crackin'—and only to hear her,—plump! ker chunk! ker splash! Spring! Lord! how she goes it!" and Sam and Andy laughed till the tears rolled down their cheeks.

"I'll make ye laugh t' other side yer mouths!" said the trader, laying about their heads with his riding-whip.

Both ducked, and ran shouting up the bank, and were on their horses before he was up.

"Good-evening, Mas'r!" said Sam, with much gravity. "I berry much spect Missis be anxious 'bout Jerry. Mas'r Haley won't want us no longer. Missis wouldn't hear of our ridin' the critters over Lizy's bridge to-night;" and, with a facetious poke into Andy's ribs, he started off, followed by the latter, at full speed,—their shouts of laughter coming faintly on the wind.

Notes

1. *Uncle Tom's Cabin* was first published serially; the present chapter appeared in the *National Era* (July 10, 1851), the source of the present text. Before

this selection opens, Mr. Shelby has sold his slaves Uncle Tom and Harry, young son of Eliza, to Dan Haley, a slave trader. A devout Christian, Tom accepts his fate as best as he can, always hoping to return to his home in Kentucky. Eliza, however, flees across the Ohio River with her son.

2. Jordan: the river in Palestine over which the Jews crossed into Canaan, the land of milk and honey, after their forty-year exodus in the desert (Exodus 3: 17)
3. Aunt Chloe: Uncle Tom's wife and Shelby's cook
4. *de novo*: anew
5. catchings: referring to Dan Haley's pursuit of Eliza and Harry
6. "And when he had opened the fifth seal, I saw under the altar the souls of them that were slain for the word of God, and for the testimony which they held:" (Revelation 6: 9)
7. soul-drivers: It is a common term for clergymen, but here it apparently refers to the slave traders.
8. "…Love your enemies, bless them that curse you, do good to them that hate you, and pray for them which despitefully use you, and persecute you;" (Matthew 5: 44)
9. Although many northern sympathizers harbored runaway slaves from the South, the law strictly prohibited this practice. Therefore, the slaves fled to neutral Canada by means of the Underground Railroad, the clandestine organization of individuals whose homes were used as "stations on the escape route."

Chapter 21

Mark Twain (1835–1910)

Samuel Langhorne Clemens was born in Florida, Missouri, on November 30, 1835; his father, John Marshall Clemens, a lawyer, originating from Virginia; his mother, Jane Lampton, from Kentucky. When he was four, his family moved to Hannibal, Missouri, a small township on the Mississippi, where he continued to live until the age of eighteen.

His formal education ended soon after his father's death in 1847. The next year, he became a printer's apprentice, working for a time on the *Missouri Courier*, under the editorship of Joseph P. Ament. In 1851, he began working for the *Hannibal Journal*, a newspaper owned by his elder brother, Orion. From 1853, he traveled widely, as a journeyman printer, in the eastern states and in the West. As a result of a steamboat journey down the Mississippi, he met Horace Bixby, the captain of the boat, and turned to a career on the river. After an apprenticeship of one and a half years, he became a licensed pilot in 1859. He left the Mississippi at the outbreak of the Civil War, and became, in swift succession, an army volunteer, a gold prospector in Nevada, a timber speculator and a journalist. He met Artemus Ward and Bret Harte during this time and turned increasingly toward a professional literary career.

While working for the Virginia City *Territorial Enterprise*, he adopted the pseudonym "Mark Twain," the way of a boatman taking soundings, and meaning two fathoms, i.e. twelve feet. The choice of name may have been characteristically ironic, since two fathoms was presumably an uncomfortable depth for a large steamboat. His first book, *The Celebrated Jumping Frog of Calaveras County* appeared in 1867. Assignments as a traveling reporter to

Chapter 21 Mark Twain

the Sandwich Islands and then to the Mediterranean and Middle East brought him success as a public lecturer and also material for his first major literary success, *Innocents Abroad* (1869). He married Olivia Langdon the following year, and in 1871 established himself, as a successful writer, in a large mansion in Hartford, Connecticut. He continued to live there for the next seventeen years. It was during this period that his most famous works were written, *Roughing It* (1872), *The Gilded Age* (1873), *The Adventures of Tom Sawyer* (1876), *Life on the Mississippi* (1883), and *Adventures of Huckleberry Finn* (1884). He combined his writing with public lecturing and foreign traveling, becoming American ambassador at large, and acquiring an international reputation as humorist-frontier-philosopher.

He indulged in frequent financial speculation, particularly in typesetting machinery and the Charles L. Webster publishing house. Although his literary reputation became increasingly secure (received an M.A. of Yale in 1888), his intellectual pessimism and despair of human nature increased with his success. *The Gilded Age*, written in collaboration with Dudley Warner, had already pointed toward his uneasy acceptance of the values of nineteenth-century American society. In the year of *Pudd'nhead Wilson* (1894), he was bankrupted by the failure of both the type-setting and publishing companies, and was compelled to restart his travels to raise the money to discharge his debts. It was during his absence on this voyage that his daughter Susy died.

In 1898, the year that he cleared his debts, he wrote three works expressing his acute pessimism: *The Man That Corrupted Hadleyburg* (published 1900), the philosophizing treatise *What Is Man?* (published 1906) and *The Mysterious Stranger* (published posthumously in 1916). From this time until his death, he maintained a bitter skepticism, relieved at times by outraged commentary on world affairs, notably on Belgian atrocities in the Congo and American behavior in the Philippines.

His last years were saddened by personal bereavement, his wife dying in 1904 and his daughter Jean in 1909. In 1906 he started preparing material for his *Autobiography*, and in 1907 received an honorary doctorate of Oxford University. He died at Redding, Connecticut, on April 21, 1910, at the age of seventy-five.

The Adventures of Tom Sawyer

The Story

Tom Sawyer, a plain American boy, lives with his younger brother Sid and Aunt Polly in St. Petersburg, a remote town on the banks of the Mississippi River. Sid is a "model" boy. He is obedient, demure, and sneaky. He leads a tedious life, fully satisfied with his school and the monotony of the little town.

Tom is quite the opposite of his brother. The stifling atmosphere of the well-bred petty-bourgeois family is too close for him and he is always on the alert to do some mischief. At school he disobeys the cruel and unjust teacher, Mr. Dobbins, and busies himself with outside matters at the lessons. Tom's bosom friend is Huck Finn, a boy deserted by his drunkard of a father, and looked upon as an outcast in the town.

But Tom is not only engaged in mischiefs and tomfooleries. He has read many books and wants to make his life just as bright as it is depicted in the stories. He devises games in which the boys play the role of brave outlaws and warlike Native Americans who are the terror of the rich and the oppressors.

One night, while testing their pluck in a graveyard, the boys involuntarily witness the murder of Dr. Robinson. An innocent man is charged with the crime. But on the day of the trial Tom fearlessly exposes the real criminal, the Injun Joe who escapes through an open window of the court-room.

Fearing revenge and pursuit, the boys go through a lot of scares, but are lucky in all their enterprises. They sally out several times at night to dig for hidden treasures near a dilapidated house three miles from town. There they almost fall into the hands of the murderer who accidentally finds a box filled with gold coins.

Shortly after the incident Tom goes to a picnic with a party of schoolmates. Exploring a cave, he gets lost with Judge Thatcher's daughter, Becky. Tom behaves like a brave boy, calms Becky's fears and finds the way out of the cave.

In a few days' time Tom and Huck return to the cave. They find the dead body of their pursuer, the Injun Joe, and the hidden treasures. Although the boys become rich, they are still possessed with the idea of piracy.

Chapter XXI
Eloquence—and the Master's Gilded Dome

Vacation was approaching. The schoolmaster, always severe, grew severer and more exacting than ever, for he wanted the school to make a good showing on "Examination" day. His rod and his ferule were seldom idle now—at least among the smaller pupils. Only the biggest boys, and young ladies of eighteen and twenty escaped lashing. Mr. Dobbins's lashings were very vigorous ones, too; for although he carried, under his wig, a perfectly bald and shiny head, he had only reached middle age and there was no sign of feebleness in his muscle. As the great day approached, all the tyranny that was in him came to the surface; he seemed to take a vindictive pleasure in punishing the least shortcomings. The consequence was, that the smaller boys spent their days in terror and suffering and their nights in plotting revenge. They threw away no opportunity to do the master a mischief. But he kept ahead all the time. The retribution that followed every vengeful success was so sweeping and majestic that the boys always retired from the field badly worsted. At last they conspired together and hit upon a plan that promised a dazzling victory. They swore-in the sign-painter's boy, told him the scheme, and asked his help. He had his own reasons for being delighted, for the master boarded in his father's family and had given the boy ample cause to hate him. The master's wife would go on a visit to the country in a few days, and there would be nothing to interfere with the plan; the master always prepared himself for great occasions by getting pretty well fuddled, and the sign-painter's boy said that when the dominie had reached the proper condition on Examination Evening he would "manage the thing" while he napped in his chair; then he would have him awakened at the right time and hurried away to school.

In the fullness of time the interesting occasion arrived. At eight in the evening the schoolhouse was brilliantly lighted, and adorned with wreaths and festoons of foliage and flowers. The master sat throned in his great chair upon a raised platform, with his blackboard behind him. He was looking tolerably mellow. Three rows of benches on each side and six rows in front of him were occupied by the dignitaries of the town and by the parents of the pupils. To his left, back of the rows of citizens, was a spacious temporary platform upon which were seated the scholars who were to take part in the exercises of the evening; rows of small boys, washed and dressed to an intolerable state of discomfort; rows of gawky big boys; snow-banks of girls and young ladies clad in lawn and muslin and conspicuously conscious of their bare arms, their grandmothers' ancient trinkets, their bits of pink and blue ribbon and the flowers in their hair. All the rest of the house was filled with non-participating scholars.

The exercises began. A very little boy stood up and sheepishly recited, "You'd scarce expect one of my age to speak in public on the stage, etc."—accompanying himself with the painfully exact and spasmodic gestures which a machine might have used—supposing the machine to be a trifle out of order. But he got through safely, though cruelly scared, and got a fine round of applause when he made his manufactured bow and retired.

A little shame-faced girl lisped "Mary had little lamb, etc.," performed a compassion-inspiring curtsy, got her meed of applause, and sat down flushed and happy.

Tom Sawyer stepped forward with conceited confidence and soared into the unquenchable and indestructible "Give me liberty or give me death" speech, with fine fury and frantic gesticulation, and broke down in the middle of it. A ghastly stage-fright seized him, his legs quaked under him and he was like to choke. True, he had the manifest sympathy of the house—but he had the house's silence, too, which was even worse than its sympathy. The master frowned, and this completed the disaster. Tom struggled a while and then retired, utterly defeated. There was a weak attempt at applause, but it died early.

"The Boy Stood on the Burning Deck" followed; also "The Assyrian Came Down," and other declamatory gems. Then there were reading exercises, and a spelling fight. The meager Latin class recited with honor. The prime feature of the evening was in order, now—original "compositions" by the young ladies. Each in her turn stepped forward to the edge of the platform, cleared her throat, held up her manuscript (tied with dainty ribbon), and proceeded to read, with labored attention to "expression" and punctuation. The themes were the same that had been illuminated upon similar occasions by their mothers before them, their grandmothers, and doubtless all their ancestors in the female line clear back to the Crusades. "Friendship" was one; "Memories of Other Days"; "Religion in History"; "Dream Land"; "The Advantages of Culture"; "Forms of Political Government Compared and Contrasted"; "Melancholy"; "Filial Love"; "Heart Longings," etc., etc.

A prevalent feature in these compositions was a nursed and petted melancholy; another was a wasteful and opulent gush of "fine language"; another was a tendency to lug in by the ears particularly prized words and phrases until they were worn entirely out; and a peculiarity that conspicuously marked and marred them was the inveterate and intolerable sermon that wagged its crippled tail at the end of each and every one of them. No matter what the subject might be, a brain-racking effort was made to squirm it into some aspect or other that the moral and religious mind could contemplate with edification. The glaring insincerity of these sermons was not sufficient to compass the banishment of the fashion from the schools, and it is not sufficient to-day; it never will be sufficient while the world stands, perhaps. There is no school in all our land where the young ladies do not feel obliged to close their compositions with a sermon; and you will find that the sermon of the most frivolous and the least religious girl in the school is always the longest and the most relentlessly pious. But enough of this. Homely truth is unpalatable.

Let us return to the "Examination." The first composition that was read was one entitled "Is this, then, Life?" Perhaps the reader can endure an extract from it:

> *In the common walks of life, with what delightful emotions does the youthful mind look forward to some anticipated scene of festivity! Imagination is busy sketching rose-tinted pictures of joy. In fancy, the voluptuous votary of fashion sees herself amid the festive throng, "the observed of all observers." Her graceful form, arrayed in snowy robes, is whirling through the mazes of the joyous dance; her eye is brightest, her step is lightest in the gay assembly.*

> *In such delicious fancies time quickly glides by, and the welcome hour arrives for her entrance into the elysian world, of which she has had such bright dreams. How fairy-like does everything appear to her enchanted vision! Each new scene is more charming than the last. But after a while she finds that beneath this goodly exterior, all is vanity: the flattery which once charmed her soul, now grates harshly upon her ear; the ball-room has lost its charms; and with wasted health and imbittered heart, she turns away with the conviction that earthly pleasures cannot satisfy the longings of the soul!*

And so forth and so on. There was a buzz of gratification from time to time during the reading, accompanied by whispered ejaculations of "How sweet!" "How eloquent!" "So true!" etc., and after the thing had closed with a peculiarly afflicting sermon the applause was enthusiastic.

Then arose a slim, melancholy girl, whose face had the "interesting" paleness that comes of pills and indigestion, and read a "poem." Two stanzas of it will do:

A Missouri Maiden's Farewell to Alabama

> Alabama, good-bye! I love thee well!
> But yet for a while do I leave thee now!
> Sad, yes, sad thoughts of thee my heart doth swell,
> And burning recollections throng my brow!
> For I have wandered through thy flowery woods;
> Have roamed and read near Tallapoosa's stream;
> Have listened to Tallassee's warring floods,
> And wooed on Coosa's side Aurora's beam.
>
> Yet shame I not to bear an o'er-full heart,
> Nor blush to turn behind my tearful eyes;
> 'Tis from no stranger land I now must part,
> 'Tis to no strangers left I yield these sighs.

Chapter 21   Mark Twain

Welcome and home were mine within this State,
Whose vales I leave—whose spires fade fast from me;
And cold must be mine eyes, and heart, and tête,
When, dear Alabama! they turn cold on thee!

There were very few there who knew what "tête" meant, but the poem was very satisfactory, nevertheless.

Next appeared a dark-complexioned, black-eyed, black-haired young lady, who paused an impressive moment, assumed a tragic expression, and began to read in a measured, solemn tone.

A Vision

Dark and tempestuous was night. Around the throne on high not a single star quivered; but the deep intonations of the heavy thunder constantly vibrated upon the ear; whilst the terrific lightning revelled in angry mood through the cloudy chambers of heaven, seeming to scorn the power exerted over its terror by the illustrious Franklin! Even the boisterous winds unanimously came forth from their mystic homes, and blustered about as if to enhance by their aid the wildness of the scene.

At such a time, so dark, so dreary, for human sympathy my very spirit sighed; but instead thereof,

"My dearest friend, my counsellor, my comforter and guide—My joy in grief, my second bliss in joy," came to my side.

She moved like one of those bright beings pictured in the sunny walks of fancy's Eden by the romantic and young, a queen of beauty unadorned save by her own transcendent loveliness. So soft was her step, it failed to make even a sound, and but for the magical thrill imparted by her genial touch, as other unobtrusive beauties, she would have glided away unperceived—unsought. A strange sadness rested upon her features, like icy tears upon the robe of December, as she pointed to the contending elements without, and bade me contemplate the two beings presented.

This nightmare occupied some ten pages of manuscript and wound up with a sermon so destructive of all hope to non-Presbyterians that it took the first prize. This composition was considered to be the very finest effort of the evening. The mayor of the village, in delivering the prize to the author of it, made a warm speech in which he said that it was by far the most "eloquent" thing he had ever listened to, and that Daniel Webster himself might well be proud of it.

It may be remarked, in passing, that the number of compositions in which the word "beauteous" was over-fondled, and human experience referred to as "life's page," was up to the usual average.

Now the master, mellow almost to the verge of geniality, put his chair aside, turned his back to the audience, and began to draw a map of America on the blackboard, to exercise the geography class upon. But he made a sad business of it with his unsteady hand, and a smothered titter rippled over the house. He knew what the matter was and set himself to right it. He sponged out lines and remade them; but he only distorted them more than ever, and the tittering was more pronounced. He threw his entire attention upon his work, now, as if determined not to be put down by the mirth. He felt that all eyes were fastened upon him; he imagined he was succeeding, and yet the tittering continued; it even manifestly increased. And well it might. There was a garret above, pierced with a scuttle over his head; and down through this scuttle came a cat, suspended around the haunches by a string; she had a rag tied about her head and jaws to keep her from mewing; as she slowly descended she curved upward and clawed at the string, she swung downward and clawed at the intangible air. The tittering rose higher and higher—the cat was within six inches of the absorbed teacher's head—down, down, a little lower, and she grabbed his wig with her desperate claws, clung to it, and was snatched up into the garret in an instant with her trophy still in her possession! And how the light did blaze abroad from the master's bald pate—

for the sign-painter's boy had *gilded* it!

That broke up the meeting. The boys were avenged. Vacation had come.

Chapter XXII
Huck Finn Quotes Scripture

Tom joined the new order of Cadets of Temperance, being attracted by the showy character of their "regalia." He promised to abstain from smoking, chewing, and profanity as long as he remained a member. Now he found out a new thing—namely, that to promise not to do a thing is the surest way in the world to make a body want to go and do that very thing. Tom soon found himself tormented with a desire to drink and swear; the desire grew to be so intense that nothing but the hope of a chance to display himself in his red sash kept him from withdrawing from the order. Fourth of July was coming; but he soon gave that up—gave it up before he had worn his shackles over forty-eight hours—and fixed his hopes upon old Judge Frazer, justice of the peace, who was apparently on his deathbed and would have a big public funeral, since he was so high an official. During three days Tom was deeply concerned about the Judge's condition and hungry for news of it. Sometimes his hopes ran high—so high that he would venture to get out his regalia and practice before the looking-glass. But the Judge had a most discouraging way of fluctuating. At last he was pronounced upon the mend—and then convalescent. Tom was disgusted; and felt a sense of injury, too. He handed in his resignation at once—and that night the Judge suffered a relapse and died. Tom resolved that he would never trust a man like that again.

The funeral was a fine thing. The Cadets paraded in a style calculated to kill the late member with envy. Tom was a free boy again, however—there was something in that. He could drink and swear, now—but found to his surprise that he did not want to. The simple fact that he could, took the desire away, and the charm of it.

Tom presently wondered to find that his coveted vacation was beginning to hang a little heavily on his hands.

He attempted a diary—but nothing happened during three days, and so he abandoned it.

The first of all the negro minstrel shows came to town, and made a sensation. Tom and Joe Harper got up a band of performers and were happy for two days.

Even the Glorious Fourth was in some sense a failure, for it rained hard, there was no procession in consequence, and the greatest man in the world (as Tom supposed), Mr. Benton, an actual United States Senator, proved an overwhelming disappointment—for he was not twenty-five feet high, nor even anywhere in the neighborhood of it.

A circus came. The boys played circus for three days afterward in tents made of rag carpeting—admission, three pins for boys, two for girls—and then circusing was abandoned.

A phrenologist and a mesmerizer came—and went again and left the village duller and drearier than ever.

There were some boys-and-girls' parties, but they were so few and so delightful that they only made the aching voids between ache the harder.

Becky Thatcher was gone to her Constantinople home to stay with her parents during vacation—so there was no bright side to life anywhere.

The dreadful secret of the murder was a chronic misery. It was a very cancer for permanency and pain.

Then came the measles.

During two long weeks Tom lay a prisoner, dead to the world and its happenings. He was very ill, he was interested in nothing. When he got upon his feet at last and moved feebly down town, a melancholy change had come over everything and every creature. There had been a "revival," and everybody had "got religion," not only the adults, but even the boys and girls. Tom went about, hoping against hope for the sight of one blessed sinful face, but disappointment crossed him everywhere. He found Joe Harper studying a Testament, and turned sadly away from the depressing spectacle. He sought Ben Rogers, and found him visiting the poor with a basket of tracts. He hunted up Jim Hollis, who called his attention to the precious blessing of his late measles as a warning. Every boy he encountered added another ton to his depression; and when, in desperation, he flew for refuge at last to the bosom of Huckleberry Finn and was received with a Scriptural quotation, his heart broke and he crept home and to bed realizing that he alone of all the town was lost, forever and forever.

And that night there came on a terrific storm, with driving rain, awful claps of thunder and blinding sheets of lightning. He covered his head with the bedclothes and waited in a horror of suspense for his doom; for he had not the shadow of a doubt that all this hubbub was about him. He believed he had taxed the forbearance of the powers above to the extremity of endurance and that this was the result. It might have seemed to him a waste of pomp and ammunition to kill a bug with a battery of artillery, but there seemed nothing incongruous about the getting up such an expensive thunderstorm as this to knock the turf from under an insect like himself.

By and by the tempest spent itself and died without accomplishing its object. The boy's first impulse was to be grateful, and reform. His second was to wait—for there might not be any more storms.

The next day the doctors were back; Tom had relapsed. The three weeks he spent on his back this time seemed an entire age. When he got abroad at last he was hardly grateful that he had been spared, remembering how lonely was his estate, how companionless and forlorn he was. He drifted listlessly down the street and found Jim Hollis acting as judge in a juvenile court that was trying a cat for murder, in the presence of her victim, a bird. He found Joe Harper and Huck Finn up an alley eating a stolen melon. Poor lads! They—like Tom—had suffered a relapse.

Chapter 22

O. Henry (1862–1910)

William Sidney Porter, whose pen name was O. Henry, was born in North Carolina, in 1862. His father was a doctor and an editor, and his mother sometimes wrote poetry. He got little education, but he was much entertained as a boy by his maiden aunt who taught him a little, but read stories to him much. Sometimes the teacher and a group of youngsters would start a game of storytelling; one began a story, the next person would take it up and add a little, then a third went on with it. Young O. Henry's part was always interesting.

When he was twenty years old he went to Texas, a land of ranches and cowboys, flocks of sheep and herds of cattle. He was fond of country life, and loved to hear the birds sing and the brooks babble. He was a good singer and belonged to a quartette which sang regularly in the churches of Austin, Texas. He worked in a drug store for some time and then in a bank. He was always careful in his work and was successful as a business employee.

But he longed for more independence and so together with a friend bought a newspaper and they published the news of the week in humorous fashion, and also short sketches, drawings, and verse. It was from this time that he began his career as a writer. He wrote stories for different magazines, and when there came a big demand for his stories, the publishers of *Ainslee's Magazine* invited him to come to New York and guaranteed him a fixed income of twelve hundred dollars a year. This seemed a big sum to him then but later he made as much as that in a week. He made a contract with the *New York World* to write a story a week, and in addition to that he wrote stories for other magazines. He received from one hundred to three hundred dollars for

Chapter 22 O. Henry

each story. It was not easy work for him to write so many stories, as he was always conscientious and painstaking to write the best he could.

He was very sociable and friendly, especially with children and poor people, and even with tramps and thieves. He would often walk and talk at all hours of the night with such people and invite them into a restaurant with him to drink coffee. Many of his stories tell about the lives of poor people in New York, as well as in other places. The title of one of his books, *The Four Million*, indicates that he considered all the people of New York City worth writing about, and not simply the upper "Four Hundred." He sympathized with their lot and hated those rich who exploited and despised them. This is especially seen in his "An Unfinished Story."

It is said that O. Henry imitated Guy de Maupassant as a model. There is much in common between these two writers. Both are gifted with a clear style and a keen observation of details, and both write about people in the poorer walks of life. But O. Henry's outlook upon life was not involved in such bitter gloom as the Frenchman's, and his works abound in good-natured humor.

His stories are usually short. The plots are exceedingly clever and interesting; humor abounds, and the end is always surprising. Often there are two endings: first an unexpected ending, then another, which is quite a different one and a still better surprise. Many of his stories contain a great deal of slang and colloquial expressions that make them hard to be understood by people outside of America. Such forms of speech are used to give what is called local color, to make the stories fit in with the characters and scenes described. O. Henry's own speech, both spoken and written, is always chaste and clear.

His own estimate of himself was always a very modest one, and he was shy and retiring in the presence of friends, yet his fame, which was great in his lifetime, so that over a million volumes of his stories were sold in America alone, is destined to become more widespread.

It is hard to tell which are his best stories, as different writers have such different opinions. Nearly every story he writes grips the attention and interest from the beginning, and all are wholesome reading. Probably his best volume is *The Four Million*, and some of his best individual stories are "A Retrieved

Reformation," "The Gift of the Magi," "A Municipal Report," "An Unfinished Story," "Phoebe," "A Lickpenny Lover," and "The Furnished Room."

The Cop and the Anthem

On his bench in Madison Square Soapy moved uneasily. When wild geese honk high of nights, and when women without sealskin coats grow kind to their husbands, and when Soapy moves uneasily on his bench in the park, you may know that winter is near at hand.

A dead leaf fell in Soapy's lap. That was Jack Frost's card. Jack is kind to the regular denizens[1] of Madison Square, and gives fair warning of his annual call. At the corners of four streets he hands his pasteboard to the North Wind, footman of the mansion of All Outdoors, so that the inhabitants thereof may make ready.

Soapy's mind became cognizant of the fact that the time had come for him to resolve himself into a singular Committee of Ways and Means to provide against the coming rigor. And therefore he moved uneasily on his bench.

The hibernatorial[2] ambitions of Soapy were not of the highest. In them were no considerations of Mediterranean cruises, of soporific[3] Southern skies or drifting in the Vesuvian Bay. Three months on the Island[4] was what his soul craved. Three months of assured board and bed and congenial company, safe from Boreas[5] and bluecoats, seemed to Soapy the essence of things desirable.

For years the hospitable Blackwell's had been his winter quarters. Just as his more fortunate fellow New Yorkers had bought their tickets to Palm Beach and the Riviera each winter, so Soapy had made his humble arrangements for his annual hegira[6] to the Island. And now the time was come. On the previous night three Sabbath newspapers, distributed beneath his coat, about his ankles and over his lap, had failed to repulse the cold as he slept on his bench near the spurting fountain in the ancient square. So the Island loomed big and timely in Soapy's mind. He scorned the provisions made in the name of charity for the city's dependents. In Soapy's opinion the Law was more benign than Philanthropy. There was an endless round of institutions, municipal and eleemosynary[7], on which he might set out and receive lodging and food accordant with the simple life. But to one of Soapy's proud spirit the gifts of charity are encumbered. If not in coin you must pay in humiliation of spirit for every benefit received at the hands of philanthropy. As Caesar had his Brutus, every bed of charity must have its toll of a bath, every loaf of bread its compensation of a private and personal inquisition. Wherefore it is better to be a guest of the law, which, though conducted by rules, does not meddle unduly with a gentleman's private affairs.

Soapy, having decided to go to the Island, at once set about accomplishing his desire. There were many easy ways of doing this. The pleasantest was to dine luxuriously at some expensive restaurant; and then, after declaring insolvency, be handed over quietly and without uproar to a policeman. An accommodating magistrate would do the rest.

Soapy left his bench and strolled out of the square and across the level sea of asphalt, where Broadway and Fifth Avenue flow together. Up Broadway he turned, and halted at a glittering café, where are gathered together nightly the choicest products of the grape, the silkworm, and the protoplasm[8].

Soapy had confidence in himself from the lowest button of his vest upward. He was shaven, and his coat was decent and his neat black, ready-tied four-in-hand had been presented to him by a lady missionary on Thanksgiving Day. If he could reach a table in the restaurant unsuspected success would be his. The portion of him that would show above the table would raise no doubt in the waiter's mind. A roasted mallard duck, thought Soapy, would be about the thing—with a bottle of Chablis[9], and then Camembert[10], a demi-tasse[11] and a cigar. One dollar for the cigar would be enough. The total would not be so high as to call forth any supreme manifestation of revenge from the café management; and yet the meat would leave him filled and happy for the journey to his winter refuge.

But as Soapy set foot inside the restaurant door the head waiter's eye fell upon his frayed trousers and decadent shoes. Strong and ready hands turned him about and conveyed him in silence and haste to the sidewalk and averted the ignoble fate of the menaced mallard.

Soapy turned off Broadway. It seemed that his route to the coveted Island was not to be an epicurean one. Some other way of entering limbo must be thought of.

At a corner of Sixth Avenue electric lights and cunningly displayed wares behind plate-glass made a shop window conspicuous. Soapy took a cobblestone and dashed it through the glass. People came running around the corner, a policeman in the lead. Soapy stood still, with his hands in his pockets, and smiled at the sight of brass buttons.

"Where's the man that done that?" inquired the officer excitedly.

"Don't you figure out that I might have had something to do with it?" said Soapy, not without sarcasm, but friendly, as one greets good fortune.

The policeman's mind refused to accept Soapy even as a clue. Men who smash windows do not remain to parley with the law's minions. They take to their heels. The policeman saw a man halfway down the block running to catch a car. With drawn club he joined in the pursuit. Soapy, with disgust in his heart, loafed along, twice unsuccessful.

On the opposite side of the street was a restaurant of no great pretensions. It catered to large appetites and modest purses. Its crockery and atmosphere were thick; its soup and napery thin. Into this place Soapy took his accusive[12] shoes and tell-tale trousers without challenge. At a table he sat and consumed beefsteak, flapjacks, doughnuts and pie. And then to the waiter he betrayed the fact that the minutest coin and himself were strangers.

"Now, get busy and call a cop," said Soapy. "And don't keep a gentleman waiting."

"No cop for youse," said the waiter, with a voice like butter cakes and an eye like the cherry in a Manhattan cocktail. "Hey, Con!"

Neatly upon his left ear on the callous pavement two waiters pitched Soapy. He arose, joint by joint, as a carpenter's rule opens, and beat the dust from his clothes. Arrest seemed but a rosy dream. The Island seemed very far away. A policeman who stood before a drug store two doors away laughed and walked down the street.

Five blocks Soapy travelled before his courage permitted him to woo capture again. This time the opportunity presented what he fatuously termed to himself a "cinch." A young woman of a modest and pleasing guise was standing before a show window gazing with sprightly interest at its display of shaving mugs and inkstands, and two yards from the window a large policeman of severe demeanor leaned against a water-plug.

It was Soapy's design to assume the role of the despicable and execrated "masher." The refined and elegant appearance of his victim and the contiguity of the conscientious cop encouraged him to believe that he would soon feel the pleasant official clutch upon his arm that would insure his winter quarters on the right little, tight little isle.

Soapy straightened the lady missionary's ready-made tie, dragged his shrinking cuffs into the open, set his hat at a killing cant and sidled toward the young woman. He made eyes at her, was taken with sudden coughs and "hems," smiled, smirked and went brazenly through the impudent and contemptible litany of the "masher." With half an eye Soapy saw that the policeman was watching him fixedly. The young woman moved away a few steps, and again bestowed her absorbed attention upon the shaving mugs. Soapy followed, boldly stepping to her side, raised his hat and said:

"Ah there, Bedelia! Don't you want to come and play in my yard?"

The policeman was still looking. The persecuted young woman had but to beckon a finger and Soapy would be practically *en route* for his insular haven. Already he imagined he could feel the cozy warmth of the station-house. The young woman faced him and, stretching out a hand, caught Soapy's coat sleeve.

"Sure, Mike," she said joyfully, "if you'll blow me to a pail of suds. I'd have spoke to you sooner, but the cop was watching."

With the young woman playing the clinging ivy to his oak Soapy walked past the policeman, overcome with gloom. He seemed doomed to liberty.

At the next corner he shook off his companion and ran. He halted in the district where by night are found the lightest streets, hearts, vows, and librettos. Women in furs and men in greatcoats moved gaily in the wintry air. A sudden fear seized Soapy that some dreadful enchantment had rendered him immune to arrest. The thought brought a little of panic upon it, and when he came upon another policeman lounging grandly in front of a transplendent[13] theatre, he caught at the immediate straw of "disorderly conduct."

On the sidewalk Soapy began to yell drunken gibberish at the top of his harsh voice. He danced, howled, raved, and otherwise disturbed the welkin[14].

The policeman twirled his club, turned his back to Soapy and remarked to a citizen:

"'Tis one of them Yale lads celebratin' the goose egg they give to the Hartford College. Noisy; but no harm. We've instructions to lave them be."

Disconsolate, Soapy ceased his unavailing racket. Would never a policeman lay hands on him? In his fancy the Island seemed an unattainable Arcadia[15]. He buttoned his thin coat against the chilling wind.

In a cigar store he saw a well-dressed man lighting a cigar at a swinging light. His silk umbrella he had set by the door on entering. Soapy stepped inside, secured the umbrella and sauntered off with it slowly. The man at the cigar light followed hastily.

"My umbrella," he said, sternly.

"Oh, is it?" sneered Soapy, adding insult to petit larceny. "Well, why don't you call a policeman? I took it. Your umbrella! Why don't you call a cop? There stands one on the corner."

The umbrella owner slowed his steps. Soapy did likewise, with a presentiment that luck would again run against him. The policeman looked at the two curiously.

"Of course," said the umbrella man—"that is—well, you know how these mistakes occur—I—if it's your umbrella I hope you'll excuse me—I picked it up this morning in a restaurant—if you recognize it as yours, why—I hope you'll—"

"Of course it's mine," said Soapy, viciously.

The ex-umbrella man retreated. The policeman hurried to assist a tall blonde in an opera cloak across the street in front of a street car that was approaching two blocks away.

Soapy walked eastward through a street damaged by improvements. He hurled the umbrella wrathfully into an excavation. He muttered against the men who wear helmets and carry clubs. Because he wanted to fall into their clutches, they seemed to regard him as a king who could do no wrong.

Chapter 22 O. Henry

At length Soapy reached one of the avenues to the east where the glitter and turmoil was but faint. He set his face down this toward Madison Square, for the homing instinct survives even when the home is a park bench.

But on an unusually quiet corner Soapy came to a standstill. Here was an old church, quaint and rambling and gabled. Through one violet-stained window a soft light glowed, where, no doubt, the organist loitered over the keys, making sure of his mastery of the coming Sabbath anthem. For there drifted out to Soapy's ears sweet music that caught and held him transfixed against the convolutions of the iron fence.

The moon was above, lustrous and serene; vehicles and pedestrians were few; sparrows twittered sleepily in the eaves—for a little while the scene might have been a country churchyard. And the anthem that the organist played cemented Soapy to the iron fence, for he had known it well in the days when his life contained such things as mothers and roses and ambitions and friends and immaculate thoughts and collars.

The conjunction of Soapy's receptive state of mind and the influences about the old church wrought a sudden and wonderful change in his soul. He viewed with swift horror the pit into which he had tumbled, the degraded days, unworthy desires, dead hopes, wrecked faculties and base motives that made up his existence.

And also in a moment his heart responded thrillingly to this novel mood. An instantaneous and strong impulse moved him to battle with his desperate fate. He would pull himself out of the mire; he would make a man of himself again; he would conquer the evil that had taken possession of him. There was time; he was comparatively young yet; he would resurrect his old eager ambitions and pursue them without faltering. Those solemn but sweet organ notes had set up a revolution in him. To-morrow he would go into the roaring down-town district and find work. A fur importer had once offered him a place as driver. He would find him to-morrow and ask for the position. He would be somebody in the world. He would—

Soapy felt a hand laid on his arm. He looked quickly around into the broad face of a policeman.

"What are you doin' here?" asked the officer.

"Nothin'," said Soapy.

"Then come along," said the policeman.

"Three months on the Island," said the Magistrate in the Police Court the next morning.

Notes
1. denizens: inhabitants
2. hibernatorial: pertaining to hibernation, wintering in close quarters
3. soporific: causing sleep
4. the Island: Blackwell's Island in the East River was once the site of a workhouse. It is now called Welfare Island.
5. Boreas: in Greek mythology, the personification of the north wind
6. hegira: the flight of Mohammed from Mecca; used here to indicate any similar flight
7. eleemosynary: charitable
8. protoplasm: the substance of animal and plant cells; here, generally, flesh and blood
9. Chablis: a white French wine
10. Camembert: a soft cheese originally made in France
11. demi-tasse: a small cup of black coffee
12. accusive: coined by O. Henry, meaning containing or expressing accusation
13. transplendent: brilliantly luxurious; another O. Henry coinage
14. welkin: sky, air
15. Arcadia: an imaginary ideal place

Chapter 23
Henry James (1843–1916)

Henry James was born in New York City, the second child of wealthy, somewhat aristocratic parents. His father, Henry James, Sr., was a philosopher and a friend of Emerson's; his brother William became a prominent philosopher and psychologist. Henry James, Sr., disapproved of most schools and, consequently, sent his sons to a variety of tutors and European schools in search of the best education for them. The children received the major part of their education at home, however, in lively conversations with their father and other children. The James family's travels in Europe were another source of education for Henry.

When he was growing up in New York, Henry was given a great deal of independence, so much in fact, that he felt isolated from other people. A quiet child among exuberant brothers and cousins, Henry was more often an observer than a participant in their activities. Henry's family lived for a time in Boston, where he became acquainted with New England authors and friends of his father, began his friendship with William Dean Howells, and attended Harvard Law School. After 1866, James lived in Europe much of the time and in 1875 decided to make it his permanent home. He lived in Paris for a year, where he met Turgenev, Flaubert, and Zola. The next year he settled in London and lived there and in the English countryside for the rest of his life. In 1915, a year before his death, to show his support for England in World War I, James became a British citizen.

In 1871 *The Atlantic* serialized James' first novel, *Watch and Ward*, with which he hoped, but failed, to achieve fame. Years later, looking back and finding such early works "hideous," James preferred to declare that his first real novel was *Roderick Hudson* (1875). The next decade saw the appearance of novels that brought him popular success: *The American* (1877), with its "international" theme of the traditionless American confronting the complexity of European life; *Daisy Miller* (1878), which one American critic described as "an outrage to American girlhood" but which brought James his first international fame; and *The Portrait of a Lady* (1881), the finest example of James' early work.

The most ambitious novels of James' second period, *The Bostonians* (1886), *The Princess Casamassima* (1886), and *The Tragic Muse* (1890), were public failures as were his attempts, in the 1890s, to write for the stage. But he continued to write short stories and novels, and while James never recovered his early popularity, his last, full-length novels, *The Wings of the Dove* (1902), *The Ambassadors* (1903), and *The Golden Bowl* (1904), exemplify the mature and formidable style of a third literary period, which critics have come to praise as "The Major Phase."

Unlike Howells, James' greatest influence was exerted not on his own age but on the one that followed. At the time of his death, James' audience was small, his impact slight. He had been attacked for criticizing his native land and for the narrow emotional and social range of his characters. And he had been ridiculed for the obscure and costive style of his final period, a style that was able to express the subtlest meanings but was based on the assumption that the reader was as well educated, as exquisitely attuned, and in as little hurry as the author. James' latest works were derided as "cathedrals of frosted glass," and at the end of his life he acknowledged that his writing had become "insurmountably unsaleable." Yet his influence has come to be immense. In twenty-two novels and over a hundred short stories, and in his critical commentaries, he made major contributions to the art of fiction itself, helping to transform the novel from its alliances with journalism and romantic storytelling into an art form of penetrating analysis of individuals confronting society, chronicles of the psychological perceptions that James himself defined as the highest form of experience.

Chapter 23   Henry James

The Portrait of a Lady

The Story

Isabel Archer, upon the death of her father, had been visited by her aunt, Mrs. Touchett. She proved so attractive to the older woman that Mrs. Touchett decided to give her the advantage of more cosmopolitan experience, and Isabel was quickly carried off to Europe so she might see something of the world of culture and fashion.

On the day the women arrived at the Touchett home in England, Isabel's sickly young cousin, Ralph Touchett, and his father were taking tea in the garden with their friend, Lord Warburton. When Isabel appeared, Warburton had been confessing to the two men his boredom and his distaste for his routine existence. The young nobleman was much taken with the American girl's grace and lively manner.

Isabel had barely settled at Gardencourt, her aunt's home, before she received a letter from an American friend, Henrietta Stackpole, a newspaper woman who was writing a series of articles on the sights of Europe. At Ralph's invitation, Henrietta went to Gardencourt to spend some time with Isabel and to obtain material for her writing.

Soon after Henrietta's arrival, Isabel heard from another American friend. Caspar Goodwood, a would-be suitor, had followed her abroad. Learning her whereabouts from Henrietta, he wrote to ask if he might see her. Isabel was much irked by his aggressiveness, and she decided not to answer his letter.

On the day she received the letter from Goodwood, Lord Warburton proposed to her. Not wishing to seem indifferent to the honor of his proposal, she asked for time to consider it. At last she decided she could not marry the young Englishman, for she wished to see considerably more of the world before she married. She was afraid that marriage to Warburton, although he was a model of kindness and thoughtfulness, would prove stifling.

Because Isabel had not seen London on her journey with Mrs. Touchett and since it was on Henrietta Stackpole's itinerary, the two young women, accompanied by Ralph Touchett, went to the capital. Henrietta quickly made the acquaintance of a Mr. Bantling, who undertook to squire her around. When Caspar Goodwood visited Isabel at her hotel, she again refused him, though his persistence made her agree that if he still wished to ask for her hand he might visit her again after two years had passed.

While the party was in London a telegram came from Gardencourt. Old Mr. Touchett was seriously ill of the gout, and his wife was much alarmed. Isabel and Ralph left on the afternoon train. Henrietta remained under the escort of her new friend.

During the time Mr. Touchett lay dying and his family was preoccupied, Isabel was forced to amuse herself with a new companion. Madame Merle, an old friend of Mrs. Touchett, had come to Gardencourt to spend a few days. She and Isabel thrown together a great deal, exchanged many confidences. Isabel admired the older woman for her ability to amuse herself, for her skill at needlework, at painting, at the piano, and for her ability to accommodate herself to any social situation. On the other hand, Madame Merle spoke enviously of Isabel's youth and intelligence, lamenting the life which had left her, at middle age, a widow with no children and no visible success in life.

When her uncle died, he left Isabel, at her cousin's instigation, one-half of his fortune. Ralph, greatly impressed with his young kinswoman's brilliance, had persuaded his father that she should be given an opportunity to fly as far and as high as she might. For himself, he knew he could not live long because of his pulmonary illness, and his legacy was enough to let him live in comfort.

As quickly as she could, Mrs. Touchett sold her London house and took Isabel to Paris with her. Ralph went south for the winter to preserve what was left of his health. In Paris the new heiress was introduced to many of her aunt's friends among American expatriates, but she was not impressed. She thought their indolent lives worthy only of contempt. Meanwhile Henrietta and Mr. Bantling had arrived in Paris, and Isabel spent much time with them and Edward Rosier. She had known Rosier when both were children and she was traveling abroad with her father. Rosier was another dilettante, living on the income from his inheritance. He explained to Isabel that he could not return to his own country because there was no occupation there worthy of a gentleman.

Chapter 23 Henry James

In February Mrs. Touchett and her niece went to the Palazzo Crescentini, the Touchett house in Florence. They stopped on the way to see Ralph, who was staying in San Remo. In Florence they were joined once more by Madame Merle.

Unknown to Isabel or her aunt, Madame Merle also visited her friend, Gilbert Osmond, another American who lived in voluntary exile outside Florence with his art collection and his young, convent-bred daughter, Pansy. Madame Merle told Osmond of Isabel's arrival in Florence saying that as the heir to a fortune, Isabel would be a valuable addition to Osmond's collection.

The heiress who had rejected two worthy suitors did not refuse the third. She was quickly captivated by the charm of the sheltered life Gilbert Osmond had created for himself. Her friends were against the match. Henrietta Stackpole, who was inclined to favor Caspar Goodwood, was convinced that Osmond was interested only in Isabel's money, as was Isabel's aunt. Mrs. Touchett had requested Madame Merle, the good friend of both parties, to discover the state of their affections; she was convinced that Madame Merle could have prevented the match. Ralph Touchett was disappointed that his cousin should have fallen to the ground from her flight so quickly. Caspar Goodwood, learning of Isabel's intended marriage when he revisited, persuaded her to reconsider her step. Isabel was indignant when commented on the fact that she did not even know her intended husband's antecedents.

After her marriage to Gilbert Osmond, Isabel and her husband established their home in Rome, in a setting completely expressive of Osmond's tastes. Before three years had passed, Isabel began to realize that her friends had not been completely wrong in their objections to her marriage. Osmond's exquisite taste had made their home one of the most popular in Rome, but his ceaseless effort to press his wife into a mold to make her a reflection of his own ideas, had not made their marriage one of the happiest.

He had succeeded in destroying a romance between Pansy and Edward Rosier, who had visited the girl's step-mother and found the daughter attractive. He had not succeeded, however, in contracting the match he desired between Pansy and Lord Warburton. Warburton had found Pansy as pleasing as Isabel had once been, but he had dropped his suit when he saw that the girl's affections lay with Rosier.

Ralph Touchett, his health growing steadily worse, gave up his wanderings on the Continent and returned to Gardencourt to die. When Isabel received a telegram from his mother telling her before his death, she felt it her duty to go to Gardencourt at once. Osmond reacted to her wish as if it were a personal insult. He expected that, as his wife, Isabel would want to remain at his side, and that she would not disobey the wish of his. He also made it plain that he disliked Ralph.

In a state of turmoil after her conversation with her husband, Isabel met the Countess Gemini, Osmond's sister. The countess, visiting the Osmonds, had seen how matters lay between her brother and Isabel. An honest soul, she had felt more sympathy for her sister-in-law than for her brother. To comfort Isabel, she told her the story of Gilbert's past. After his first wife had died, he and Madame Merle had an affair that lasted six or seven years. During that time Madame Merle, a widow, had borne him a child, Pansy. Changing his residence, Osmond had been able to pretend to his new circle of friends that the original Mrs. Osmond had died in giving birth to the child.

With this news fresh in her mind, and still determined to go to England, Isabel stopped to say goodbye to Pansy, who was staying in a convent where her father had sent her to recuperate from her affair with Rosier. There, too, she met Madame Merle. Madame Merle, with her keen perception, had no difficulty realizing that Isabel knew her secret. When she remarked that Isabel would never need to see her again, that she would go to America, Isabel was certain Madame Merle would also find in America much to her own advantage.

Isabel was in time to see her cousin before his death. She stayed on briefly at Gardencourt after the funeral, long enough to bid goodbye to Lord Warburton, who had come to offer condolences to her aunt, and to reject a third offer from Caspar Goodwood, who knew of her husband's treatment. When she left to start her journey back to Italy, Isabel knew what she must do. Her first duty was not to herself, but to put her house in order.

Chapter VI

Isabel Archer was a young person of many theories; her imagination was remarkably active. It had been her fortune to possess a finer mind than most of the persons among whom her lot was cast; to have a larger perception of surrounding facts and to care for knowledge that was tinged with the unfamiliar. It is true that among her contemporaries she passed for a young woman of extraordinary profundity; for these excellent people never withheld their admiration from a reach of intellect of which they themselves were not conscious, and spoke of Isabel as a prodigy of learning, a creature reported to have read the classic authors—in translations. Her paternal aunt, Mrs. Varian, once spread the rumour that Isabel was writing a book—Mrs. Varian having a reverence for books, and averred that the girl would distinguish herself in print. Mrs. Varian thought highly of literature, for which she entertained that esteem that is connected with a sense of privation. Her own large house, remarkable for its assortment of mosaic tables and decorated ceilings, was unfurnished with a library, and in the way of printed volumes contained nothing but half a dozen novels in paper on a shelf in the apartment of one of the Miss Varians. Practically, Mrs. Varian's acquaintance with literature was confined to *The New York Interviewer*; as she very justly said, after you had read the *Interviewer* you had lost all faith in culture. Her tendency, with this, was rather to keep the *Interviewer* out of the way of her daughters; she was determined to bring them up properly, and they read nothing at all. Her impression with regard to Isabel's labours was quite illusory; the girl had never attempted to write a book and had no desire for the laurels of authorship. She had no talent for expression and too little of the consciousness of genius; she only had a general idea that people were right when they treated her as if she were rather superior. Whether or no she were superior, people were right in admiring her if they thought her so; for it seemed to her often that her mind moved more quickly than theirs, and this encouraged an impatience that might easily be confounded with superiority. It may be affirmed without delay that Isabel was probably very liable to the sin of self-esteem; she often surveyed with complacency the field of her own nature; she was in the habit of taking for granted, on scanty evidence, that she was right; she treated herself to occasions of homage. Meanwhile her errors and delusions were frequently such as a biographer interested in preserving the dignity of his subject must shrink from specifying. Her thoughts were a tangle of vague outlines which had never been corrected by the judgement of people speaking with authority. In matters of opinion she had had her own way, and it had led her into a thousand ridiculous zigzags. At moments she discovered she was grotesquely wrong, and then she treated herself to a week of passionate humility. After this she held her head higher than ever again; for it was of no use, she had an unquenchable desire to think well of herself. She had a theory that it was only under this provision life was worth living; that one should be one of the best, should be conscious of a fine organisation (she couldn't help knowing her organisation was fine), should move in a realm of light, of natural wisdom, of happy impulse, of inspiration gracefully chronic. It was almost as unnecessary to cultivate doubt of one's self as to cultivate doubt of one's best friend: one should try to be one's own best friend and to give one's self, in this manner, distinguished company. The girl had a certain nobleness of imagination which rendered her a good many services and played her a great many tricks. She spent half her time in thinking of beauty and bravery and magnanimity; she had a fixed determination to regard the world as a place of brightness, of free expansion, of irresistible action: she held it must be detestable to be afraid or ashamed. She had an infinite hope that she should never do anything wrong. She had resented so strongly, after discovering them, her mere errors of feeling (the discovery always made her tremble as if she had escaped from a trap which might have caught her and smothered her) that the chance of inflicting a sensible injury upon another person, presented only as a contingency, caused her at moments to hold her breath. That always struck her as the worst thing that could happen to her. On the whole, reflectively, she was in no uncertainty about the things that were wrong. She had no love of their look, but when she fixed them hard she recognised them. It was wrong to be mean, to be jealous, to be false, to be cruel; she had seen very little of the evil of the world, but she had seen women who lied and who tried to hurt each other. Seeing such things had quickened her high spirit; it seemed indecent not to scorn them. Of course the danger of a high spirit was the danger of inconsistency—the danger of keeping up the flag after the place has surrendered; a sort of behaviour so crooked as to be almost a dishonour to the flag. But Isabel, who knew little of the sorts of artillery to which young women are exposed, flattered herself that such contradictions would never be noted in her own conduct. Her life should always be in harmony with the most pleasing impression she should produce; she would be what she appeared, and she would appear what she was. Sometimes she went so far as to wish that she might find herself some day in a difficult position, so that she should have the pleasure of being as heroic as the occasion demanded. Altogether, with her meagre knowledge, her inflated ideals, her confidence at once innocent and dogmatic, her temper at once exacting and indulgent, her mixture of curiosity and fastidiousness, of vivacity and indifference, her desire to look very well and to be if possible even better, her determination to see, to try, to know, her combination of the delicate, desultory, flame-like spirit and the eager and personal creature of conditions: she would be an easy victim of scientific criticism if she were not intended to awaken on the reader's part an impulse more tender and more purely expectant.

It was one of her theories that Isabel Archer was very fortunate in being independent, and that she ought to make some very enlightened use of that state. She never called it the state of solitude, much less of singleness; she thought such descriptions weak, and, besides, her sister Lily constantly urged her to come and abide. She had a friend whose acquaintance she had made shortly before her father's death, who offered so high an example of useful activity that Isabel always thought of her as a model. Henrietta Stackpole had the advantage of an admired ability; she was thoroughly launched in journalism, and her letters to the *Interviewer*, from Washington, Newport, the White Mountains and other places, were universally quoted. Isabel pronounced them with confidence "ephemeral," but she esteemed the courage, energy and good-humour of the writer, who, without parents and without property, had adopted three of the children of an infirm and widowed sister and was paying their school-bills out of the proceeds of her literary labour. Henrietta was in the van of progress and had clear-cut views on most subjects; her cherished desire had long been to come to Europe and write a series of letters to the *Interviewer* from the radical point of view—an enterprise the less difficult as she knew perfectly in advance what her opinions would be and to how many objections most European institutions lay open. When she heard that Isabel was coming she wished to start at once; thinking, naturally, that it would be delightful the two should travel together. She had been obliged, however, to postpone this enterprise. She thought Isabel a glorious creature, and had spoken of her covertly in some of her letters, though she never mentioned the fact to her friend, who would not have taken pleasure in it and was not a regular student of the *Interviewer*. Henrietta, for Isabel, was chiefly a proof that a woman might suffice to herself and be happy. Her resources were of the obvious kind; but even if one had not the journalistic talent and a genius for guessing, as Henrietta said, what the public was going to want, one was not therefore to conclude that one had no vocation, no beneficent aptitude of any sort, and resign one's self to being frivolous and hollow. Isabel was stoutly determined not to be hollow. If one should wait with the right patience one would find some happy work to one's hand. Of course, among her theories, this young lady was not without a collection of views on the subject of marriage. The first on the list was a conviction of the vulgarity of thinking too much of it. From lapsing into eagerness on this point she earnestly prayed she might be delivered; she held that a woman ought to be able to live to herself, in the absence of exceptional flimsiness, and that it was perfectly possible to be happy without the society of a more or less coarse-minded person of another sex. The girl's prayer was very sufficiently answered; something pure and proud that there was in her—something cold and dry an unappreciated suitor with a taste for analysis might have called it—had hitherto kept her from any great vanity of conjecture on the article of possible husbands. Few of the men she saw seemed worth a ruinous expenditure, and it made her smile to think that one of them should present himself as an incentive to hope and a reward of patience. Deep in her soul—it was the deepest thing there—lay a belief that if a certain light should dawn she could give herself completely; but this image, on the whole, was too formidable to be attractive. Isabel's thoughts hovered about it, but they seldom rested on it long; after a little it ended in alarms. It often seemed to her that she thought too much

Chapter 23 Henry James

about herself; you could have made her colour, any day in the year, by calling her a rank egoist. She was always planning out her development, desiring her perfection, observing her progress. Her nature had, in her conceit, a certain garden-like quality, a suggestion of perfume and murmuring boughs, of shady bowers and lengthening vistas, which made her feel that introspection was, after all, an exercise in the open air, and that a visit to the recesses of one's spirit was harmless when one returned from it with a lapful of roses. But she was often reminded that there were other gardens in the world than those of her remarkable soul, and that there were moreover a great many places which were not gardens at all—only dusky pestiferous tracts, planted thick with ugliness and misery. In the current of that repaid curiosity on which she had lately been floating, which had conveyed her to this beautiful old England and might carry her much further still, she often checked herself with the thought of the thousands of people who were less happy than herself—a thought which for the moment made her fine, full consciousness appear a kind of immodesty. What should one do with the misery of the world in a scheme of the agreeable for one's self? It must be confessed that this question never held her long. She was too young, too impatient to live, too unacquainted with pain. She always returned to her theory that a young woman whom after all every one thought clever should begin by getting a general impression of life. This impression was necessary to prevent mistakes, and after it should be secured she might make the unfortunate condition of others a subject of special attention.

England was a revelation to her, and she found herself as diverted as a child at a pantomime. In her infantile excursions to Europe she had seen only the Continent, and seen it from the nursery window; Paris, not London, was her father's Mecca, and into many of his interests there his children had naturally not entered. The images of that time moreover had grown faint and remote, and the old-world quality in everything that she now saw had all the charm of strangeness. Her uncle's house seemed a picture made real; no refinement of the agreeable was lost upon Isabel; the rich perfection of Gardencourt at once revealed a world and gratified a need. The large, low rooms, with brown ceilings and dusky corners, the deep embrasures and curious casements, the quiet light on dark, polished panels, the deep greenness outside, that seemed always peeping in, the sense of well-ordered privacy in the centre of a "property"—a place where sounds were felicitously accidental, where the tread was muffed by the earth itself and in the thick mild air all friction dropped out of contact and all shrillness out of talk—these things were much to the taste of our young lady, whose taste played a considerable part in her emotions. She formed a fast friendship with her uncle, and often sat by his chair when he had had it moved out to the lawn. He passed hours in the open air, sitting with folded hands like a placid, homely household god, a god of service, who had done his work and received his wages and was trying to grow used to weeks and months made up only of off-days. Isabel amused him more than she suspected—the effect she produced upon people was often different from what she supposed—and he frequently gave himself the pleasure of making her chatter. It was by this term that he qualified her conversation, which had much of the "point" observable in that of the young ladies of her country, to whom the ear of the world is more directly presented than to their sisters in other lands. Like the mass of American girls Isabel had been encouraged to express herself; her remarks had been attended to; she had been expected to have emotions and opinions. Many of her opinions had doubtless but a slender value, many of her emotions passed away in the utterance; but they had left a trace in giving her the habit of seeming at least to feel and think, and in imparting moreover to her words when she was really moved that prompt vividness which so many people had regarded as a sign of superiority. Mr. Touchett used to think that she reminded him of his wife when his wife was in her teens. It was because she was fresh and natural and quick to understand, to speak—so many characteristics of her niece—that he had fallen in love with Mrs. Touchett. He never expressed this analogy to the girl herself, however; for if Mrs. Touchett had once been like Isabel, Isabel was not at all like Mrs. Touchett. The old man was full of kindness for her; it was a long time, as he said, since they had had any young life in the house; and our rustling, quickly-moving, clear-voiced heroine was as agreeable to his sense as the sound of flowing water. He wanted to do something for her and wished she would ask it of him. She would ask nothing but questions;

it is true that of these she asked a quantity. Her uncle had a great fund of answers, though her pressure sometimes came in forms that puzzled him. She questioned him immensely about England, about the British constitution, the English character, the state of politics, the manners and customs of the royal family, the peculiarities of the aristocracy, the way of living and thinking of his neighbours; and in begging to be enlightened on these points she usually enquired whether they corresponded with the descriptions in the books. The old man always looked at her a little with his fine dry smile while he smoothed down the shawl spread across his legs.

"The books?" he once said; "well, I don't know much about the books. You must ask Ralph about that. I've always ascertained for myself—got my information in the natural form. I never asked many questions even; I just kept quiet and took notice. Of course I've had very good opportunities—better than what a young lady would naturally have. I'm of an inquisitive disposition, though you mightn't think it if you were to watch me: however much you might watch me I should be watching you more. I've been watching these people for upwards of thirty-five years, and I don't hesitate to say that I've acquired considerable information. It's a very fine country on the whole—finer perhaps than what we give it credit for on the other side. Several improvements I should like to see introduced; but the necessity of them doesn't seem to be generally felt as yet. When the necessity of a thing is generally felt they usually manage to accomplish it; but they seem to feel pretty comfortable about waiting till then. I certainly feel more at home among them than I expected to when I first came over; I suppose it's because I've had a considerable degree of success. When you're successful you naturally feel more at home."

"Do you suppose that if I'm successful I shall feel at home?" Isabel asked.

"I should think it very probable, and you certainly will be successful. They like American young ladies very much over here; they show them a great deal of kindness. But you mustn't feel too much at home, you know."

"Oh, I'm by no means sure it will *satisfy* me," Isabel judicially emphasised. "I like the place very much, but I'm not sure I shall like the people."

"The people are very good people; especially if you like them."

"I've no doubt they're good," Isabel rejoined; "but are they pleasant in society? They won't rob me nor beat me; but will they make themselves agreeable to me? That's what I like people to do. I don't hesitate to say so, because I always appreciate it. I don't believe they're very nice to girls; they're not nice to them in the novels."

"I don't know about the novels," said Mr. Touchett. "I believe the novels have a great deal but I don't suppose they're very accurate. We once had a lady who wrote novels staying here; she was a friend of Ralph's and he asked her down. She was very positive, quite up to everything; but she was not the sort of person you could depend on for evidence. Too free a fancy—I suppose that was it. She afterwards published a work of fiction in which she was understood to have given a representation—something in the nature of a caricature, as you might say—of my unworthy self. I didn't read it, but Ralph just handed me the book with the principal passages marked. It was understood to be a description of my conversation; American peculiarities, nasal twang, Yankee notions, stars and stripes. Well, it was not at all accurate; she couldn't have listened very attentively. I had no objection to her giving a report of my conversation, if she liked; but I didn't like the idea that she hadn't taken the trouble to listen to it. Of course I talk like an American—I can't talk like a Hottentot. However I talk, I've made them understand me pretty well over here. But I don't talk like the old gentleman in that lady's novel. He wasn't an American; we wouldn't have him over there at any price. I just mention the fact to show you that they're not always accurate. Of course, as I've no daughters, and as Mrs. Touchett resides in Florence, I haven't had much chance to notice about the young ladies. It sometimes appears as if the young women in the lower class were not very well treated; but I guess their position is better in the upper and even to some extent in the middle."

"Gracious," Isabel exclaimed; "how many classes have they? About fifty, I suppose."

"Well, I don't know that I ever counted them. I never took much notice of the classes. That's the advantage of being an American here; you don't belong to any class."

"I hope so," said Isabel. "Imagine one's belonging to an English class!"

"Well, I guess some of them are pretty comfortable—especially towards the top. But for me there are only two classes: the people I trust and the people I don't. Of those two, my dear Isabel, you belong to the first."

"I'm much obliged to you," said the girl quickly. Her way of taking compliments seemed sometimes rather dry; she got rid of them as rapidly as possible. But as regards this she was sometimes misjudged; she was thought insensible to them, whereas in fact she was simply unwilling to show how infinitely they pleased her. To show that was to show too much. "I'm sure the English are very conventional," she added.

"They've got everything pretty well fixed," Mr. Touchett admitted. "It's all settled beforehand—they don't leave it to the last moment."

"I don't like to have everything settled beforehand," said the girl. "I like more unexpectedness."

Her uncle seemed amused at her distinctness of preference. "Well, it's settled beforehand that you'll have great success," he rejoined. "I suppose you'll like that."

"I shall not have success if they're too stupidly conventional. I'm not in the least stupidly conventional. I'm just the contrary. That's what they won't like."

"No, no, you're all wrong," said the old man. "You can't tell what they'll like. They're very inconsistent; that's their principal interest."

"Ah well," said Isabel, standing before her uncle with her hands clasped about the belt of her black dress and looking up and down the lawn—"that will suit me perfectly!"

Chapter VII

The two amused themselves, time and again, with talking of the attitude of the British public as if the young lady had been in a position to appeal to it; but in fact the British public remained for the present profoundly indifferent to Miss Isabel Archer, whose fortune had dropped her, as her cousin said, into the dullest house in England. Her gouty uncle received very little company, and Mrs. Touchett, not having cultivated relations with her husband's neighbours, was not warranted in expecting visits from them. She had, however, a peculiar taste; she liked to receive cards. For what is usually called social intercourse she had very little relish; but nothing pleased her more than to find her hall-table whitened with oblong morsels of symbolic pasteboard. She flattered herself that she was a very just woman, and had mastered the sovereign truth that nothing in this world is got for nothing. She had played no social part as mistress of Gardencourt, and it was not to be supposed that, in the surrounding country, a minute account should be kept of her comings and goings. But it is by no means certain that she did not feel it to be wrong that so little notice was taken of them and that her failure (really very gratuitous) to make herself important in the neighbourhood had not much to do with the acrimony of her allusions to her husband's adopted country. Isabel presently found herself in the singular situation of defending the British constitution against her aunt; Mrs. Touchett having formed the habit of sticking pins into this venerable instrument. Isabel always felt an impulse to pull out the pins; not that she imagined they inflicted any damage on the tough old parchment, but because it seemed to her her aunt might make better use of her sharpness. She was very critical herself—it was incidental to her age, her sex and her nationality; but she was very sentimental as well, and there was something in Mrs. Touchett's dryness that set her own moral fountains flowing.

"Now what's your point of view?" she asked of her aunt. "When you criticise everything here you should have a point of view. Yours doesn't seem to be American—you thought everything over there so disagreeable. When I criticise I have mine; it's thoroughly American!"

"My dear young lady," said Mrs. Touchett, "there are as many points of view in the world as there are people of sense to take them. You may say that doesn't make them very numerous! American? Never in the world; that's shockingly narrow. My point of view, thank God, is personal!"

Isabel thought this a better answer than she admitted; it was a tolerable description of her own manner of judging, but it would not have sounded well for her to say so. On the lips of a person less advanced in life and less enlightened by experience than Mrs. Touchett such a declaration would savour of immodesty, even of arrogance. She risked it nevertheless in talking with Ralph, with whom she talked a great deal and with whom her conversation was of a sort that gave a large licence to extravagance. Her cousin used, as the phrase is, to chaff her; he very soon established with her a reputation for treating everything as a joke, and he was not a man to neglect the privileges such a reputation conferred. She accused him of an odious want of seriousness, of laughing at all things, beginning with himself. Such slender faculty of reverence as he possessed centred wholly upon his father; for the rest, he exercised his wit indifferently upon his father's son, this gentleman's weak lungs, his useless life, his fantastic mother, his friends (Lord Warburton in especial), his adopted, and his native country, his charming new-found cousin. "I keep a band of music in my ante-room," he said once to her. "It has orders to play without stopping; it renders me two excellent services. It keeps the sounds of the world from reaching the private apartments, and it makes the world think that dancing's going on within." It was dance-music indeed that you usually heard when you came within ear-shot of Ralph's band; the liveliest waltzes seemed to float upon the air. Isabel often found herself irritated by this perpetual fiddling; she would have liked to pass through the ante-room, as her cousin called it, and enter the private apartments. It mattered little that he had assured her they were a very dismal place; she would have been glad to undertake to sweep them and set them in order. It was but half-hospitality to let her remain outside; to punish him for which Isabel administered innumerable taps with the ferule of her straight young wit. It must be said that her wit was exercised to a large extent in self-defence, for her cousin amused himself with calling her "Columbia" and accusing her of a patriotism so heated that it scorched. He drew a caricature of her in which she was represented as a very pretty young woman dressed, on the lines of the prevailing fashion, in the folds of the national banner. Isabel's chief dread in life at this period of her development was that she should appear narrow-minded; what she feared next afterwards was that she should really be so. But she nevertheless made no scruple of abounding in her cousin's sense and pretending to sigh for the charms of her native land. She would be as American as it pleased him to regard her, and if he chose to laugh at her she would give him plenty of occupation. She defended England against his mother, but when Ralph sang its praises on purpose, as she said, to work her up, she found herself able to differ from him on a variety of points. In fact, the quality of this small ripe country seemed as sweet to her as the taste of an October pear; and her satisfaction was at the root of the good spirits which enabled her to take her cousin's chaff and return it in kind. If her good-humour flagged at moments it was not because she thought herself ill-used, but because she suddenly felt sorry for Ralph. It seemed to her he was talking as a blind and had little heart in what he said. "I don't know what's the matter with you," she observed to him once; "but I suspect you're a great humbug."

"That's your privilege," Ralph answered, who had not been used to being so crudely addressed.

"I don't know what you care for; I don't think you care for anything. You don't really care for England when you praise it; you don't care for America even when you pretend to abuse it."

"I care for nothing but you, dear cousin," said Ralph.

"If I could believe even that, I should be very glad."

"Ah well, I should hope so!" the young man exclaimed.

Isabel might have believed it and not have been far from the truth. He thought a great deal about her; she was constantly present to his mind. At a time when his thoughts had been a good deal of a burden to him her sudden arrival, which promised nothing and was an open-handed gift of fate, had refreshed and quickened them, given them wings and something to fly for. Poor Ralph had been for many weeks steeped in melancholy; his outlook, habitually sombre, lay under the shadow of a deeper cloud. He had grown anxious about his father, whose gout, hitherto confined to his legs, had begun to ascend into regions more vital. The old man had been gravely ill in the spring, and the doctors had whispered to Ralph that another attack would be less easy to deal with. Just now he appeared disburdened of pain, but Ralph could not rid himself of a suspicion that this was a subterfuge of the enemy, who was waiting to take him off his guard. If the manoeuvre should succeed there would be little hope of any great resistance. Ralph had always taken for granted that his father would survive him—that his own name would be the first grimly called. The father and son had been close companions, and the idea of being left alone with the remnant of a tasteless life on his hands was not gratifying to the young man, who had always and tacitly counted upon his elder's help in making the best of a poor business. At the prospect of losing his great motive Ralph lost indeed his one inspiration. If they might die at the same time it would be all very well; but without the encouragement of his father's society he should barely have patience to await his own turn. He had not the incentive of feeling that he was indispensable to his mother; it was a rule with his mother to have no regrets. He bethought himself of course that it had been a small kindness to his father to wish that, of the two, the active rather than the passive party should know the felt wound; he remembered that the old man had always treated his own forecast of an early end as a clever fallacy, which he should be delighted to discredit so far as he might by dying first. But of the two triumphs, that of refuting a sophistical son and that of holding on a while longer to a state of being which, with all abatements, he enjoyed, Ralph deemed it no sin to hope the latter might be vouchsafed to Mr. Touchett.

These were nice questions, but Isabel's arrival put a stop to his puzzling over them. It even suggested there might be a compensation for the intolerable ennui of surviving his genial sire. He wondered whether he were harbouring "love" for this spontaneous young woman from Albany; but he judged that on the whole he was not. After he had known her for a week he quite made up his mind to this, and every day he felt a little more sure. Lord Warburton had been right about her; she was a really interesting little figure. Ralph wondered how their neighbour had found it out so soon; and then he said it was only another proof of his friend's high abilities, which he had always greatly admired. If his cousin were to be nothing more than an entertainment to him, Ralph was conscious she was an entertainment of a high order. "A character like that," he said to himself—"a real little passionate force to see at play is the finest thing in nature. It's finer than the finest work of art—than a Greek bas-relief, than a great Titian, than a Gothic cathedral. It's very pleasant to be so well treated where one had least looked for it. I had never been more blue, more bored, than for a week before she came; I had never expected less that anything pleasant would happen. Suddenly I receive a Titian, by the post, to hang on my wall—a Greek bas-relief to stick over my chimney-piece. The key of a beautiful edifice is thrust into my hand, and I'm told to walk in and admire. My poor boy, you've been sadly ungrateful, and now you had better keep very quiet and never grumble again." The sentiment of these reflextions was very just; but it was not exactly true that Ralph Touchett had had a key put into his hand. His cousin was a very brilliant girl, who would take, as he said, a good deal of knowing; but she needed the knowing, and his attitude with regard to her, though it was contemplative and critical, was not judicial. He surveyed the edifice from the outside and admired it greatly; he looked in at the windows and received an impression of proportions equally fair. But he felt that he saw it only by glimpses and that he had not yet stood under the roof. The door was fastened, and though he had keys in his pocket he had a conviction that none of them would fit. She was intelligent and generous; it was a fine free nature; but what was she going to do with herself? This question was irregular, for with most women one had no occasion to ask it. Most women did with themselves nothing at all; they waited, in attitudes more or less gracefully passive, for a man to come that way and furnish them with a destiny. Isabel's originality was that she gave one an impression of having intentions of her own. "Whenever she executes them," said Ralph, "may I be there to see!"

It devolved upon him of course to do the honours of the place. Mr. Touchett was confined to his chair, and his wife's position was that of rather a grim visitor; so that in the line of conduct that opened itself to Ralph duty and inclination were harmoniously mixed. He was not a great walker, but he strolled about the grounds with his cousin—a pastime for which the weather remained favourable with a persistency not allowed for in Isabel's somewhat lugubrious prevision of the climate; and in the long afternoons, of which the length was but the measure of her gratified eagerness, they took a boat on the river, the dear little river, as Isabel called it, where the opposite shore seemed still a part of the foreground of the landscape; or drove over the country in a phaeton—a low, capacious, thick-wheeled phaeton formerly much used by Mr. Touchett, but which he had now ceased to enjoy. Isabel enjoyed it largely and, handling the reins in a manner which approved itself to the groom as

Chapter 23   Henry James

"knowing," was never weary of driving her uncle's capital horses through winding lanes and byways full of the rural incidents she had confidently expected to find; past cottages thatched and timbered, past ale-houses latticed and sanded, past patches of ancient common and glimpses of empty parks, between hedgerows made thick by midsummer. When they reached home they usually found tea had been served on the lawn and that Mrs. Touchett had not shrunk from the extremity of handing her husband his cup. But the two for the most part sat silent; the old man with his head back and his eyes closed, his wife occupied with her knitting and wearing that appearance of rare profundity with which some ladies consider the movement of their needles.

One day, however, a visitor had arrived. The two young persons, after spending an hour on the river, strolled back to the house and perceived Lord Warburton sitting under the trees and engaged in conversation, of which even at a distance the desultory character was appreciable, with Mrs. Touchett. He had driven over from his own place with a portmanteau and had asked, as the father and son often invited him to do, for a dinner and a lodging. Isabel, seeing him for half an hour on the day of her arrival, had discovered in this brief space that she liked him; he had indeed rather sharply registered himself on her fine sense and she had thought of him several times. She had hoped she should see him again—hoped too that she should see a few others. Gardencourt was not dull; the place itself was sovereign, her uncle was more and more a sort of golden grandfather, and Ralph was unlike any cousin she had ever encountered—her idea of cousins having tended to gloom. Then her impressions were still so fresh and so quickly renewed that there was as yet hardly a hint of vacancy in the view. But Isabel had need to remind herself that she was interested in human nature and that her foremost hope in coming abroad had been that she should see a great many people. When Ralph said to her, as he had done several times, "I wonder you find this endurable; you ought to see some of the neighbours and some of our friends, because we have really got a few, though you would never suppose it"—when he offered to invite what he called a "lot of people" and make her acquainted with English society, she encouraged the hospitable impulse and promised in advance to hurl herself into the fray. Little, however, for the present, had come of his offers, and it may be confided to the reader that if the young man delayed to carry them out it was because he found the labour of providing for his companion by no means so severe as to require extraneous help. Isabel had spoken to him very often about "specimens"; it was a word that played a considerable part in her vocabulary; she had given him to understand that she wished to see English society illustrated by eminent cases.

"Well now, there's a specimen," he said to her as they walked up from the riverside and he recognised Lord Warburton.

"A specimen of what?" asked the girl.

"A specimen of an English gentleman."

"Do you mean they're all like him?"

"Oh no; they're not all like him."

"He's a favourable specimen then," said Isabel; "because I'm sure he's nice."

"Yes, he's very nice. And he's very fortunate."

The fortunate Lord Warburton exchanged a handshake with our heroine and hoped she was very well. "But I needn't ask that," he said, "since you've been handling the oars."

"I've been rowing a little," Isabel answered; "but how should you know it?"

"Oh, I know *he* doesn't row; he's too lazy," said his lordship, indicating Ralph Touchett with a laugh.

"He has a good excuse for his laziness," Isabel rejoined, lowering her voice a little.

"Ah, he has a good excuse for everything!" cried Lord Warburton, still with his sonorous mirth.

"My excuse for not rowing is that my cousin rows so well," said Ralph. "She does everything well. She touches nothing that she doesn't adorn!"

"It makes one want to be touched, Miss Archer," Lord Warburton declared.

"Be touched in the right sense and you'll never look the worse for it," said Isabel, who, if it pleased her to hear it said that her accomplishments were numerous, was happily able to reflect that such complacency was not the indication of a feeble mind, inasmuch as there were several things in which she excelled. Her desire to think well of herself had at least the element of humility that it always needed to be supported by proof.

Lord Warburton not only spent the night at Gardencourt, but he was persuaded to remain over the second day; and when the second day was ended he determined to postpone his departure till the morrow. During this period he addressed many of his remarks to Isabel, who accepted this evidence of his esteem with a very good grace. She found herself liking him extremely; the first impression he had made on her had had weight, but at the end of an evening spent in his society she scarce fell short of seeing him—though quite without luridity—as a hero of romance. She retired to rest with a sense of good fortune, with a quickened consciousness of possible felicities. "It's very nice to know two such charming people as those," she said, meaning by "those" her cousin and her cousin's friend. It must be added moreover that an incident had occurred which might have seemed to put her good-humour to the test. Mr. Touchett went to bed at half-past nine o'clock, but his wife remained in the drawing-room with the other members of the party. She prolonged her vigil for something less than an hour, and then, rising, observed to Isabel that it was time they should bid the gentlemen good-night. Isabel had as yet no desire to go to bed; the occasion wore, to her sense, a festive character, and feasts were not in the habit of terminating so early. So, without further thought, she replied, very simply—

"Need I go, dear aunt? I'll come up in half an hour."

"It's impossible I should wait for you," Mrs. Touchett answered.

"Ah, you needn't wait! Ralph will light my candle," Isabel gaily engaged.

"I'll light your candle; do let me light your candle, Miss Archer!" Lord Warburton exclaimed. "Only I beg it shall not be before midnight."

Mrs. Touchett fixed her bright little eyes upon him a moment and transferred them coldly to her niece. "You can't stay alone with the gentlemen. You're not—you're not at your blest Albany, my dear."

Isabel rose, blushing. "I wish I were," she said.

"Oh, I say, mother!" Ralph broke out.

"My dear Mrs. Touchett!" Lord Warburton murmured.

"I didn't make your country, my lord," Mrs. Touchett said majestically. "I must take it as I find it."

"Can't I stay with my own cousin?" Isabel enquired.

"I'm not aware that Lord Warburton is your cousin."

"Perhaps I had better go to bed!" the visitor suggested. "That will arrange it."

Mrs. Touchett gave a little look of despair and sat down again. "Oh, if it's necessary I'll stay up till midnight."

Ralph meanwhile handed Isabel her candlestick. He had been watching her; it had seemed to him her temper was involved—an accident that might be interesting. But if he had expected anything of a flare he was disappointed, for the girl simply laughed a little, nodded good-night and withdrew accompanied by her aunt. For himself he was annoyed at his mother, though he thought she was right. Above-stairs the two ladies separated at Mrs. Touchett's door. Isabel had said nothing on her way up.

"Of course you're vexed at my interfering with you," said Mrs. Touchett.

Isabel considered. "I'm not vexed, but I'm surprised—and a good deal mystified. Wasn't it proper I should remain in the drawing-room?"

"Not in the least. Young girls here—in decent houses—don't sit alone with the gentlemen late at night."

"You were very right to tell me then," said Isabel. "I don't understand it, but I'm very glad to know it."

"I shall always tell you," her aunt answered, "whenever I see you taking what seems to me too much liberty."

"Pray do; but I don't say I shall always think your remonstrance just."

"Very likely not. You're too fond of your own ways."

"Yes, I think I'm very fond of them. But I always want to know the things one shouldn't do."

"So as to do them?" asked her aunt.

"So as to choose," said Isabel.

Chapter 24

Jack London (1876–1916)

Jack London (original name John Griffith London) was born on January 12, 1876, the illegitimate son of W. H. Chaney, a talented and self-taught man who became an astrologer, and Flora Wellman, an eccentric woman from a wealthy Ohio family who was both a spiritualist and music teacher. London, who never saw his real father, took the name of his stepfather. He grew up in extreme poverty: From earliest youth he supported himself with menial and dangerous jobs, experiencing profoundly the struggle for survival that most other writers and intellectuals knew only from observation or books. By the time he was eighteen he had worked in a cannery and as an oyster pirate, seaman, jute mill worker, and coal shoveler. After crossing much of the continent as a member of Coxey's Army (an organized group of the unemployed who, following the panic of 1893, carried their call for economic reform to Washington, D.C.), he was jailed for thirty days for vagrancy. At this point he determined to educate himself in order to improve his own condition and that of others.

With an intellectual energy that matched his physical strength, London quickly completed high school and spent a semester reading prodigiously as a special student at the University of California. Temperament rather than logic led him to embrace the hopeful socialism of Marx on the one hand and the rather darker views of Nietzsche and Darwinism on the other. That is, London believed at the same time in the inevitable triumph of the strongest individuals. London's sincere intellectual and personal involvement in the socialist movement is recorded in such novels and polemical works as *The People of the Abyss* (1903), *The Iron Heel* (1908), *The War of the Classes*

(1905), and *Revolution* (1910); his competing, deeply felt commitment to the fundamental reality of the law of survival and the will to power is dramatized in his most popular novels, *The Call of the Wild* (1903) and *The Sea Wolf* (1904). Wolf Larsen, the ruthless, amoral protagonist of the latter book, best realizes the ideal of the "superman." The contradiction between these competing beliefs is most vividly projected in the patently autobiographical novel *Martin Eden* (1909), a central document for London scholars.

London had been writing sporadically for five years, but his professional career began after he spent the winter of 1897–1898 in the Klondike in a futile search for gold. Within two years, by the time he published his first collection of stories, *The Son of the Wolf* (1900), he was on his way to becoming the highest paid author of his time. By his twenty-seventh birthday *The Call of the Wild* had made him rich.

London frankly disliked his profession: He wrote for money, but he was also a methodical and careful craftsman who produced a minimum of 1,000 publishable words a day, six days a week. He wrote on many subjects, from agronomy to penal reform, from astral projection to warfare. The most enduringly popular of his stories involved the primitive (and melodramatic) struggle of strong and weak individuals in the context of irresistible natural forces such as the wild sea or the arctic wastes. At a time when America's frontier was closing and President Theodore Roosevelt was urging the strenuous life, London adapted the physical ruggedness and psychological independence of Rudyard Kipling's heroes to the American experience in *The Call of the Wild*, *The Sea Wolf*, and *White Fang* (1906). Like his contemporaries Stephen Crane and Frank Norris (and like Ernest Hemingway a generation later), London was fascinated by the way violence tested and defined human character, though he was much more interested in ideas than Crane and less sentimental than Norris. Thus, in *The Law of Life*, the tribal patriarch's death is depicted as an illustration of the law that all living things die rather than in terms of the particular psychological state of the individual facing his end.

London continued to write until his death in 1916 from a "gastrointestinal type of uremia," widely supposed to have been suicide. But the bulk of his best works had been done by 1910. He had written too much too fast, with too little concern for the stylistic and formal refinement and subtlety of characterization that rank high with critics. He had not, moreover, reconciled his contradictory views of man's nature and destiny. But London's stories of man in and against nature continue to be popular all over the world. In them, London strips everything down to the symbolic starkness of dream, to a primordial simplicity that has the strange and compelling power of ancient myth.

The Sea Wolf

The Story

When the ship in which he was a passenger sank in a collision off the coast of California, Humphrey Van Weyden was picked up by the crew of Wolf Larsen's ship, the *Ghost*, a sailing vessel headed for seal hunting ranges in the Bering Sea. Wolf Larsen was a brute. Van Weyden witnessed the inhuman treatment of a sick mate who died shortly afterward. He saw a cabin boy badly beaten. In his own interview with the captain, he fared little better. Instead of promising to help him return to San Francisco, Wolf demanded that Van Weyden sign as cabin boy and stay with his ship.

The crew set to work taking in the topsails and jibs. From that moment Hump, as the crew called Van Weyden, learned life the hard way. He had to get his sea legs and he had to learn the stoical indifference to pain and suffering which the sailors seemed to have mastered already. As cabin boy, he peeled potatoes and washed greasy pots and pans. Mugridge, the cook, abused him and robbed him of his money.

Only one man, Louis, seemed to share Hump's feelings about the captain and his ship. Louis predicted many deaths would result from this voyage. He said that Wolf Larsen was a violent, dangerous man, that the crew and seal hunters were vicious outcasts. Wolf did seem mad. He varied from moods of wild exultation to spells of extreme depression. In his cabin were classic books of literature, and when he spoke he chose either to use excellent English or the lingo of the sailors. Sometimes he amused himself by arguing with Hump. He claimed that life was without meaning.

During a southeaster Hump badly dislocated his knee, and Wolf unexpectedly allowed Hump to rest for three days while he talked to him about philosophy and literature. When Hump returned to the galley, the cook was whetting his knife. In return, Hump obtained a knife and began whetting it also. His actions so frightened the cowardly cook that Hump was no longer the victim of his abuse.

Louis talked of the coming season with the seals. Moreover, he hinted that trouble would come if the *Macedonia*, a sealing steamer, came near. Captained by Death Larsen, the brother and enemy of Wolf, the *Macedonia* was a certain menace. As a prelude to things to come, an outbreak of fury took place aboard the *Ghost*. First, Wolf Larsen and the mate beat a seaman named Johnson to a pulp because he complained of ill treatment; then Leach, the former cabin boy, beat the cook. Later two hunters exchanged shots, severely wounding each other, and Wolf beat them because they had crippled themselves before the hunting season began. Afterward Wolf suffered from one of his periodic headaches. To Hump, life on shipboard was a tremendous experience in human cruelty and viciousness.

A few days later the men tried to mutiny. In the row which followed, Johansen, the mate, was drowned and Wolf was nearly killed. While Hump dressed Wolf's wounds, Wolf promoted him to mate in Johansen's place. Both Leach and Johnson would have killed Wolf in a second, but he remained too wary of them.

At the seal hunting grounds a terrific storm cost them the lives of four men. The ship itself was beaten, its sails torn to shreds and portions of the deck swept into the sea.

When Leach and Johnson deserted in a small skiff, Wolf started out in pursuit. On the morning of the third day an open boat was sighted. The boat contained a young woman and four men, survivors from a sinking steamer. Wolf took them aboard, planning to make sailors of the men as he had of Hump. Shortly afterward the *Ghost* overtook Johnson and Leach. Refusing to pick them up, Wolf let them struggle to get aboard until their small craft capsized. He watched them drown without comment and then ordered the ship's course set for a return to the seal hunting grounds.

The woman survivor was Maud Brewster, a rich woman and a poet, as weak physically for a woman as Hump had been for a man. Wolf resented the intimacy which sprang up at once between Maud Brewster and Hump, but he took out his resentment by deciding to give the cook the first bath the cook had ever been known to take.

At his orders Mugridge was thrown into the water with a tow rope slung about his middle. First, however, the cook fled madly about the ship, causing one man to break a leg and another to be injured in a fall. Before Wolf was ready to bring Mugridge back aboard ship, a shark bit off the cook's right foot at the ankle. Dragged aboard, Mugridge in his fury tried to bite Wolf's leg, and the captain almost strangled him. Then Hump bandaged the wounded man's leg. Maud Brewster looked on, nearly fainting.

The *Macedonia* appeared one day and robbed Wolf's hunters of their day's catch of seals by cutting off the line of approach to the *Ghost*. In revenge, Wolf set his men to work capturing hunters from the *Macedonia*. When the *Macedonia* gave chase, Wolf sailed his ship into a fog bank.

That night Wolf tried to seize Maud, but Hump, awakening, ran his knife into Wolf's shoulder. At the same time, Wolf was overcome by one of his headaches, this seizure accompanied by blindness. Hump helped him to his bunk and under cover of darkness he and Maud made their escape in an open boat. After days of tossing they came to a small island. Using supplies they had taken from the *Ghost*, they set about making themselves houses and gathering food for the coming winter.

One morning Hump saw the wreck of the *Ghost* lying offshore. Going aboard, he discovered Wolf alone, his crew having deserted him to go aboard Death Larsen's ship. Wolf seemed nearly insane, and had only a sick man's desire to sleep. Hump stole some pistols and food which he took to the island.

Hump, planning to repair the masts of the *Ghost*, began work on the crippled ship. That night Wolf undid all Hump's work, and cast the masts off the vessel.

Hump and Maud began anew to refit the ship. One day Wolf attempted to murder Hump, but during the struggle he had one of his spasms and fainted. While he was still unconscious, they handcuffed him and shut him in the hold.

Then they moved aboard the *Ghost* and the work of refitting the vessel went forward. Wolf became more than a prisoner. He had a stroke which paralyzed the right side of his body.

Hump continued to repair the vessel. At last it was able to sail. Wolf Larsen finally lost the use of his muscles and lay in a coma. When he died, Hump and Maud buried him at sea. By that time they were deeply in love. When a United States revenue cutter discovered them one day, they felt that their dangerous Odyssey was at an end. But they were about to begin another, less perilous journey, together.

Chapter XXI

The chagrin Wolf Larsen felt from being ignored by Maud Brewster and me in the conversation at table had to express itself in some fashion, and it fell to Thomas Mugridge to be the victim. He had not mended his ways nor his shirt, though the latter he contended he had changed. The garment itself did not bear out the assertion, nor did the accumulations of grease on stove and pot and pan attest a general cleanliness.

"I've given you warning, Cooky," Wolf Larsen said, "and now you've got to take your medicine."

Mugridge's face turned white under its sooty veneer, and when Wolf Larsen called for a rope and a couple of men, the miserable Cockney[1] fled wildly out of the galley and dodged and ducked about the deck with the grinning crew in pursuit. Few things could have been more to their liking than to give him a tow over the side, for to the forecastle he had sent messes and concoctions of the vilest order. Conditions favoured the undertaking. The *Ghost* was slipping through the water at no more than three miles an hour, and the sea was fairly calm. But Mugridge had little stomach for a dip in it. Possibly he had seen men towed before. Besides, the water was frightfully cold, and his was anything but a rugged constitution.

As usual, the watches below and the hunters turned out for what

Chapter 24 Jack London

promised sport. Mugridge seemed to be in rabid fear of the water, and he exhibited a nimbleness and speed we did not dream he possessed. Cornered in the right-angle of the poop and galley, he sprang like a cat to the top of the cabin and ran aft. But his pursuers forestalling him, he doubled back across the cabin, passed over the galley, and gained the deck by means of the steerage-scuttle. Straight forward he raced, the boat-puller Harrison at his heels and gaining on him. But Mugridge, leaping suddenly, caught the jib-boom-lift. It happened in an instant. Holding his weight by his arms, and in mid-air doubling his body at the hips, he let fly with both feet. The oncoming Harrison caught the kick squarely in the pit of the stomach, groaned involuntarily, and doubled up and sank backward to the deck.

Hand-clapping and roars of laughter from the hunters greeted the exploit, while Mugridge, eluding half of his pursuers at the foremast, ran aft and through the remainder like a runner on the football field. Straight aft he held, to the poop and along the poop to the stern. So great was his speed that as he curved past the corner of the cabin he slipped and fell. Nilson was standing at the wheel, and the Cockney's hurtling body struck his legs. Both went down together, but Mugridge alone arose. By some freak of pressures, his frail body had snapped the strong man's leg like a pipe-stem.

Parsons took the wheel, and the pursuit continued. Round and round the decks they went, Mugridge sick with fear, the sailors hallooing and shouting directions to one another, and the hunters bellowing encouragement and laughter. Mugridge went down on the fore-hatch under three men; but he emerged from the mass like an eel, bleeding at the mouth, the offending shirt ripped into tatters, and sprang for the main-rigging. Up he went, clear up, beyond the ratlines, to the very masthead.

Half-a-dozen sailors swarmed to the crosstrees after him, where they clustered and waited while two of their number, Oofty-Oofty and Black (who was Latimer's boat-steerer), continued up the thin steel stays, lifting their bodies higher and higher by means of their arms.

It was a perilous undertaking, for, at a height of over a hundred feet from the deck, holding on by their hands, they were not in the best of positions to protect themselves from Mugridge's feet. And Mugridge kicked savagely, till the Kanaka[2], hanging on with one hand, seized the Cockney's foot with the other. Black duplicated the performance a moment later with the other foot. Then the three writhed together in a swaying tangle, struggling, sliding, and falling into the arms of their mates on the crosstrees.

The aërial battle was over, and Thomas Mugridge, whining and gibbering, his mouth flecked with bloody foam, was brought down to deck. Wolf Larsen rove a bowline in a piece of rope and slipped it under his shoulders. Then he was carried aft and flung into the sea. Forty,—fifty,—sixty feet of line ran out, when Wolf Larsen cried "Belay[3]!" Oofty-Oofty took a turn on a bitt[4], the rope tautened, and the *Ghost*, lunging onward, jerked the cook to the surface.

It was a pitiful spectacle. Though he could not drown, and was nine-lived[5] in addition, he was suffering all the agonies of half-drowning. The *Ghost* was going very slowly, and when her stern lifted on a wave and she slipped forward she pulled the wretch to the surface and gave him a moment in which to breathe; but between each lift the stern fell, and while the bow lazily climbed the next wave the line slacked and he sank beneath.

I had forgotten the existence of Maud Brewster, and I remembered her with a start as she stepped lightly beside me. It was her first time on deck since she had come aboard. A dead silence greeted her appearance.

"What is the cause of the merriment?" she asked.

"Ask Captain Larsen," I answered composedly and coldly, though inwardly my blood was boiling at the thought that she should be witness to such brutality.

She took my advice and was turning to put it into execution, when her eyes lighted on Oofty-Oofty, immediately before her, his body instinct with alertness and grace as he held the turn of the rope.

"Are you fishing?" she asked him.

He made no reply. His eyes, fixed intently on the sea astern, suddenly flashed.

"Shark ho, sir!" he cried.

"Heave in! Lively! All hands tail on![6]" Wolf Larsen shouted, springing himself to the rope in advance of the quickest.

Mugridge had heard the Kanaka's warning cry and was screaming madly. I could see a black fin cutting the water and making for him with greater swiftness than he was being pulled aboard. It was an even toss[7] whether the shark or we would get him, and it was a matter of moments. When Mugridge was directly beneath us, the stern descended the slope of a passing wave, thus giving the advantage to the shark. The fin disappeared. The belly flashed white in a swift upward rush. Almost equally swift, but not quite, was Wolf Larsen. He threw his strength into one tremendous jerk. The Cockney's body left the water; so did part of the shark's. He drew up his legs, and the man-eater seemed no more than barely to touch one foot, sinking back into the water with a splash. But at the moment of contact Thomas Mugridge cried out. Then he came in like a fresh-caught fish on a line, clearing the rail generously and striking the deck in a heap, on hands and knees, and rolling over.

But a fountain of blood was gushing forth. The right foot was missing, amputated neatly at the ankle. I looked instantly to Maud Brewster. Her face was white, her eyes dilated with horror. She was gazing, not at Thomas Mugridge, but at Wolf Larsen. And he was aware of it, for he said, with one of his short laughs:

"Man-play, Miss Brewster. Somewhat rougher, I warrant, than what you have been used to, but still—man-play. The shark was not in the reckoning. It—"

But at this juncture, Mugridge, who had lifted his head and ascertained the extent of his loss, floundered over on the deck and buried his teeth in Wolf Larsen's leg. Wolf Larsen stooped, coolly, to the Cockney, and pressed with thumb and finger at the rear of the jaws and below the ears. The jaws opened with reluctance, and Wolf Larsen stepped free.

"As I was saying," he went on, as though nothing unwonted had happened, "the shark was not in the reckoning. It was—ahem—shall we say Providence?"

She gave no sign that she had heard, though the expression of her eyes changed to one of inexpressible loathing as she started to turn away. She no more than started, for she swayed and tottered, and reached her hand weakly out to mine. I caught her in time to save her from falling, and helped her to a seat on the cabin. I thought she must faint outright, but she controlled herself.

"Will you get a tourniquet[8], Mr. Van Weyden," Wolf Larsen called to me.

I hesitated. Her lips moved, and though they formed no words, she commanded me with her eyes, plainly as speech, to go to the help of the unfortunate man. "Please," she managed to whisper, and I could but obey.

By now I had developed such skill at surgery that Wolf Larsen, with a few words of advice, left me to my task with a couple of sailors for assistants. For his task he elected a vengeance on the shark. A heavy swivel-hook, baited with fat salt-pork, was dropped overside; and by the time I had compressed the severed veins and arteries, the sailors were singing and heaving in the offending monster. I did not see it myself, but my assistants, first one and then the other, deserted me for a few moments to run amidships and look at what was going on. The shark, a sixteen-footer, was hoisted up against the main-rigging. Its jaws were pried apart to their greatest extension, and a stout stake, sharpened at both ends, was so inserted that when the pries were removed the spread jaws were fixed upon it. This accomplished, the hook was cut out. The shark dropped back into the sea, helpless, yet with its full strength, doomed—to lingering starvation—a living death less meet[9] for it than for the man who devised the punishment.

Notes

1. Cockney: a native of London, used slightly and generally with allusion to peculiarities of pronunciation
2. Kanaka: a native of the South Sea Islands
3. belay: stop there, halt
4. bitt: a strong post of wood or iron to which cables are made fast
5. nine-lived: having nine lives as the cat is humorously said to have, hence, not easy to kill
6. All hands grasp the "tail"! tail—a rope spliced around a block so as to leave a long end by which the block may be attached to any object

7. It was an even toss…: The chances were equal…
8. tourniquet: a device for arresting bleeding
9. meet: suitable, fit, proper

🌿 Martin Eden

The Story

The hero of the novel is Martin Eden, a plain, rough sailor. Once he happens to save in a hand-to-hand fight with a group of hoodlums a young man named Arthur Morse. The grateful Arthur introduces Martin to his family. It is a typical bourgeois family with a narrow philistine outlook, and outward respectability.

Martin is dazzled by the seeming culture of the Morses. He naively believes high society to be the realm of spiritual beauty, pure and noble aspirations and full intellectual life. He falls in love and idolizes Arthur's sister Ruth whom he considers to be the personification of all these qualities.

Inspired by love, Martin determines to make his way in the world and become Ruth's equal. He reads a lot; with inhuman perseverance he masters the rudiments of sciences and crams two years of high school into three months of studies. When he runs out of money he sets out as a common sailor in a ship bound for the South Seas. While on board, Martin is inspired with a new idea—to become a writer. Upon his return to Oakland, Martin lives in poverty, devoting every minute of his time to writing and studying. His only rest is his occasional visits to the Morses.

His first stories are turned down by the publishers, but he keeps on sending them.

In the meanwhile Martin and Ruth become engaged to be married despite the most stubborn opposition of her parents who are shocked at the idea of a rough sailor becoming one of their family.

Desirous of encouragement in his work, Martin shows some of his stories to Ruth, but meets with bitter disappointment; she takes him for an impractical dreamer and urges him to give up writing and accept a job at her father's office. But Martin persists in his efforts. His visits to the Morses convince him gradually that he has been under the wrong impression as regards the "beauty and noble thinking" of high society. He scandalizes their sense of respectability by his blunt and straightforward criticism. The Morses shut the door of their house on Martin and force Ruth to cancel her engagement with him.

This is a fateful blow to Martin, and he stops writing. But he continues to send his old rejected stories to the printing houses, and suddenly the tide changes and they are accepted, one after another.

Eden becomes famous and receives enormous fees for his publications. His popularity grows to such an extent that people vie with each other to be introduced to him, but neither fame nor wealth can change his apathetic outlook on life.

The Morses, hearing of Martin's brilliant career, withdraw their opposition to his union with Ruth. She even visits Martin to reconcile with him, but all in vain, as he feels complete aversion toward the life of which she is part and parcel. He is wholly disillusioned with everything in life, and feeling an insistent urge to escape from this world, sails on a liner to the South Seas.

Unable to bear any longer the aching weariness of an aimless life, Martin Eden commits suicide.

Chapter I

The one opened the door with a latch-key and went in, followed by a young fellow who awkwardly removed his cap. He wore rough clothes that smacked of the sea, and he was manifestly out of place in the spacious hall in which he found himself. He did not know what to do with his cap, and was stuffing it into his coat pocket when the other took it from him. The act was done quietly and naturally, and the awkward young fellow appreciated it. "He understands," was his thought. "He'll see me through all right."

He walked at the other's heels with a swing to his shoulders, and his legs spread unwittingly, as if the level floors were tilting up and sinking down to the heave and lunge of the sea. The wide rooms seemed too narrow for his rolling gait, and to himself he was in terror lest his broad shoulders should collide with the doorways or sweep the bric-a-brac from the low mantel. He recoiled from side to side between the various objects and multiplied the hazards that in reality lodged only in his mind. Between a grand piano and a centre-table piled high with books was space for a half a dozen to walk abreast, yet he essayed it with trepidation. His heavy arms hung loosely at his sides. He did not know what to do with those arms and hands, and when, to his excited vision, one arm seemed liable to brush against the books on the table, he lurched away like a frightened horse, barely missing the piano stool. He watched the easy walk of the other in front of him, and for the first time realized that his walk was different from that of other men. He experienced a momentary pang of shame that he should walk so uncouthly. The sweat burst through the skin of his forehead in tiny beads, and he paused and mopped his bronzed face with his handkerchief.

"Hold on, Arthur, my boy," he said, attempting to mask his anxiety with facetious utterance. "This is too much all at once for yours truly. Give me a chance to get my nerve. You know I didn't want to come, an' I guess your fam'ly ain't hankerin' to see me neither."

"That's all right," was the reassuring answer. "You mustn't be frightened at us. We're just homely people—Hello, there's a letter for me."

He stepped back to the table, tore open the envelope, and began to read, giving the stranger an opportunity to recover himself. And the stranger understood and appreciated. His was the gift of sympathy, understanding; and beneath his alarmed exterior that sympathetic process went on. He mopped his forehead dry and glanced about him with a controlled face, though in the eyes there was an expression such as wild animals betray when they fear the trap. He was surrounded by the unknown, apprehensive of what might happen, ignorant of what he should do, aware that he walked and bore himself awkwardly, fearful that every attribute and power of him was similarly afflicted. He was keenly sensitive, hopelessly self-conscious, and the amused glance that the other stole privily at him over the top of the letter burned into him like a dagger-thrust. He saw the glance, but he gave no sign, for among the things he had learned was discipline. Also, that dagger-thrust went to his pride. He cursed himself for having come, and at the same time resolved that, happen what would, having come, he would carry it through. The lines of his face hardened, and into his eyes came a fighting light. He looked about more unconcernedly, sharply observant, every detail of the pretty interior registering itself on his brain. His eyes were wide apart; nothing in their field of vision escaped; and as they drank in the beauty before them the fighting light died out and a warm glow took its place. He was responsive to beauty, and here was cause to respond.

An oil painting caught and held him. A heavy surf thundered and burst over an outjutting rock; lowering storm-clouds covered the sky; and, outside the line of surf, a pilot-schooner, close-hauled, heeled over till every detail of her deck was visible, was surging along against a stormy sunset sky. There was beauty, and it drew him irresistibly. He forgot his awkward walk and came closer to the painting, very close. The beauty faded out of the canvas. His face expressed his bepuzzlement. He stared at what seemed a careless daub of paint, then stepped away. Immediately all the beauty flashed back into the canvas. "A trick picture," was his thought, as he dismissed it, though in the midst of the multitudinous impressions he was receiving he found time to feel a prod of indignation that so much beauty should be sacrificed to make a trick. He did not know painting. He had been brought up on chromos and lithographs that were always definite and sharp, near or far. He had seen oil paintings, it was true, in the show windows of shops, but the glass of the windows had prevented his eager eyes from approaching too near.

He glanced around at his friend reading the letter and saw the books on the table. Into his eyes leaped a wistfulness and a yearning as promptly as the yearning leaps into the eyes of a starving man at sight of food. An impulsive stride, with one lurch to right and left of the shoulders, brought him to the table, where he began affectionately handling the books. He glanced at the titles and the authors' names, read fragments of text, caressing the volumes with his eyes and hands, and, once, recognized a book he had read. For the rest, they were strange books and strange authors. He chanced upon a volume of Swinburne and began reading steadily, forgetful of where he was, his face glowing. Twice he closed the book on his forefinger to look at the name of the author. Swinburne! He would remember that name. That fellow had eyes, and he had certainly seen color and flashing light. But who was Swinburne? Was

Chapter 24 Jack London

he dead a hundred years or so, like most of the poets? Or was he alive still, and writing? He turned to the title-page…yes, he had written other books; well, he would go to the free library the first thing in the morning and try to get hold of some of Swinburne's stuff. He went back to the text and lost himself. He did not notice that a young woman had entered the room. The first he knew was when he heard Arthur's voice saying:—

"Ruth, this is Mr. Eden."

The book was closed on his forefinger, and before he turned he was thrilling to the first new impression, which was not of the girl, but of her brother's words. Under that muscled body of his he was a mass of quivering sensibilities. At the slightest impact of the outside world upon his consciousness, his thoughts, sympathies, and emotions leapt and played like lambent flame. He was extraordinarily receptive and responsive, while his imagination, pitched high, was ever at work establishing relations of likeness and difference. "Mr. Eden," was what he had thrilled to—he who had been called "Eden," or "Martin Eden," or just "Martin," all his life. And "*Mister!*" It was certainly going some, was his internal comment. His mind seemed to turn, on the instant, into a vast camera obscura, and he saw arrayed around his consciousness endless pictures from his life, of stoke-holes and forecastles, camps and beaches, jails and boozing-kens, fever-hospitals and slum streets, wherein the thread of association was the fashion in which he had been addressed in those various situations.

And then he turned and saw the girl. The phantasmagoria of his brain vanished at sight of her. She was a pale, ethereal creature, with wide, spiritual blue eyes and a wealth of golden hair. He did not know how she was dressed, except that the dress was as wonderful as she. He likened her to a pale gold flower upon a slender stem. No, she was a spirit, a divinity, a goddess; such sublimated beauty was not of the earth. Or perhaps the books were right, and there were many such as she in the upper walks of life. She might well be sung by that chap Swinburne. Perhaps he had had somebody like her in mind when he painted that girl, Iseult, in the book there on the table. All this plethora of sight, and feeling, and thought occurred on the instant. There was no pause of the realities wherein he moved. He saw her hand coming out to his, and she looked him straight in the eyes as she shook hands, frankly, like a man. The women he had known did not shake hands that way. For that matter, most of them did not shake hands at all. A flood of associations, visions of various ways he had made the acquaintance of women, rushed into his mind and threatened to swamp it. But he shook them aside and looked at her. Never had he seen such a woman. The women he had known! Immediately, beside her, on either hand, ranged the women he had known. For an eternal second he stood in the midst of a portrait gallery, wherein she occupied the central place, while about her were limned many women, all to be weighed and measured by a fleeting glance, herself the unit of weight and measure. He saw the weak and sickly faces of the girls of the factories, and the simpering, boisterous girls from the south of Market. There were women of the cattle camps, and swarthy cigarette-smoking women of Old Mexico. These, in turn, were crowded out by Japanese women, doll-like, stepping mincingly on wooden clogs; by Eurasians, delicate featured, stamped with degeneracy; by full-bodied South-Sea-Island women, flower-crowned and brown-skinned. All these were blotted out by a grotesque and terrible nightmare brood—frowsy, shuffling creatures from the pavements of Whitechapel, gin-bloated hags of the stews, and all the vast hell's following of harpies, vile-mouthed and filthy, that under the guise of monstrous female form prey upon sailors, the scrapings of the ports, the scum and slime of the human pit.

"Won't you sit down, Mr. Eden?" the girl was saying. "I have been looking forward to meeting you ever since Arthur told us. It was brave of you—"

He waved his hand deprecatingly and muttered that it was nothing at all, what he had done, and that any fellow would have done it. She noticed that the hand he waved was covered with fresh abrasions, in the process of healing, and a glance at the other loose-hanging hand showed it to be in the same condition. Also, with quick, critical eye, she noted a scar on his cheek, another that peeped out from under the hair of the forehead, and a third that ran down and disappeared under the starched collar. She repressed a smile at sight of the red line that marked the chafe of the collar against the bronzed neck. He was evidently unused to stiff collars. Likewise her feminine eye took in the clothes he wore, the cheap and unaesthetic cut, the wrinkling of the coat across the shoulders, and the series of wrinkles in the sleeves that advertised bulging biceps muscles.

While he waved his hand and muttered that he had done nothing at all, he was obeying her behest by trying to get into a chair. He found time to admire the ease with which she sat down, then lurched toward a chair facing her, overwhelmed with consciousness of the awkward figure he was cutting. This was a new experience for him. All his life, up to then, he had been unaware of being either graceful or awkward. Such thoughts of self had never entered his mind. He sat down gingerly on the edge of the chair, greatly worried by his hands. They were in the way wherever he put them. Arthur was leaving the room, and Martin Eden followed his exit with longing eyes. He felt lost, alone there in the room with that pale spirit of a woman. There was no barkeeper upon whom to call for drinks, no small boy to send around the corner for a can of beer and by means of that social fluid start the amenities of friendship flowing.

"You have such a scar on your neck, Mr. Eden," the girl was saying. "How did it happen? I am sure it must have been some adventure."

"A Mexican with a knife, miss," he answered, moistening his parched lips and clearing his throat. "It was just a fight. After I got the knife away, he tried to bite off my nose."

Baldly as he had stated it, in his eyes was a rich vision of that hot, starry night at Salina Cruz, the white strip of beach, the lights of the sugar steamers in the harbor, the voices of the drunken sailors in the distance, the jostling stevedores, the flaming passion in the Mexican's face, the glint of the beast-eyes in the starlight, the sting of the steel in his neck, and the rush of blood, the crowd and the cries, the two bodies, his and the Mexican's, locked together, rolling over and over and tearing up the sand, and from away off somewhere the mellow tinkling of a guitar. Such was the picture, and he thrilled to the memory of it, wondering if the man could paint it who had painted the pilot-schooner on the wall. The white beach, the stars, and the lights of the sugar steamers would look great, he thought, and midway on the sand the dark group of figures that surrounded the fighters. The knife occupied a place in the picture, he decided, and would show well, with a sort of gleam, in the light of the stars. But of all this no hint had crept into his speech. "He tried to bite off my nose," he concluded.

"Oh," the girl said, in a faint, far voice, and he noticed the shock in her sensitive face.

He felt a shock himself, and a blush of embarrassment shone faintly on his sunburned cheeks, though to him it burned as hotly as when his cheeks had been exposed to the open furnace-door in the fire-room. Such sordid things as stabbing affrays were evidently not fit subjects for conversation with a lady. People in the books, in her walk of life, did not talk about such things—perhaps they did not know about them, either.

There was a brief pause in the conversation they were trying to get started. Then she asked tentatively about the scar on his cheek. Even as she asked, he realized that she was making an effort to talk his talk, and he resolved to get away from it and talk hers.

"It was just an accident," he said, putting his hand to his cheek. "One night, in a calm, with a heavy sea running, the main-boom-lift carried away, an' next the tackle. The lift was wire, an' it was threshin' around like a snake. The whole watch was tryin' to grab it, an' I rushed in an' got swatted."

"Oh," she said, this time with an accent of comprehension, though secretly his speech had been so much Greek to her and she was wondering what a *lift* was and what *swatted* meant.

"This man Swineburne," he began, attempting to put his plan into execution and pronouncing the *i* long.

"Who?"

"Swineburne," he repeated, with the same mispronunciation. "The poet."

"Swinburne," she corrected.

"Yes, that's the chap," he stammered, his cheeks hot again. "How long since he died?"

"Why, I haven't heard that he was dead." She looked at him curiously. "Where did you make his acquaintance?"

"I never clapped eyes on him," was the reply. "But I read some of his poetry out of that book there on the table just before you come in. How do you like his poetry?"

Chapter 24 Jack London

And thereat she began to talk quickly and easily upon the subject he had suggested. He felt better, and settled back slightly from the edge of the chair, holding tightly to its arms with his hands, as if it might get away from him and buck him to the floor. He had succeeded in making her talk her talk, and while she rattled on, he strove to follow her, marvelling at all the knowledge that was stowed away in that pretty head of hers, and drinking in the pale beauty of her face. Follow her he did, though bothered by unfamiliar words that fell glibly from her lips and by critical phrases and thought-processes that were foreign to his mind, but that nevertheless stimulated his mind and set it tingling. Here was intellectual life, he thought, and here was beauty, warm and wonderful as he had never dreamed it could be. He forgot himself and stared at her with hungry eyes. Here was something to live for, to win to, to fight for—ay, and die for. The books were true. There were such women in the world. She was one of them. She lent wings to his imagination, and great, luminous canvases spread themselves before him, whereon loomed vague, gigantic figures of love and romance, and of heroic deeds for woman's sake— for a pale woman, a flower of gold. And through the swaying, palpitant vision, as through a fairy mirage, he stared at the real woman, sitting there and talking of literature and art. He listened as well, but he stared, unconscious of the fixity of his gaze or of the fact that all that was essentially masculine in his nature was shining in his eyes. But she, who knew little of the world of men, being a woman, was keenly aware of his burning eyes. She had never had men look at her in such fashion, and it embarrassed her. She stumbled and halted in her utterance. The thread of argument slipped from her. He frightened her, and at the same time it was strangely pleasant to be so looked upon. Her training warned her of peril and of wrong, subtle, mysterious, luring; while her instincts rang clarion-voiced through her being, impelling her to hurdle caste and place and gain to this traveller from another world, to this uncouth young fellow with lacerated hands and a line of raw red caused by the unaccustomed linen at his throat, who, all too evidently, was soiled and tainted by ungracious existence. She was clean, and her cleanness revolted; but she was woman, and she was just beginning to learn the paradox of woman.

"As I was saying—what was I saying?" She broke off abruptly and laughed merrily at her predicament.

"You was saying that this man Swinburne failed bein' a great poet because—an' that was as far as you got, miss," he prompted, while to himself he seemed suddenly hungry, and delicious little thrills crawled up and down his spine at the sound of her laughter. Like silver, he thought to himself, like tinkling silver bells; and on the instant, and for an instant, he was transported to a far land, where under pink cherry blossoms, he smoked a cigarette and listened to the bells of the peaked pagoda calling straw-sandalled devotees to worship.

"Yes, thank you," she said. "Swinburne fails, when all is said, because he is, well, indelicate. There are many of his poems that should never be read. Every line of the really great poets is filled with beautiful truth, and calls to all that is high and noble in the human. Not a line of the great poets can be spared without impoverishing the world by that much."

"I thought it was great," he said hesitatingly, "the little I read. I had no idea he was such a—a scoundrel. I guess that crops out in his other books."

"There are many lines that could be spared from the book you were reading," she said, her voice primly firm and dogmatic.

"I must 'a' missed 'em," he announced. "What I read was the real goods. It was all lighted up an' shining, an' it shun right into me an' lighted me up inside, like the sun or a searchlight. That's the way it landed on me, but I guess I ain't up much on poetry, miss."

He broke off lamely. He was confused, painfully conscious of his inarticulateness. He had felt the bigness and glow of life in what he had read, but his speech was inadequate. He could not express what he felt, and to himself he likened himself to a sailor, in a strange ship, on a dark night, groping about in the unfamiliar running rigging. Well, he decided, it was up to him to get acquainted in this new world. He had never seen anything that he couldn't get the hang of when he wanted to and it was about time for him to want to learn to talk the things that were inside of him so that she could understand. *She* was bulking large on his horizon.

"Now Longfellow—" she was saying.

"Yes, I've read 'm," he broke in impulsively, spurred on to exhibit and make the most of his little store of book knowledge, desirous of showing her that he was not wholly a stupid clod. "'The Psalm of Life,' 'Excelsior,' an'...I guess that's all."

She nodded her head and smiled, and he felt, somehow, that her smile was tolerant, pitifully tolerant. He was a fool to attempt to make a pretence that way. That Longfellow chap most likely had written countless books of poetry.

"Excuse me, miss, for buttin' in that way. I guess the real facts is that I don't know nothin' much about such things. It ain't in my class. But I'm goin' to make it in my class."

It sounded like a threat. His voice was determined, his eyes were flashing, the lines of his face had grown harsh. And to her it seemed that the angle of his jaw had changed; its pitch had become unpleasantly aggressive. At the same time a wave of intense virility seemed to surge out from him and impinge upon her.

"I think you could make it in—in your class," she finished with a laugh. "You are very strong."

Her gaze rested for a moment on the muscular neck, heavy corded, almost bull-like, bronzed by the sun, spilling over with rugged health and strength. And though he sat there, blushing and humble, again she felt drawn to him. She was surprised by a wanton thought that rushed into her mind. It seemed to her that if she could lay her two hands upon that neck that all its strength and vigor would flow out to her. She was shocked by this thought. It seemed to reveal to her an undreamed depravity in her nature. Besides, strength to her was a gross and brutish thing. Her ideal of masculine beauty had always been slender gracefulness. Yet the thought still persisted. It bewildered her that she should desire to place her hands on that sunburned neck. In truth, she was far from robust, and the need of her body and mind was for strength. But she did not know it. She knew only that no man had ever affected her before as this one had, who shocked her from moment to moment with his awful grammar.

"Yes, I ain't no invalid," he said. "When it comes down to hard-pan, I can digest scrap-iron. But just now I've got dyspepsia. Most of what you was sayin' I can't digest. Never trained that way, you see. I like books and poetry, and what time I've had I've read 'em, but I've never thought about 'em the way you have. That's why I can't talk about 'em. I'm like a navigator adrift on a strange sea without chart or compass. Now I want to get my bearin's. Mebbe you can put me right. How did you learn all this you've ben talkin'?"

"By going to school, I fancy, and by studying," she answered.

"I went to school when I was a kid," he began to object.

"Yes; but I mean high school, and lectures, and the university."

"You've gone to the university?" he demanded in frank amazement. He felt that she had become remoter from him by at least a million miles.

"I'm going there now. I'm taking special courses in English."

He did not know what "English" meant, but he made a mental note of that item of ignorance and passed on.

"How long would I have to study before I could go to the university?" he asked.

She beamed encouragement upon his desire for knowledge, and said: "That depends upon how much studying you have already done. You have never attended high school? Of course not. But did you finish grammar school?"

"I had two years to run, when I left," he answered. "But I was always honorably promoted at school."

The next moment, angry with himself for the boast, he had gripped the arms of the chair so savagely that every finger-end was stinging. At the same moment he became aware that a woman was entering the room. He saw the girl leave her chair and trip swiftly across the floor to the newcomer. They kissed each other, and, with arms around each other's waists, they advanced toward him. That must be her mother, he thought. She was a tall, blonde woman, slender, and stately, and beautiful. Her gown was what he might expect in such a house. His eyes delighted in the graceful lines of it. She and her dress together reminded him of women on the stage. Then he remembered seeing similar grand ladies and gowns entering the London theatres while he stood and watched and the policemen shoved him back into the drizzle beyond the awning. Next his mind leaped to the Grand Hotel at Yokohama, where, too, from the sidewalk, he had seen grand ladies.

Chapter 24 Jack London

Then the city and the harbor of Yokohama, in a thousand pictures, began flashing before his eyes. But he swiftly dismissed the kaleidoscope of memory, oppressed by the urgent need of the present. He knew that he must stand up to be introduced, and he struggled painfully to his feet, where he stood with trousers bagging at the knees, his arms loose-hanging and ludicrous, his face set hard for the impending ordeal.

Chapter 25

Theodore Dreiser (1871–1945)

Theodore Herman Albert Dreiser was born in Terre Haute, Indiana, on August 27, 1871, the twelfth of thirteen children. His gentle and devoted mother was illiterate; his German immigrant father was severe and distant. From the former he seems to have absorbed a quality of compassionate wonder; from the latter he seems to have inherited moral earnestness and the capacity to persist in the face of failure, disappointment, and despair.

Dreiser's childhood was decidedly unhappy. The large family moved from house to house in Indiana dogged by poverty, insecurity, and internal division. One of his brothers became a famous popular songwriter under the name of Paul Dresser, but other brothers and sisters drifted into drunkenness, promiscuity, and squalor. Dreiser as a youth was as ungainly, confused, shy, and full of vague yearnings as most of his fictional protagonists, male and female. In this as in many other ways, Dreiser's novels are direct projections of his inner life as well as careful transcriptions of his expriences.

From the age of fifteen Dreiser was essentially on his own, earning meager support from a variety of menial jobs. A high school teacher staked him to a year at Indiana University in 1889, but Dreiser's education was to come from experience and from independent reading and thinking. This education began in 1892 when he wangled his first newspaper job with the *Chicago Globe*. Over the next decade, as an itinerant journalist, Dreiser slowly groped his way to authorship, testing what he knew from direct experience against what he was learning from reading Charles Darwin, Ernst Haeckel, Thomas Huxley, and Herbert Spencer, those late-nineteenth-century scientists and social scientists who lent support to the view that nature and society had

Chapter 25 Theodore Dreiser

no divine sanction.

Sister Carrie (1900), which traced the material rise of Carrie Meeber and the tragic decline of G.W. Hurstwood, was Dreiser's first novel. Because it depicted social transgressions by characters who felt no remorse and largely escaped punishment, and because it used "strong" language and used names of living persons, it was virtually suppressed by its publisher, who printed but refused to promote the book. Since its reissue in 1907 it has steadily risen in popularity and scholarly acceptance as one of the key works in the Dreiser canon. Indeed, though turn-of-the-century readers found Dreiser's point of view crude and immoral, his influence on the fiction of the first quarter of the twentieth century is perhaps greater than any other writer's. In this early period some of his best short fictions were written, among them *Nigger Jeff* and *Butcher Rogaum's Daughter*.

In the first years of the twentieth century Dreiser suffered a breakdown. With the help of his brother Paul, however, he eventually recovered and by 1904 was on the way to several successful years as an editor, the last of them as editorial director of the Butterick Publishing Company. In 1910 he resigned to write *Jannie Gerhardt* (1911), the first of a long succession of books that marked his turn to writing as a full-time career.

In *The Financier* (1912), *The Titan* (1914), and *The Stoic* (not published until 1947), Dreiser shifted from the pathos of helpless protagonists to the power of those unusual individuals who assumed dominant roles in business and society. The protagonist of this "Trilogy of Desire" (as Dreiser described it), Frank Cowperwood, is modeled after the Chicago speculator Charles T. Yerkes. These novels of the businessman as buccaneer introduced, even more explicitly than had *Sister Carrie*, the notion that men of high sexual energy were financially successful, a theme that is carried over into the rather weak autobiographical novel *The "Genius"* (1915).

The identification of potency with money is at the heart of Dreiser's greatest and most successful novel, *An American Tragedy* (1925). The center of this immense novel's thick texture of biographical circumstance, social fact, and industrial detail is a young man who acts as if the only way he can be truly fulfilled is by acquiring wealth—through marriage if necessary.

During the last two decades of his life Dreiser turned entirely away from fiction and toward political activism and polemical writing. He visited the Soviet Union in 1927 and published *Dreiser Looks at Russia* the following year. In the 1930s, like many other American intellectuals and writers, Dreiser was increasingly attracted by the philosophical program of the Communist Party. Unable to believe in traditional religious credos, yet unable to give up his strong sense of justice, he continued to seek a way to reconcile his determinism with his compassionate sense of the mystery of life.

In his lifetime Dreiser was controversial as a man and as a writer. He was accused, with some justice by conventional standards, of being immoral in his personal behavior, a poor thinker, and a dangerous political radical; his style was said (by critics more than by fellow authors) to be ponderous and his narrative sense weak. As time passes, however, Dreiser has been recognized as a profound and prescient critic of debased American values and as a powerful novelist.

Sister Carrie

The Story

When Carrie Meeber left her hometown in Wisconsin, she had nothing but a few dollars and a certain unspoiled beauty and charm. Young, inexperienced, she was going to Chicago to live with her sister and to find work. While on the train, she met Charles Drouet, a genial, flashy traveling salesman. Before the train pulled into the station, they had exchanged addresses, and Drouet promised to call on Carrie at the sister's house.

When she arrived at her sister's home, Carrie discovered that her life there would be far from the happy, carefree existence of which she had dreamed. The Hansons were hard-working people, grim and penny-pinching, allowing themselves no pleasures, and living a dull, conventional life. It was clear to Carrie that Drouet could not possibly call there, not only because of the unattractive atmosphere, but also because the Hansons were sure to object to him. She wrote and told him that he was not to call, that she would get in touch with him later.

Chapter 25 Theodore Dreiser

Meanwhile Carrie went job-hunting and finally found work in a small shoe factory. Of her first wages, all but fifty cents went to her sister and brother-in-law. Then she fell ill and lost her job. Once again she had to look for work. Day after day she trudged the streets, without success. It seemed as if she would have to go back to Wisconsin, and the Hansons encouraged her to do so. If she could not bring in money, they did not want her.

One day, while Carrie was looking for work, she met Drouet and told him her troubles. He offered her money which, with reluctance, she finally accepted. The money was for clothes she needed, but she did not know how to explain the source of the money to her sister. Drouet solved the problem by suggesting that he rent a room for her, where she could keep her clothing. A few days later Carrie went to live with Drouet, who had promised to marry her as soon as he had completed a business deal.

In the meantime Drouet introduced her to a friend, G. W. Hurstwood. Hurstwood had a good job as the manager of a saloon, a comfortable home, a wife, and two grown children. More than twice Carrie's age, he nevertheless accepted Drouet's suggestion that he look in on her while the salesman was out of town on one of his trips. Before long Hurstwood was passionately in love with her. When Drouet came back, he discovered from a chambermaid that Carrie and Hurstwood had been going out together frequently. A scene followed. Carrie was furious when Drouet told her that Hurstwood was already married. She blamed Drouet for her folly, saying that he should have told her that Hurstwood was a married man.

Meanwhile, Mrs. Hurstwood had become suspicious of her husband. Drouet had secured for Carrie a part in a theatrical entertainment which a local lodge was presenting. Hurstwood, hearing that Carrie was to appear, persuaded many of his friends to go with him to the show. Mrs. Hurstwood learned of the affair and heard, too, that her husband had been seen riding with an unknown woman. She confronted Hurstwood and told him that she intended to sue for divorce. Faced with social and financial ruin, Hurstwood was in despair. One night he discovered that his employer's safe was open. He robbed it of several thousand dollars and went to Carrie's apartment. Drouet had just deserted her. Pretending that Drouet had been hurt, Hurstwood succeeded in getting Carrie on a train bound for Montreal. In Montreal Hurstwood was approached by an agent of his former employer, who urged him to return the money and to settle the issue quietly. Hurstwood returned all but a relatively small sum.

Under the name of Wheeler, he and Carrie were married, Carrie being all the while under the impression that the ceremony was legal. Then they left for New York. There Hurstwood looked for work, but with no success. Finally he bought a partnership in a small tavern. After a time the partnership was dissolved and he lost all his money. Every day he went looking for work. Gradually he grew less eager for a job, and began staying at home all day. When bills piled up, he and Carrie moved to a new apartment to escape their creditors.

Carrie set out to find work and was lucky enough to get a job as a chorus girl. With a friend, she took an apartment and left Hurstwood to himself. Soon Carrie became a well-known actress, and a local hotel invited her to become a guest there, at a nominal expense. Carrie had many friends and admirers. She had money and all the comforts and luxuries which appealed to a small-town girl.

Hurstwood had not fared so well. He could find no work. Once he worked as a scab, during some labor troubles, but he left that job because it was too hazardous. He became a bum, living in Bowery flophouses and begging on the streets. One day he went to see Carrie. She gave him some money, largely because she had seen Drouet and had learned for the first time of Hurstwood's theft in Chicago. She believed that Hurstwood had kept his disgrace a secret in order to spare her feelings.

Although Carrie was a toast of the town, she was not happy in spite of her success. She was invited to give performances abroad. In the meantime Hurstwood died and, unknown to Carrie, was buried in the potter's field. As Carrie was sailing for London, Hurstwood's ex-wife, daughter, and prospective son-in-law were coming into the city, eager for pleasure and social success, a success made possible by the daughter's coming marriage and by Hurstwood's divorce settlement, which had given the family all of his property.

Chapter I
The Magnet Attracting: A Waif Amid Forces

When Caroline Meeber boarded the afternoon train for Chicago, her total outfit consisted of a small trunk, a cheap imitation alligator-skin satchel, a small lunch in a paper box, and a yellow leather snap purse, containing her ticket, a scrap of paper with her sister's address in Van Buren Street, and four dollars in money. It was in August, 1889. She was eighteen years of age, bright, timid, and full of the illusions of ignorance and youth. Whatever touch of regret at parting characterised her thoughts, it was certainly not for advantages now being given up. A gush of tears at her mother's farewell kiss, a touch in her throat when the cars clacked by the flour mill where her father worked by the day, a pathetic sigh as the familiar green environs of the village passed in review, and the threads which bound her so lightly to girlhood and home were irretrievably broken.

To be sure there was always the next station, where one might descend and return. There was the great city, bound more closely by these very trains which came up daily. Columbia City was not so very far away, even once she was in Chicago. What, pray, is a few hours—a few hundred miles? She looked at the little slip bearing her sister's address and wondered. She gazed at the green landscape, now passing in swift review, until her swifter thoughts replaced its impression with vague conjectures of what Chicago might be.

When a girl leaves her home at eighteen, she does one of two things. Either she falls into saving hands and becomes better, or she rapidly assumes the cosmopolitan standard of virtue and becomes worse. Of an intermediate balance, under the circumstances, there is no possibility. The city has its cunning wiles, no less than the infinitely smaller and more human tempter. There are large forces which allure with all the soulfulness of expression possible in the most cultured human. The gleam of a thousand lights is often as effective as the persuasive light in a wooing and fascinating eye. Half the undoing of the unsophisticated and natural mind is accomplished by forces wholly superhuman. A blare of sound, a roar of life, a vast array of human hives, appeal to the astonished senses in equivocal terms. Without a counsellor at hand to whisper cautious interpretations, what falsehoods may not these things breathe into the unguarded ear! Unrecognised for what they are, their beauty, like music, too often relaxes, then weakens, then perverts the simpler human perceptions.

Caroline, or Sister Carrie, as she had been half affectionately termed by the family, was possessed of a mind rudimentary in its power of observation and analysis. Self-interest with her was high, but not strong. It was, nevertheless, her guiding characteristic. Warm with the fancies of youth, pretty with the insipid prettiness of the formative period, possessed of a figure promising eventual shapeliness and an eye alight with certain native intelligence, she was a fair example of the middle American class—two generations removed from the emigrant. Books were beyond her interest—knowledge a sealed book. In the intuitive graces she was still crude. She could scarcely toss her head gracefully. Her hands were almost ineffectual. The feet, though small, were set flatly. And yet she was interested in her charms, quick to understand the keener pleasures of life, ambitious to gain in material things. A half-equipped little knight she was, venturing to reconnoitre the mysterious city and dreaming wild dreams of some vague, far-off supremacy, which should make it prey and subject—the proper penitent, grovelling at a woman's slipper.

"That," said a voice in her ear, "is one of the prettiest little resorts in Wisconsin."

"Is it?" she answered nervously.

The train was just pulling out of Waukesha. For some time she had been conscious of a man behind. She felt him observing her mass of hair. He had been fidgeting, and with natural intuition she felt a certain interest growing in that quarter. Her maidenly reserve, and a certain sense of what was conventional under the circumstances, called her to forestall and deny this familiarity, but the daring and magnetism of the individual, born of past experiences and triumphs, prevailed. She answered.

He leaned forward to put his elbows upon the back of her seat and proceeded to make himself volubly agreeable.

"Yes, that is a great resort for Chicago people. The hotels are swell. You are not familiar with this part of the country, are you?"

Chapter 25   Theodore Dreiser

"Oh, yes, I am," answered Carrie. "That is, I live at Columbia City. I have never been through here, though."

"And so this is your first visit to Chicago," he observed.

All the time she was conscious of certain features out of the side of her eye. Flush, colourful cheeks, a light moustache, a grey fedora hat. She now turned and looked upon him in full, the instincts of self-protection and coquetry mingling confusedly in her brain.

"I didn't say that," she said.

"Oh," he answered, in a very pleasing way and with an assumed air of mistake, "I thought you did."

Here was a type of the travelling canvasser for a manufacturing house—a class which at that time was first being dubbed by the slang of the day "drummers." He came within the meaning of a still newer term, which had sprung into general use among Americans in 1880, and which concisely expressed the thought of one whose dress or manners are calculated to elicit the admiration of susceptible young women—a "masher." His suit was of a striped and crossed pattern of brown wool, new at that time, but since become familiar as a business suit. The low crotch of the vest revealed a stiff shirt bosom of white and pink stripes. From his coat sleeves protruded a pair of linen cuffs of the same pattern, fastened with large, gold plate buttons, set with the common yellow agates known as "cat's-eyes." His fingers bore several rings—one, the ever-enduring heavy seal—and from his vest dangled a neat gold watch chain, from which was suspended the secret insignia of the Order of Elks. The whole suit was rather tight-fitting, and was finished off with heavy-soled tan shoes, highly polished, and the grey fedora hat. He was, for the order of intellect represented, attractive, and whatever he had to recommend him, you may be sure was not lost upon Carrie, in this, her first glance.

Lest this order of individual should permanently pass, let me put down some of the most striking characteristics of his most successful manner and method. Good clothes, of course, were the first essential, the things without which he was nothing. A strong physical nature, actuated by a keen desire for the feminine, was the next. A mind free of any consideration of the problems or forces of the world and actuated not by greed, but an insatiable love of variable pleasure. His method was always simple. Its principal element was daring, backed, of course, by an intense desire and admiration for the sex. Let him meet with a young woman once and he would approach her with an air of kindly familiarity, not unmixed with pleading, which would result in most cases in a tolerant acceptance. If she showed any tendency to coquetry he would be apt to straighten her tie, or if she "took up" with him at all, to call her by her first name. If he visited a department store it was to lounge familiarly over the counter and ask some leading questions. In more exclusive circles, on the train or in waiting stations, he went slower. If some seemingly vulnerable object appeared he was all attention—to pass the compliments of the day, to lead the way to the parlor car, carrying her grip, or, failing that, to take a seat next her with the hope of being able to court her to her destination. Pillows, books, a footstool, the shade lowered; all these figured in the things which he could do. If, when she reached her destination he did not alight and attend her baggage for her, it was because, in his own estimation, he had signally failed.

A woman should some day write the complete philosophy of clothes. No matter how young, it is one of the things she wholly comprehends. There is an indescribably faint line in the matter of man's apparel which somehow divides for her those who are worth glancing at and those who are not. Once an individual has passed this faint line on the way downward he will get no glance from her. There is another line at which the dress of a man will cause her to study her own. This line the individual at her elbow now marked for Carrie. She became conscious of an inequality. Her own plain blue dress, with its black cotton tape trimmings, now seemed to her shabby. She felt the worn state of her shoes.

"Let's see," he went on, "I know quite a number of people in your town. Morgenroth the clothier and Gibson the dry goods man."

"Oh, do you?" she interrupted, aroused by memories of longings their show windows had cost her.

At last he had a clew to her interest, and followed it deftly. In a few minutes he had come about into her seat. He talked of sales of clothing, his travels, Chicago, and the amusements of that city.

"If you are going there, you will enjoy it immensely. Have you relatives?"

"I am going to visit my sister," she explained.

"You want to see Lincoln Park," he said, "and Michigan Boulevard. They are putting up great buildings there. It's a second New York—great. So much to see—theatres, crowds, fine houses—oh, you'll like that."

There was a little ache in her fancy of all he described. Her insignificance in the presence of so much magnificence faintly affected her. She realised that hers was not to be a round of pleasure, and yet there was something promising in all the material prospect he set forth. There was something satisfactory in the attention of this individual with his good clothes. She could not help smiling as he told her of some popular actress of whom she reminded him. She was not silly, and yet attention of this sort had its weight.

"You will be in Chicago some little time, won't you?" he observed at one turn of the now easy conversation.

"I don't know," said Carrie vaguely—a flash vision of the possibility of her not securing employment rising in her mind.

"Several weeks, anyhow," he said, looking steadily into her eyes.

There was much more passing now than the mere words indicated. He recognised the indescribable thing that made up for fascination and beauty in her. She realised that she was of interest to him from the one standpoint which a woman both delights in and fears. Her manner was simple, though for the very reason that she had not yet learned the many little affectations with which women conceal their true feelings. Some things she did appeared bold. A clever companion—had she ever had one—would have warned her never to look a man in the eyes so steadily.

"Why do you ask?" she said.

"Well, I'm going to be there several weeks. I'm going to study stock at our place and get new samples. I might show you 'round."

"I don't know whether you can or not. I mean I don't know whether I can. I shall be living with my sister, and—"

"Well, if she minds, we'll fix that." He took out his pencil and a little pocket note-book as if it were all settled. "What is your address there?"

She fumbled her purse which contained the address slip.

He reached down in his hip pocket and took out a fat purse. It was filled with slips of paper, some mileage books, a roll of greenbacks. It impressed her deeply. Such a purse had never been carried by any one attentive to her. Indeed, an experienced traveller, a brisk man of the world, had never come within such close range before. The purse, the shiny tan shoes, the smart new suit, and the air with which he did things, built up for her a dim world of fortune, of which he was the centre. It disposed her pleasantly toward all he might do.

He took out a neat business card, on which was engraved Bartlett, Caryoe & Company, and down in the left-hand corner, Chas. H. Drouet.

"That's me," he said, putting the card in her hand and touching his name. "It's pronounced Drew-eh. Our family was French, on my father's side."

She looked at it while he put up his purse. Then he got out a letter from a bunch in his coat pocket. "This is the house I travel for," he went on, pointing to a picture on it, "corner of State and Lake." There was pride in his voice. He felt that it was something to be connected with such a place, and he made her feel that way.

"What is your address?" he began again, fixing his pencil to write.

She looked at his hand.

"Carrie Meeber," she said slowly. "Three hundred and fifty-four West Van Buren Street, care S. C. Hanson."

He wrote it carefully down and got out the purse again. "You'll be at home if I come around Monday night?" he said.

"I think so," she answered.

How true it is that words are but the vague shadows of the volumes we mean. Little audible links, they are, chaining together great inaudible feelings and purposes. Here were these two, bandying little phrases, drawing purses, looking at cards, and both unconscious of how inarticulate all their real feelings were. Neither was wise enough to be sure of the working of the mind of the other. He could not tell how his luring succeeded. She could not realise that she was drifting, until he secured her address. Now she felt that she had yielded something—he, that he had gained a victory. Already they felt

Chapter 25 Theodore Dreiser

that they were somehow associated. Already he took control in directing the conversation. His words were easy. Her manner was relaxed.

They were nearing Chicago. Signs were everywhere numerous. Trains flashed by them. Across wide stretches of flat, open prairie they could see lines of telegraph poles stalking across the fields toward the great city. Far away were indications of suburban towns, some big smokestacks towering high in the air.

Frequently there were two-story frame houses standing out in the open fields, without fence or trees, lone outposts of the approaching army of homes.

To the child, the genius with imagination, or the wholly untravelled, the approach to a great city for the first time is a wonderful thing. Particularly if it be evening—that mystic period between the glare and gloom of the world when life is changing from one sphere or condition to another. Ah, the promise of the night. What does it not hold for the weary! What old illusion of hope is not here forever repeated! Says the soul of the toiler to itself, "I shall soon be free. I shall be in the ways and the hosts of the merry. The streets, the lamps, the lighted chamber set for dining, are for me. The theatre, the halls, the parties, the ways of rest and the paths of song—these are mine in the night." Though all humanity be still enclosed in the shops, the thrill runs abroad. It is in the air. The dullest feel something which they may not always express or describe. It is the lifting of the burden of toil.

Sister Carrie gazed out of the window. Her companion, affected by her wonder, so contagious are all things, felt anew some interest in the city and pointed out its marvels.

"This is Northwest Chicago," said Drouet. "This is the Chicago River," and he pointed to a little muddy creek, crowded with the huge masted wanderers from far-off waters nosing the black-posted banks. With a puff, a clang, and a clatter of rails it was gone. "Chicago is getting to be a great town," he went on. "It's a wonder. You'll find lots to see here."

She did not hear this very well. Her heart was troubled by a kind of terror. The fact that she was alone, away from home, rushing into a great sea of life and endeavour, began to tell. She could not help but feel a little choked for breath—a little sick as her heart beat so fast. She half closed her eyes and tried to think it was nothing, that Columbia City was only a little way off.

"Chicago! Chicago!" called the brakeman, slamming open the door. They were rushing into a more crowded yard, alive with the clatter and clang of life. She began to gather up her poor little grip and closed her hand firmly upon her purse. Drouet arose, kicked his legs to straighten his trousers, and seized his clean yellow grip.

"I suppose your people will be here to meet you?" he said. "Let me carry your grip."

"Oh, no," she said. "I'd rather you wouldn't. I'd rather you wouldn't be with me when I meet my sister."

"All right," he said in all kindness. "I'll be near, though, in case she isn't here, and take you out there safely."

"You're so kind," said Carrie, feeling the goodness of such attention in her strange situation.

"Chicago!" called the brakeman, drawing the word out long. They were under a great shadowy train shed, where the lamps were already beginning to shine out, with passenger cars all about and the train moving at a snail's pace. The people in the car were all up and crowding about the door.

"Well, here we are," said Drouet, leading the way to the door. "Good-bye, till I see you Monday."

"Good-bye," she answered, taking his proffered hand.

"Remember, I'll be looking till you find your sister."

She smiled into his eyes.

They filed out, and he affected to take no notice of her. A lean-faced, rather commonplace woman recognised Carrie on the platform and hurried forward.

"Why, Sister Carrie!" she began, and there was a perfunctory embrace of welcome.

Carrie realised the change of affectional atmosphere at once. Amid all the maze, uproar, and novelty she felt cold reality taking her by the hand. No world of light and merriment. No round of amusement. Her sister carried with her most of the grimness of shift and toil.

Chapter 25 Theodore Dreiser

"Why, how are all the folks at home?" she began; "how is father, and mother?"

Carrie answered, but was looking away. Down the aisle, toward the gate leading into the waiting-room and the street, stood Drouet. He was looking back. When he saw that she saw him and was safe with her sister he turned to go, sending back the shadow of a smile. Only Carrie saw it. She felt something lost to her when he moved away. When he disappeared she felt his absence thoroughly. With her sister she was much alone, a lone figure in a tossing, thoughtless sea.

Part V
Twentieth-Century Literature

The United States began the twentieth century with a population of less than 76,000,000, almost two thirds of it rural. The expansion of the railroads after the Civil War had reduced the provincial isolation of the nation—by 1900 the United States had 200,000 miles of railroad tracks, more than all of Europe—yet the dominant symbol of mobility and industrialism that was to transform America had only begun to appear: In all the land there were only 8,000 horseless carriages and a mere 150 miles of paved country roads.

Three quarters of a century later the population had almost tripled. The vast majority of Americans lived in large urban centers. They owned 120,000,000 automobiles that congested 3,000,000 miles of roads and streets; more of the American land was paved than remained in virgin wilderness. The nation's wealth and its technological achievements on earth and in space had astonished the world.

In 1900 the American arts were poised on the brink of a turbulent modernity. In little more than two decades American painters, architects, composers, poets, playwrights, and novelists would adopt a variety of avant-garde doctrines so revolutionary as to exhaust the traditional vocabulary of the arts and require the creation of completely new descriptive terms: futurism, expressionism, postimpressionism, dadaism, cubism, imagism, and surrealism.

In the years preceding World War I, nineteenth-century realism and naturalism remained vital forces in American literature. Henry James, now living in England, published two of his greatest novels, *The Ambassadors* (1903) and *The Golden Bowl* (1904). The literary naturalists Stephen Crane and Frank Norris died in the first years of the century, but Theodore Dreiser's *Sister Carrie*, a commercial and critical failure when first published in 1900, was reissued in 1907 and won high praise for its grim, naturalistic portrayal of American society. Early in the century Ezra Pound and T. S. Eliot published works that would change the nature of American poetry, but their impact (and that of other modernist writers) on the general reading public was slight. The genteel tradition and popular romanticism still dominated the nation's literary tastes. The best-selling American books in the first decades of the twentieth century were historical romances.

Part V   Twentieth-Century Literature

The growth of mass-circulation periodicals created a rich marketplace for popular writers. By the 1920s general-audience magazines with circulations in the millions were paying as much as six thousand dollars for a short story and sixty thousand dollars for a serial. During the depression years of the 1930s the profitable mass market for literature temporarily declined, but after World War II it expanded enormously with the growth of the population, the increase of wealth and education, the expansion of mass distribution book clubs, and the technological advances in printing that made possible the publishing of vast numbers of inexpensive paperbacks.

Early in the century a rising number of "little magazines" brought numerous avant-garde writers to the attention of a limited but sophisticated audience. The most influential was *Poetry: A Magazine of Verse*, founded in Chicago by Harriet Monroe in 1912. Its first issue contained two poems by Ezra Pound. In 1915 it printed T. S. Eliot's "The Love Song of J. Alfred Prufrock." Within a few years it had published works by Edwin Arlington Robinson, Carl Sandburg, and Robert Frost, followed soon after by Robinson Jeffers, Wallace Stevens, and Hart Crane. Their works often forced changes in the traditional relationships between poets and their audiences, requiring readers armed with modernist sympathies and advanced intellectual understanding.

Although the form and direction of modern American literature had clearly begun to emerge in the first decades of the century, the First World War (1914–1918) stands as a great dividing line between the nineteenth century and contemporary America. World War I had its origins in the political turmoil of the early 1900s and in the vain rivalries of imperial powers that once had seemed to be the glory of their age. For the United States the war began as a crusade for purity and democracy, and at its end, President Woodrow Wilson proclaimed that Americans had gained everything for which they had fought. But out of the war's catastrophes and appalling waste came little more than a sense of the failure of political leaders and a belief in the futility of hope. No abiding solutions to the world's problems had been found, and the years following the war soon brought the resurgence of nationalism and the rise of new totalitarianism that would in turn produce a second world war less than a quarter of a century later.

Writers of the first postwar era self-consciously acknowledged that they were a "Lost Generation," devoid of faith and alienated from a civilization. Yet in the decade of the 1920s American literature achieved a new diversity and reached its greatest heights. The publication in 1922 of T. S. Eliot's *The Waste Land*, the most significant American poem of the twentieth century, helped to establish a modern tradition of literature rich with learning and allusive thought. In 1920 Sinclair Lewis published his memorable denunciation of American small-town provincialism in *Main Street*, and in the same year Theodore Dreiser began writing his masterpiece of naturalism, *An American Tragedy* (1925); F. Scott Fitzgerald summarized the experiences and attitudes of the decade in his short stories and in his novel *The Great Gatsby* (1925). Ernest Hemingway wrote *The Sun Also Rises* (1926) and *A Farewell to Arms* (1929), and William Faulkner published one of the most influential American novels of the age, *The Sound and the Fury* (1929).

After the First World War a group of new American dramatists emerged, and the American theater ceased to be wholly dependent on the dramatic traditions of Europe. Experimental playwrights, hostile to outworn and timid theatrical convention, created works of tragedy, stark realism, and social protest. In the "new American theater," plots, dialogue, staging, and acting differed radically from the bland dramatic farce of an earlier day. Plays by "advanced" dramatists won large audiences and drew widespread critical acclaim. Early in the 1920s the most prominent of the new American playwrights, Eugene O'Neill, established an international reputation with such plays as *The Emperor Jones* (1920), *Anna Christie* (1921) and *The Hairy Ape* (1922).

The years between 1920 and 1930 were a time of new directions and new achievements in all the arts. Numerous museums and galleries for modern art were established. The American skyscraper became the pre-eminent achievement of twentieth-century architecture. The American motion picture industry rose to world dominance. The Jazz music of American blacks—the most influential art form to originate in the United States—spread throughout the world. And with the slow disintegration of old prejudices came the

"Harlem Renaissance," a burst of literary achievement in the 1920s by black playwrights, poets, and novelists who presented new insights into the American experience and prepared the way for the emergence of numerous black writers after mid-century.

With the end of the decade came the stock market crash of 1929 and the Great Depression of the 1930s, cataclysmic events that shattered public complacency and transformed American society. The abrupt end of prosperity weakened the nation's confidence in its government and its political leaders. American artists of all kinds produced works of political and social criticism. Painters created harsh visions of American life on farms and in cities. Photographers recorded the miseries of poverty and want. John Steinbeck and other writers described the sweat-drenched lives of factory workers and migrant farmers in journalistic reports, in short stories, and in such memorable novels as *The Grapes of Wrath* (1939).

The social upheavals and the literary concerns of the Great Depression years ended with the prosperity and turmoil brought by the Second World War (1939–1945). After the war a new generation of American authors appeared, writing in the skeptical, ironic tradition of the earlier realists and naturalists. The writers of the fifties used a prose style modeled on the works of Ernest Hemingway and F. Scott Fitzgerald, narrative techniques derived from William Faulkner, and psychological insights taken from the writings of Sigmund Freud and his followers. In the 1960s and 1970s America's prose writers turned increasingly to experimental techniques, to absurd humor, and to mocking examination of the irrational and the disordered.

Chapter 26

Ezra Pound (1885–1972)

Ezra Loomis Pound was born in Hailey, Idaho, on October 30, 1885. He attended the University of Pennsylvania and then Hamilton College, from which he graduated in 1905. He returned to the University of Pennsylvania for graduate study in Romance languages. He took an M.A. in 1906, spent the summer abroad, and returned to Pennsylvania on a fellowship for another year of study in Renaissance literature. In 1908 he again went abroad, and by 1920 regarded himself as a permanent expatriate.

By 1912, he was the author of seven volumes which identified him as a distinct poetic personality, who combined a command of the older tradition with impressive and often daring originality. When Harriet Monroe in 1912 issued from Chicago the prospectus for her new magazine, *Poetry: A Magazine of Verse*, Pound characteristically proposed himself as its foreign correspondent.

He was a prolific essayist for the little magazines of New York, London, and Paris, which then constituted a large and exciting literary world. He unselfishly and persistently championed the experimental and often unpopular artists whom he approved—George Antheil, the musician; Henri Gaudier-Brzeska, pioneer abstractionist sculptor, killed in World War I; and James Joyce, among others. Most important of all, perhaps, was the advice and encouragement which he gave to T. S. Eliot, who had candidly acknowledged the value of Pound's assistance in the final revision of *The Waste Land* (1922) and in connection with other poems of that period. Both poets of independent power and interests, they became the early leaders in restoring to poetry the use of literary reference as an imaginative instrument.

Chapter 26 Ezra Pound

Such referential figures of speech assume that the poet and his readers share a common cultural inheritance. In the present age of increasing complexity, diffuseness, and specialization of knowledge, both Pound and Eliot required of their readers a familiarity with the classics, the productions of the Italian and English Renaissance, and specialized areas of Continental literature, including the works of the French symbolists. After *The Waste Land*, Eliot's poetry became somewhat less difficult in this respect, while Pound's continued to draw fundamentally upon his formidably recondite culture. A large part of his work consists of "reconstructions" in modern English of poems from earlier literatures, chiefly Greek, Latin, Italian, Provencal, and Chinese. Among his reconstructions, his *Homage to Sextus Propertius* is a masterpiece. He called the often-expanded volume of his poems his *Personae*, or "masks," referring to the conventionalized masks of the Greek drama.

A final obstacle for the reader is the violence of Pound's distrust of capitalism and his allegiance to the Utopian concept of "social credit." Nevertheless, *Hugh Selwyn Mauberley* (1920), considered as a satire of the materialistic forces involved in World War I, is a masterpiece. In *The Cantos*, begun in 1917, the satire became intensified. The progressive series, exceeding the proposed limit of one hundred poems, are loosely connected cantos, like Dante's *La Divina Commedia* in three sections, but representing a comedy human, not divine, dealing with the wreck of civilizations by reason of the infidelity of mankind in the three epochs—the ancient world, the Renaissance, and the modern period. With *The Pisan Cantos* of 1948 and *Section: Rock-Drill* (1955), Cantos I to XCV had all been published except for two. By 1959 they numbered CIX, badly needing explication. A considerable number contain lyrical passages of genuine power; they are in places supremely witty, and many of their topical references are shrewd and valuable. But their complexity renders them controversial. Somewhat resembling *Finnegans Wake* in structure, Pound's vast poem now has a position similar to that of Joyce's novel. Pound's critics have developed a voluminous commentary concerning *The Cantos*, which, like Joyce's work, employs the complex association of scholarly lore, anthropology, modern history and personages, private history and witticisms, and obscure literary interpolations in various languages, including Chinese ideograms.

In 1924 Pound left Paris for Rapallo, Italy, attracted by Mussolini's faithless promises of democratic state socialism. During World War II, Pound, on behalf of the Italian government, conducted radio broadcasts beamed at the American troops. He was returned to the United States as a citizen accused of treason, but on examination he was declared insane. After the treason charges were dismissed in 1958, Pound returned to Italy, where he died in 1972.

A Virginal[1]

No, no! Go from me. I have left her lately.
I will not spoil my sheath with lesser brightness,
For my surrounding air hath a new lightness;
Slight are her arms, yet they have bound me straitly
And left me cloaked as with a gauze of æther;   5
As with sweet leaves; as with subtle clearness.
Oh, I have picked up magic in her nearness
To sheathe me half in half the things that sheathe her.
No, no! Go from me. I have still the flavour,
Soft as spring wind that's come from birchen bowers.   10
Green come the shoots, aye April in the branches,
As winter's wound with her sleight hand she staunches,
Hath of the trees a likeness of the savour:
As white their bark, so white this lady's hours.

Note
1. The title of this sonnet signifies a small spinet, a musical instrument popular in the sixteenth and seventeenth centuries.

🌿 **Salutation the Second** (excerpt)

You were praised, my books,
>because I had just come from the country;
I was twenty years behind the times
>so you found an audience ready.
I do not disown you, 5
>do not you disown your progeny.

Here they stand without quaint devices,
Here they are with nothing archaic about them.
Observe the irritation in general:

"Is this," they say, "the nonsense 10
>that we expect of poets?"
"Where is the Picturesque?"
>"Where is the vertigo of emotion?"
"No! his first work was the best."
>"Poor Dear! he has lost his illusions." 15

Go, little naked and impudent songs,
Go with a light foot!

🌿 **A Pact**

I make a pact with you, Walt Whitman—
I have detested you long enough.
I come to you as a grown child
Who has had a pig-headed father;
I am old enough now to make friends. 5
It was you that broke the new wood,
Now is a time for carving.
We have one sap and one root—
Let there be commerce between us.

In a Station of the Metro[1]

The apparition of these faces in the crowd;
Petals on a wet, black bough.

Note

1. metro: Paris subway

The River-Merchant's Wife: A Letter[1]

While my hair was still cut straight across my forehead
I played about the front gate, pulling flowers.
You came by on bamboo stilts, playing horse,
You walked about my seat, playing with blue plums.
And we went on living in the village of Chōkan[2]:   5
Two small people, without dislike or suspicion.

At fourteen I married My Lord you.
I never laughed, being bashful.
Lowering my head, I looked at the wall.
Called to, a thousand times, I never looked back.   10

At fifteen I stopped scowling,
I desired my dust to be mingled with yours
Forever and forever and forever.
Why should I climb the look out?

At sixteen you departed,   15
You went into far Ku-tō-en[3], by the river of swirling eddies,
And you have been gone five months.
The monkeys make sorrowful noise overhead.

You dragged your feet when you went out.
By the gate now, the moss is grown, the different mosses,   20
Too deep to clear them away!
The leaves fall early this autumn, in wind.
The paired butterflies are already yellow with August
Over the grass in the West garden;
They hurt me. I grow older.   25
If you are coming down through the narrows of the river Kiang,
Please let me know beforehand,
And I will come out to meet you
           As far as Chō-fū-Sa[4].

Notes

1. This is an adaptation from the Chinese poem of Li Po (701–762 A.D.), named Rihaku in Japanese. Pound found the material in the papers of Ernest Fenollosa and used Japanese paraphrases in making the translation with the result that the proper names are their Japanese equivalents. Among Pound's alterations are the substitution of blue for green (line 4), and of the image of walking on bamboo stilts for that of riding a bamboo horse (line 3).
2. the village of Chōkan: suburb of Nanjing
3. Ku-tō-en: name of a gigantic rock up the Yangtze River
4. Chō-fū-Sa: a beach several hundred miles away from Nanjing

Chapter 27

Edwin Arlington Robinson (1869–1935)

Edwin Arlington Robinson was one of the most productive of the new poets in the late years of the nineteenth century. He was born in 1869 in the village of Head Tide, Maine, but grew up in Gardiner, Maine, which later became "Tilbury Town," the title of an early collection of Robinson's poetry, and the background for a series of vivid character sketches in verse. He graduated from high school in Gardiner, entered Harvard, then left two years later to devote his life to poetry.

Robinson began his career as a poet in bleakness and poverty. He lived in difficult circumstances in New York City, working at various odd jobs. Sometime around 1904 one of his early books, *Captain Craig*, came to the attention of President Theodore Roosevelt. The President, learning of the poet's difficulties, in 1905 gave Robinson a clerk's job in the Customs House in New York. The position was not a particularly high-paying one, but the new job had the desired effect of allowing Robinson to devote much more of his time to poetry.

In the following years, Robinson's powerful, realistic poems continued to impress a growing audience. By 1910 he was able to devote himself completely to writing. He produced a large body of work, became one of the most widely read poets, and was honored with the Pulitzer Prize in 1922, 1925, and 1928.

Robinson's approach to characterization, and his diction and themes, reflect the new movements in poetry. "Richard Cory" and "Miniver Cheevy" are good examples of his realistic attitudes. Among his later poems, one of the finest is a brilliant commentary on Shakespeare's character called "Ben Jonson Entertains a Man from Stratford." Robinson was also interested in the

Chapter 27 Edwin Arlington Robinson

Arthurian legends, and in his long works *Merlin*, *Lancelot*, and *Tristram*, he wrote the most extensive poems based on these stories since Tennyson. While the English poet dwelt mainly on the pageantry and romance of King Arthur's court, Robinson typically explored the dark, hidden faults in human character that led to the decline and fall of the Round Table.

Robinson's poems sometimes appear to be simple, yet the surface simplicity often serves to conceal an intricacy and subtlety of thought. Like Robert Frost, Robinson is also noted for his use of a dry, sometimes biting, New England humor. Robinson's skill as a poet has continued to earn even greater praise in recent years.

The House on the Hill[1].

They are all gone away,
    The House is shut and still,
There is nothing more to say.

Through broken walls and gray
    The winds blow bleak and shrill: 5
They are all gone away.

Nor is there one to-day
    To speak them good or ill:
There is nothing more to say.

Why is it then we stray   10
    Around the sunken sill?
They are all gone away.

And our poor fancy-play
    For them is wasted skill:
There is nothing more to say.   15

There is ruin and decay
   In the House on the Hill:
They are all gone away,
There is nothing more to say.

Note

1. The form of the poem is that of the villanelle, a French form of 19 lines employing only two rhymes. A slightly different version was first published in *The New York Globe* in 1894.

Richard Cory

Whenever Richard Cory went down town,
We people on the pavement looked at him:
He was a gentleman from sole to crown,
Clean favored, and imperially slim.

And he was always quietly arrayed, 5
And he was always human when he talked;
But still he fluttered pulses when he said,
"Good-morning," and he glittered when he walked.

And he was rich—yes, richer than a king—
And admirably schooled in every grace: 10
In fine, we thought that he was everything
To make us wish that we were in his place.

So on we worked, and waited for the light,
And went without the meat, and cursed the bread;
And Richard Cory, one calm summer night, 15
Went home and put a bullet through his head.

Chapter 27   Edwin Arlington Robinson

🦌 Miniver Cheevy

Miniver Cheevy, child of scorn,
    Grew lean while he assailed the seasons;
He wept that he was ever born,
    And he had reasons.

Miniver loved the days of old   5
    When swords were bright and steeds were prancing;
The vision of a warrior bold
    Would set him dancing.

Miniver sighed for what was not,
    And dreamed, and rested from his labors;   10
He dreamed of Thebes and Camelot,
    And Priam's neighbors.[1]

Miniver mourned the ripe renown
    That made so many a name so fragrant;
He mourned Romance, now on the town,   15
    And Art, a vagrant.

Miniver loved the Medici[2],
    Albeit he had never seen one;
He would have sinned incessantly
    Could he have been one.   20

Miniver cursed the commonplace
    And eyed a khaki suit with loathing;
He missed the mediæval grace
    Of iron clothing.

Miniver scorned the gold he sought,   25

> But sore annoyed was he without it;
> Miniver thought, and thought, and thought,
> And thought about it.
>
> Miniver Cheevy, born too late,
> Scratched his head and kept on thinking;   30
> Miniver coughed, and called it fate,
> And kept on drinking.

Notes

1. Thebes was an ancient city in Boeotia, rival of Athens and Sparta for supremacy in Greece and the setting of Sophocles' tragedies about Oedipus; Camelot is the legendary court of King Arthur and the knights of the Round Table; the neighbors of King Priam in Homer's *Iliad* are his heroic compatriots in the doomed city of Troy.
2. the Medici: family of wealthy merchants, statesmen, and art patrons in Renaissance Florence

Chapter 28

Robert Frost (1874–1963)

Robert Frost was born in San Francisco and spent his early childhood in the Far West. At the death of his father, when Frost was eleven, the family moved to Salem, New Hampshire. After graduating from high school as valedictorian and class poet in 1892, Frost entered Dartmouth College but soon left to work at odd jobs and to write poetry. In 1897 he tried college again—Harvard—but he left at the end of two years, having acquired an enduring dislike for academic convention.

For the next twelve years Frost eked out a minimal living by teaching and farming while continuing to write his poems. In 1912 he decided to venture everything on a literary career. Leaving New Hampshire, he sailed for England, where he hoped "to write poetry without further scandal to friends or family." In London, he soon found a publisher, and his first book, *A Boy's Will* (1913), brought him to the attention of influential critics, among them the American expatriate Ezra Pound, who praised Frost as an authentic poet.

Following the publication of a second volume of poems, *North of Boston* (1914), Frost returned home, determined to win recognition in his native land. To support himself he taught in colleges and gave poetry readings throughout much of the United States. His fame grew with the appearance of a succession of books: *Mountain Interval* (1916), *New Hampshire* (1923), *West-Running Brook* (1928), *A Further Range* (1936), *A Witness Tree* (1942), *Steeple Bush* (1947), *In the Clearing* (1962). By the end of his life he had become a national bard; he received honorary degrees from forty-four colleges and universities and won four Pulitzer Prizes; the United States Senate passed resolutions honoring his birthdays, and when he was eighty-seven he read his poetry at the inauguration of President John F. Kennedy.

Frost had rejected the revolutionary poetic principles of his contemporaries, choosing instead "the old-fashioned way to be new." He employed the plain speech of rural New Englanders and preferred the short, traditional forms of lyric and narrative. As a poet of nature he had obvious affinities with romantic writers, notably Wordsworth and Emerson. He saw nature as a storehouse of analogy and symbol, announcing, "I'm always saying something that's just the edge of something more," but he had little faith in religious dogma or speculative thought. His concern with nature reflected deep moral uncertainties, and his poetry, for all its apparent simplicity, often probes mysteries of darkness and irrationality in the bleak and chaotic landscapes of an indifferent universe where men stand alone, unaided and perplexed.

After Apple-Picking

My long two-pointed ladder's sticking through a tree
Toward heaven still,
And there's a barrel that I didn't fill
Beside it, and there may be two or three
Apples I didn't pick upon some bough.   5
But I am done with apple-picking now.
Essence of winter sleep is on the night,
The scent of apples: I am drowsing off.
I cannot rub the strangeness from my sight
I got from looking through a pane of glass   10
I skimmed this morning from the drinking trough
And held against the world of hoary grass.
It melted, and I let it fall and break.
But I was well
Upon my way to sleep before it fell,   15
And I could tell
What form my dreaming was about to take.
Magnified apples appear and disappear,

Stem end and blossom end,
And every fleck of russet showing clear. 20
My instep arch not only keeps the ache,
It keeps the pressure of a ladder-round.
I feel the ladder sway as the boughs bend.
And I keep hearing from the cellar bin
The rumbling sound 25
Of load on load of apples coming in.
For I have had too much
Of apple-picking: I am overtired
Of the great harvest I myself desired.
There were ten thousand thousand fruit to touch, 30
Cherish in hand, lift down, and not let fall.
For all
That struck the earth,
No matter if not bruised or spiked with stubble,
Went surely to the cider-apple heap 35
As of no worth.
One can see what will trouble
This sleep of mine, whatever sleep it is.
Were he not gone,
The woodchuck could say whether it's like his 40
Long sleep, as I describe its coming on,
Or just some human sleep.

The Road Not Taken

Two roads diverged in a yellow wood,
And sorry I could not travel both
And be one traveler, long I stood
And looked down one as far as I could
To where it bent in the undergrowth; 5

Then took the other, as just as fair,
And having perhaps the better claim,
Because it was grassy and wanted wear;
Though as for that, the passing there
Had worn them really about the same,   10

And both that morning equally lay
In leaves no step had trodden black.
Oh, I kept the first for another day!
Yet knowing how way leads on to way,
I doubted if I should ever come back.   15

I shall be telling this with a sigh
Somewhere ages and ages hence:
Two roads diverged in a wood, and I—
I took the one less traveled by,
And that has made all the difference.   20

Stopping by Woods on a Snowy Evening

Whose woods these are I think I know.
His house is in the village, though;
He will not see me stopping here
To watch his woods fill up with snow.

My little horse must think it queer   5
To stop without a farmhouse near
Between the woods and frozen lake
The darkest evening of the year.

He gives his harness bells a shake
To ask if there is some mistake.   10
The only other sound's the sweep

Of easy wind and downy flake.

The woods are lovely, dark and deep,
But I have promises to keep,
And miles to go before I sleep, 15
And miles to go before I sleep.

Departmental

An ant on the tablecloth
Ran into a dormant moth
Of many times his size.
He showed not the least surprise.
His business wasn't with such. 5
We gave it scarcely a touch,
And was off on his duty run.
Yet if he encountered one
Of the hive's enquiry squad
Whose work is to find out God 10
And the nature of time and space,
He would put him onto the case.
Ants are a curious race;
One crossing with hurried tread
The body of one of their dead 15
Isn't given a moment's arrest—
Seems not even impressed.
But he no doubt reports to any
With whom he crosses antennae,
And they no doubt report 20
To the higher-up at court.
Then word goes forth in Formic[1]:
"Death's come to Jerry McCormic,
Our selfless forager Jerry.

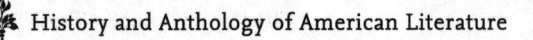

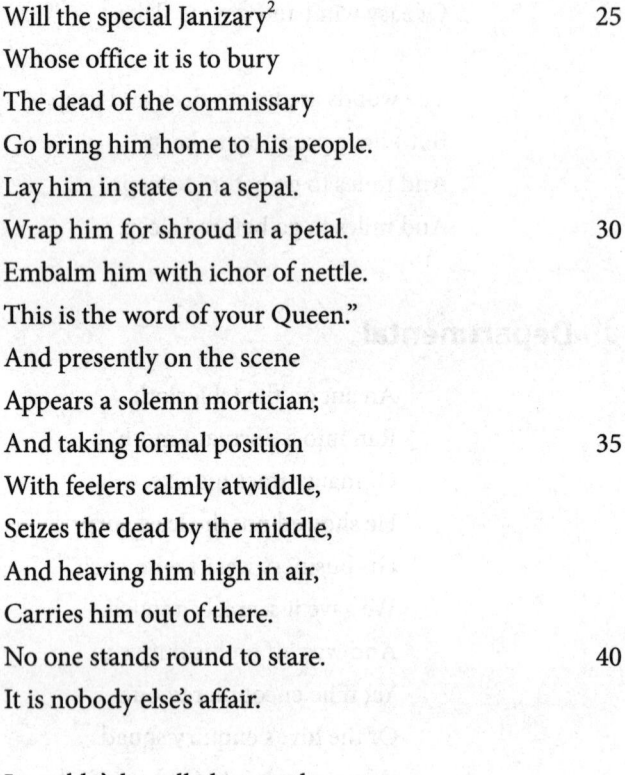

Will the special Janizary[2] 25
Whose office it is to bury
The dead of the commissary
Go bring him home to his people.
Lay him in state on a sepal.
Wrap him for shroud in a petal. 30
Embalm him with ichor of nettle.
This is the word of your Queen."
And presently on the scene
Appears a solemn mortician;
And taking formal position 35
With feelers calmly atwiddle,
Seizes the dead by the middle,
And heaving him high in air,
Carries him out of there.
No one stands round to stare. 40
It is nobody else's affair.

It couldn't be called ungentle.
But how thoroughly departmental.

Notes
1. Formic: acid emitted by ants
2. Janizary: troop of Turkish infantry soldiers

Design

I found a dimpled spider, fat and white,
On a white heal-all[1], holding up a moth
Like a white piece of rigid satin cloth—
Assorted characters of death and blight

Mixed ready to begin the morning right, 5
Like the ingredients of a witches' broth—
A snow-drop spider, a flower like a froth,
And dead wings carried like a paper kite.

What had that flower to do with being white,
The wayside blue and innocent heal-all? 10
What brought the kindred spider to that height,
Then steered the white moth thither in the night?
What but design of darkness to appall?—
If design govern in a thing so small.

Note

1. heal-all: an albino version of the common field flower *Prunella vulgaris*, whose hooded blossom is normally violet or blue, whose leaves are either toothed or toothless, and which was once widely used as a medicine

The Most of It

He thought he kept the universe alone;
For all the voice in answer he could wake
Was but the mocking echo of his own
From some tree-hidden cliff across the lake.
Some morning from the boulder-broken beach 5
He would cry out on life, that what it wants
Is not its own love back in copy speech,
But counter-love, original response.
And nothing ever came of what he cried
Unless it was the embodiment that crashed 10
In the cliff's talus[1] on the other side,
And then in the far distant water splashed,

>But after a time allowed for it to swim,
>Instead of proving human when it neared
>And someone else additional to him, 15
>As a great buck it powerfully appeared,
>Pushing the crumpled water up ahead,
>And landed pouring like a waterfall,
>And stumbled through the rocks with horny tread,
>And forced the underbrush—and that was all. 20

Note

1. talus: sloping bank of rock fragments at the foot of a cliff

Chapter 29
Carl Sandburg (1878–1967)

Like his contemporary Robert Frost, Carl Sandburg lived to enjoy enormous popular acclaim; by the end of his life he had become a familiar figure to national television audiences who listened to him read his poems, sing folk ballads, and relate anecdotes about Lincoln. But unlike Frost, Sandburg never gained the broad approval of the literary establishment, the critics whom Sandburg in turn accused of taking snobbish pride in the fact that "the average truck driver...can't understand them."

Sandburg was the son of Swedish immigrants who settled in Galesburg, Illinois; his father was a machinist's blacksmith. Sandburg had irregular schooling and worked as an itinerant laborer and jack-of-all-trades in the Midwest before enlisting in the army during the Spanish-American War and serving as correspondent for the *Galesburg Evening Mail*. After the war he attended Lombard College, working for the fire department to support himself, but withdrew without a degree in 1902. He worked as advertising writer, roving reporter, and organizer for the Social Democratic Party in Wisconsin, and he married the sister of famed photographer Edward Steichen in 1908. He served as secretary to the socialist mayor of Milwaukee (1910–1912) and wrote editorials for the *Milwaukee Leader* before moving to Chicago in 1913. He had published a pamphlet of poems privately in Galesburg in 1904, and *Poetry* magazine published his poem "Chicago" in 1914.

The poems that made Sandburg famous appeared in four volumes: *Chicago Poems* (1916), *Cornhuskers* (1918), *Smoke and Steel* (1920), and *Slabs of the Sunburnt West* (1922). With the precedent of Whitman behind them, they present a sweeping panorama of American life, encompassing prairie, eastern, and western landscapes as well as vignettes of the modern city. They celebrate, from the standpoint of a populist radical, the lives of outcasts, the contributions of immigrants and common people to urban culture, and the occupations of those who have survived or been sacrificed in the rise of industrial civilization. Sandburg's language draws on the colorful diction of immigrants and the lingo of urban dwellers, but unvarnished directness of statement takes precedence over subtleties of imagery or rhythm in his verse, even in such poems as "Cool Tombs," where the consistency of tone is impressive, or in "Flash Crimson," where the techniques of symbolism are used. Sandburg avoided regular stanza patterns and traditional blank verse and wrote an utterly free verse, developing Whitman's long line but moderating its rhetorical impact and intensity, and composing what are often in effect prose paragraphs. As one who undertook as a spokesman for the common people to inscribe "public speech," he was proud late in his career to "favor simple poems for simple people."

His most ambitious attempt to accomplish that aim was *The People, Yes* (1936), consisting of prose vignettes, anecdotes, and verse, which drew on his studies of American folksongs that preoccupied his attention after the publication of *The American Songbag* in 1927. Indeed, from 1918 on, other professional activities took precedence over his verse. He was a columnist, editorial writer, and feature writer on the *Chicago Daily News* from 1918 to 1933, and he published an account of *The Chicago Race Riots* in 1919. He published *Rootabaga Stories* (for children) and two sequels between 1922 and 1930, and his biographies include *Steichen the Photographer* (1929) and *Mary Lincoln* (1932). His major work in prose was a monumental and celebratory biography of Abraham Lincoln, beginning with the two-volume *The Prairie Years* (1926) and culminating in *The War Years* (1939), a four-volume work which won the Pulitzer Prize in 1940.

Chicago

> Hog Butcher for the World,
> Tool Maker, Stacker of Wheat,

Chapter 29 Carl Sandburg

    Player with Railroads and the Nation's Freight Handler;
    Stormy, husky, brawling,
    City of the Big Shoulders: 5

They tell me you are wicked and I believe them, for I have seen your painted
    women under the gas lamps luring the farm boys.
And they tell me you are crooked and I answer: Yes, it is true I have seen
    the gunman kill and go free to kill again.
And they tell me you are brutal and my reply is: On the faces of women   10
    and children I have seen the marks of wanton hunger.
And having answered so I turn once more to those who sneer at this my
    city, and I give them back the sneer and say to them:
Come and show me another city with lifted head singing so proud to be
    alive and coarse and strong and cunning.   15
Flinging magnetic curses amid the toil of piling job on job, here is a tall
    bold slugger set vivid against the little soft cities;
Fierce as a dog with tongue lapping for action, cunning as a savage pitted
    against the wilderness,
    Bareheaded,   20
    Shoveling,
    Wrecking,
    Planning,
    Building, breaking, rebuilding,
Under the smoke, dust all over his mouth, laughing with white teeth,   25
Under the terrible burden of destiny laughing as a young man laughs,
Laughing even as an ignorant fighter laughs who has never lost a battle,
Bragging and laughing that under his wrist is the pulse, and under his
    ribs the heart of the people,
                      Laughing!   30
Laughing the stormy, husky, brawling laughter of Youth, half-naked,
    sweating, proud to be Hog Butcher, Tool Maker, Stacker of Wheat,
    Player with Railroads and Freight Handler to the Nation.

The Harbor

    Passing through huddled and ugly walls
    By doorways where women
    Looked from their hunger-deep eyes,
    Haunted with shadows of hunger-hands,
    Out from the huddled and ugly walls,   5
    I came sudden, at the city's edge,
    On a blue burst of lake,
    Long lake waves breaking under the sun
    On a spray-flung curve of shore;
    And a fluttering storm of gulls,   10
    Masses of great gray wings
    And flying white bellies
    Veering and wheeling free in the open.

Fog

    The fog comes
    on little cat feet.

    It sits looking
    over harbor and city
    on silent haunches   5
    and then moves on.

Cool Tombs

When Abraham Lincoln was shoveled into the tombs, he forgot the copperheads and the assassin…in the dust, in the cool tombs.[1]

And Ulysses Grant lost all thought of con men and Wall Street, cash and collateral turned ashes…in the dust, in the cool tombs.[2]

Chapter 29   Carl Sandburg

    Pocahontas' body, lovely as a poplar, sweet as a red haw in November or a   5
        pawpaw in May, did she wonder? does she remember?…in the dust,
        in the cool tombs?[3]

    Take any streetful of people buying clothes and groceries, cheering a hero
        or throwing confetti and blowing tin horns…tell me if the lovers are
        losers…tell me if any get more than the lovers…in the dust…in the   10
        cool tombs.

Notes

1. President Abraham Lincoln (1809–1865) was opposed by southern sympathizers in the North, called copperheads, and assassinated by John Wilkes Booth.
2. The second administration of President Ulysses S. Grant (1822–1885) was riddled with bribery and political corruption. After leaving office Grant was exploited in business and underwent bankruptcy.
3. Pocahontas (ca. 1595–1617), daughter of the Indian chief Powhatan, intervened to save the life of Captain John Smith. The red haw is a type of American hawthorn tree; "pawpaw" is colloquial for the fruit of the papaya tree.

Flash Crimson

I shall cry God to give me a broken foot.

I shall ask for a scar and a slashed nose.

I shall take the last and the worst.

I shall be eaten by gray creepers in a bunkhouse where no runners of the
    sun come and no dogs live.   5

And yet—of all "and yets" this is the bronze strongest—

I shall keep one thing better than all else; there is the blue steel of a great
    star of early evening in it; it lives longer than a broken foot or any scar.

The broken foot goes to a hole dug with a shovel or the bone of a nose may
    whiten on a hilltop—and yet—"and yet"—   10

There is one crimson pinch of ashes left after all; and none of the shifting
    winds that whip the grass and none of the pounding rains that beat
    the dust, know how to touch or find the flash of this crimson.

I cry God to give me a broken foot, a scar, or a lousy death.

I who have seen the flash of this crimson, I ask God for the last and worst.   15

The People, Yes (excerpt)

            The people will live on.
    The learning and blundering people will live on.
        They will be tricked and sold and again sold
    And go back to the nourishing earth for rootholds,
        The people so peculiar in renewal and comeback,   5
        You can't laugh off their capacity to take it.
    The mammoth rests between his cyclonic dramas.

    The people so often sleepy, weary, enigmatic,
    is a vast huddle with many units saying:
        "I earn my living.   10
        I make enough to get by
        and it takes all my time.
        If I had more time
        I could do more for myself
        and maybe for others.   15
        I could read and study

and talk things over
and find out about things.
It takes time.
I wish I had the time." 20

The people is a tragic and comic two-face:
hero and hoodlum: phantom and gorilla twist-
ing to moan with a gargoyle mouth: "They
buy me and sell me…it's a game…
sometime I'll break loose…" 25

   Once having marched
Over the margins of animal necessity,
Over the grim line of sheer subsistence
   Then man came
To the deeper rituals of his bones, 30
To the lights lighter than any bones,
To the time for thinking things over,
To the dance, the song, the story,
Or the hours given over to dreaming,
   Once having so marched. 35

Between the finite limitations of the five senses
and the endless yearnings of man for the beyond
the people hold to the humdrum bidding of work and food
while reaching out when it comes their way
for lights beyond the prisms of the five senses, 40
for keepsakes lasting beyond any hunger or death.
   This reaching is alive.
The panderers and liars have violated and smutted it.
   Yet this reaching is alive yet
     for lights and keepsakes. 45

The people know the salt of the sea
and the strength of the winds
lashing the corners of the earth.
The people take the earth
as a tomb of rest and a cradle of hope.   50
Who else speaks for the Family of Man?
They are in tune and step
with constellations of universal law.

The people is a polychrome,
a spectrum and a prism   55
held in a moving monolith,
a console organ of changing themes,
a clavilux[1] of color poems
wherein the sea offers fog
and the fog moves off in rain   60
and the labrador sunset shortens
to a nocturne of clear stars
serene over the shot spray
of northern lights.

The steel mill sky is alive.   65
The fire breaks white and zigzag
shot on a gun-metal gloaming.
Man is a long time coming.
Man will yet win.
Brother may yet line up with brother: 70

This old anvil laughs at many broken hammers.
There are men who can't be bought.
The fireborn are at home in fire.
The stars make no noise.
You can't hinder the wind from blowing.   75

Time is a great teacher.
Who can live without hope?

In the darkness with a great bundle of grief
    the people march.
In the night, and overhead a shovel of stars for   80
    keeps[2], the people march:
        "Where to? what next?"

Notes
1. clavilux: organ-like console keyed to colored lights instead of music
2. for keeps: for all time

Chapter 30

Wallace Stevens (1879–1955)

Wallace Stevens created his poetry as a gifted nonprofessional, less concerned about promoting his literary reputation than about perfecting what he wrote. This passion for perfection is apparent in his disciplined thought, his intense and brilliant craftsmanship, and the meticulous propriety of his language, upon which he imposed the double burden of his wit and his faith that the clarification of the inner significance of an idea is a high function. His work is primarily motivated by the belief that "ideas of order," that is, true ideas, correspond with an innate order in nature and the universe, and that it is the high privilege of individuals and mankind to discover this correspondence. Hence, many of his best poems derive their emotional power from reasoned revelation. This philosophical intention is supported by the titles Stevens gave to his volumes—for example, *Harmonium*, *Ideas of Order*, and *Parts of a World*.

Stevens spent his boyhood in his birthplace, Reading, Pennsylvania. His father was a prosperous attorney. Stevens' earliest ambition was to be a writer, and after three years at Harvard, where he published poems in the *Harvard Advocate*, he went to New York in 1900 for a try at journalism. But the following year, on his father's advice, he entered the New York Law School. Admitted to the bar in 1904, he worked for several law firms before marrying and moving to Connecticut, where he eventually rose to the position of vice-president of the Hartford Accident and Indemnity Company.

During his years in New York, with the modernist movement gaining momentum, Stevens became acquainted with a number of young writers and artists in New York City, among them the poets William Carlos Williams and Marianne Moore. Stevens also began submitting his own poems to the little magazines and, for a time, tried writing for the experimental theater. It was not until 1923, however, that Stevens, at the age of forty-four, was finally persuaded to publish a book of poems, *Harmonium*. The book's poor reception and its author's growing business responsibilities almost led him to abandon poetry. For over a decade he published little, but with the reprinting of *Harmonium* (1931) and with the resulting increase in critical attention, Stevens began his years of steady publication.

In 1935 he published *Ideas of Order*. Then followed *The Man with the Blue Guitar* (1937), *Parts of a World* (1942), *Transport to Summer* (1947), and *The Auroras of Autumn* (1950). These, along with a collection of his occasional lectures on poetry, *The Necessary Angel* (1951), established him as a major American poet. For the publication of his *Collected Poems* (1954) he received the National Book Award and the Pulitzer Prize. After his death, his previously uncollected works appeared in *Opus Posthumous* (1957), and his *Letters* was published in 1966.

From the beginning it was evident that *Harmonium* was part of a revolution in American poetry. Although some of its best poems, including "Sunday Morning," were relatively traditional in form, the book baffled even the most sophisticated. In rebellion against the "stale intelligence" of the past and out "to make a new intelligence prevail," Stevens invoked the comic, the strange, the bizarre. He adopted a variety of experimental styles, created poetic surfaces of Frenchified elegance, exotic imagery, odd sounds, curious analogies, and inscrutable titles. For many readers it seemed that Stevens had carried originality to the point of mere eccentricity, and he was called a "dandy," a "virtuoso of the insane," a writer of "near nonsense." But beneath his gaudiest surfaces, Stevens' abiding concerns were clearly present. He confronted the contemporary abandonment of traditional values and sought to come to terms with the confusions of his time. The problem of the interrelation between the ideal and the real became a constant theme in his later poetry and led him to elaborate a series of oppositions between inner and outer worlds—between subject and object, perceiver and perceived, fiction and fact, or as he most often phrased it, between "imagination and reality." These contraries meet ultimately in his concept of a "supreme fiction," a modern mythology he offered as a replacement for the mythologies of the past, a new vision with "which men could propose to themselves a fulfillment." Although he constantly dealt with the nature of poetry, Stevens became in his later work increasingly meditative and philosophical, an intellectual elitist, at times difficult and obscure, who wrote, as he admitted, "for a gallery of one's own."

Peter Quince at the Clavier

I

Just as my fingers on these keys
Make music, so the selfsame sounds
On my spirit make a music, too.

Music is feeling, then, not sound;
And thus it is that what I feel,   5
Here in this room, desiring you,

Thinking of your blue-shadowed silk,
Is music. It is like the strain
Waked in the elders by Susanna.[1]

Of a green evening, clear and warm,   10
She bathed in her still garden, while
The red-eyed elders watching, felt

The basses of their beings throb
In witching chords, and their thin blood
Pulse pizzicati of Hosanna.   15

II

In the green water, clear and warm,
Susanna lay.

She searched
The touch of springs,
And found   20
Concealed imaginings.
She sighed,
For so much melody.

Upon the bank, she stood
In the cool   25
Of spent emotions.
She felt, among the leaves,
The dew
Of old devotions.

She walked upon the grass,   30
Still quavering.
The winds were like her maids,
On timid feet,
Fetching her woven scarves,
Yet wavering.   35

A breath upon her hand
Muted the night.
She turned—
A cymbal crashed,
And roaring horns.   40

III

Soon, with a noise like tambourines,
Came her attendant Byzantines.

They wondered why Susanna cried
Against the elders by her side;

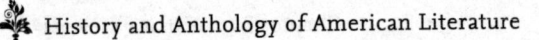

And as they whispered, the refrain   45
Was like a willow swept by rain.

Anon, their lamps' uplifted flame
Revealed Susanna and her shame.

And then, the simpering Byzantines
Fled, with a noise like tambourines.   50

IV

Beauty is momentary in the mind—
The fitful tracing of a portal;
But in the flesh it is immortal.
The body dies; the body's beauty lives.
So evenings die, in their green going,   55
A wave, interminably flowing.
So gardens die, their meek breath scenting
The cowl of winter, done repenting.
So maidens die, to the auroral
Celebration of a maiden's choral.   60
Susanna's music touched the bawdy strings
Of those white elders; but, escaping,
Left only Death's ironic scraping.
Now, in its immortality, it plays
On the clear viol of her memory,   65
And makes a constant sacrament of praise.

Note

1. A reference to the story of Daniel and Susanna in the Apocrypha of the Bible. Two elders were obsessed with lust for Susanna. When rejected by her they falsely charged her with fornication. When questioned by Daniel their lies were exposed, and they were put to death.

Chapter 30   Wallace Stevens

🌿 Anecdote of the Jar

I placed a jar in Tennessee,
And round it was, upon a hill.
It made the slovenly wilderness
Surround that hill.

The wilderness rose up to it,   5
And sprawled around, no longer wild.
The jar was round upon the ground
And tall and of a port in air.

It took dominion everywhere.
The jar was gray and bare.   10
It did not give of bird or bush,
Like nothing else in Tennessee.

🌿 The Emperor of Ice-Cream

Call the roller of big cigars,
The muscular one, and bid him whip
In kitchen cups concupiscent curds.
Let the wenches dawdle in such dress
As they are used to wear, and let the boys   5
Bring flowers in last month's newspapers.
Let be be finale of seem.
The only emperor is the emperor of ice-cream.

Take from the dresser of deal[1],
Lacking the three glass knobs, that sheet   10
On which she embroidered fantails once
And spread it so as to cover her face.
If her horny feet protrude, they come

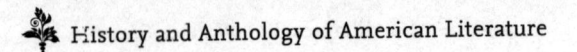

> To show how cold she is, and dumb.
> Let the lamp affix its beam. 15
> The only emperor is the emperor of ice-cream.

Note
1. deal: pine, or other inexpensive wood

Chapter 31

T. S. Eliot (1888–1965)

T. S. Eliot was born in St. Louis, Missouri, on September 26, 1888, of New England stock, his grandfather Eliot having gone west as a Unitarian minister. He studied at private academies, entered Harvard at eighteen, and there attained the M.A. degree in 1910. A student of languages and belles-lettres, especially the writings of the Elizabethans and the metaphysical poets and the literature of the Italian Renaissance, he was also attracted to the study of philosophy, taught at Harvard by such men as Irving Babbitt and George Santayana. In the winter of 1910 he went to the University of Paris, where he was influenced by the lectures of the philosopher Henri Bergson. Again at Harvard (1911–1914), he studied Sanskrit and Oriental philosophy in the graduate school, and in 1914 was awarded a traveling fellowship for study in Germany.

At Merton College, Oxford, in 1915, he again studied philosophy. That year he married the daughter of a British artist. For two years he taught in English academies, while bringing to fruition his first book of poems. In 1917, he published *Prufrock and Other Observations*. Few poets in their first book have so prophetically suggested the direction and power of what was to follow. "The Love Song of J. Alfred Prufrock" still holds its place in the development of Eliot's poetry as a whole; like much of his later work it concerns various aspects of the frustration and enfeeblement of individual character as seen in perspective with the decay of states, peoples, and religious faith.

From 1918 to 1924 Eliot was in the service of Lloyd's Bank in London. In 1920 his fourth volume, *Poems*, with "Gerontion" as its leading poem, again developed the same general pattern of ideas. It is remarkable that he excluded almost no poem of his early volumes from his later collected works. In 1920 also appeared *The Sacred Wood*, containing, among other essays, "Tradition and the Individual Talent," the earliest statement of his aesthetics. The aesthetic principle which he first elaborated in this essay provided a useful instrument for modern criticism. It relates primarily to the individual work of art, the poem conceived as a made object, an organic thing in itself, whose concrete elements are true correlatives of the artist's imagination and experience with respect to that poem. The degree to which fusion and concentration of intellect, feeling, and experience were achieved was Eliot's criterion for judging the poem. Such ideas he developed in other essays have been influential in promoting the intrinsic analysis of poetry.

Also in 1920, Eliot began *The Waste Land*, one of the major works of modern literature. Its subject, the apparent failure of Western civilization which World War I seemed to demonstrate, set the tone of his poetry until 1930. Such poems as "The Love Song of J. Alfred Prufrock" and "Gerontion" had suggested the spiritual debility of the modern individual and his culture while in satirical counterpoint his Sweeney poems had symbolized the rising tide of anticultural infidelity and human baseness. It is likely that in his abundant use of literary reference in *The Waste Land* he was influenced by Pound, a close friend whose advice, as Eliot declared, he followed strictly in cutting and concentrating the poem. *The Waste Land* is the acknowledged masterpiece of its sort. It also introduced a form—the orchestration of related themes in successive movements—which he used again in "The Hollow Men" (1925), *Ash-Wednesday* (1930), and his later masterpieces, *Four Quartets* (1936–1942; 1943).

The Waste Land appeared as a volume in New York and London in 1922, but it had been published earlier that year in *The Criterion*, an influential London literary quarterly which Eliot edited from 1922 through 1939. His second volume of criticism, *Homage to John Dryden* (1924) was much admired for its critical method. In 1925 Eliot became a member of the board of the publishing firm now known as Faber and Faber, and he was long in that association. In 1927 he was confirmed in the Anglican Church and became a

British subject.

A year later, in connection with the publication of the critical volume *For Lancelot Andrewes* (1928), he described himself as "a royalist in politics, a classicist in literature, and an Anglo-Catholic in religion"; and he had manifested an increasing reliance upon authority and tradition. His later poetry took a positive turn toward faith in life, in strong contrast with the desperation of *The Waste Land*. This was demonstrated by *Ash-Wednesday*, a poem of mystical conflict between faith and doubt, beautiful in its language if difficult in its symbolism. In 1932, in *Sweeney Agonistes*, he brought Sweeney to a deserved and gruesome death in a strange play that fascinates the attention by mingling penitence with musical comedy. In "The Hollow Men" he satirized the straw men, the Guy Fawkes men, whose world would end "not with a bang, but a whimper"; also in this period he produced the "Ariel Poems," including the exquisite "Marina" (1930). *Murder in the Cathedral* (1935), a poetic tragedy on the betrayal of Thomas à Becket, has been successfully performed, and is a drama of impressive spiritual power. His *Collected Poems, 1909-1935* (1936), and the collected *Essays, Ancient and Modern*, which in the same year gave perspective to his criticism, brought to an end this first period of spiritual exploration.

Eliot's next major accomplishment, the *Four Quartets*, originated during his visit to the United States (1932–1934), his first return to his native country in seventeen years. During this period he wrote the small "Landscapes," some of them drawn from American scenes, which were spiritually connected with the theme of the *Quartets*. His lectures at Harvard University in 1932 resulted in the influential volume *The Use of Poetry and the Use of Criticism* (1933). In 1934 he lectured at the University of Virginia, and produced the study of orthodoxy and faith entitled *After Strange Gods: A Primer of Modern Heresy*. Presumably it was during this year that he conceived the subject of "Burnt Norton," the first of the *Quartets*.

The four poems that eventually resulted provide a reasoned philosophical discussion of the foundations of Christian faith, involving the nature of time, the significance of history, the religious psychology of man, and the nature of his experience; most importantly, perhaps, they attempt, by means of lofty poetic feeling and metaphysical insight, to suggest the actuality and meaning of such Christian mysteries as Incarnation and Pentecost. The four poems, which had all been previously published, were brought together in *Four Quartets* (1943).

Eliot dramatized domestic life in terms of his philosophy. *The Family Reunion* (1939) was not generally considered successful as drama. *The Cocktail Party* (1949), *The Confidential Clerk* (1953), and *The Elder Statesman* (1958) created interest as experimental theater.

Few men of letters have been more fully honored in their own day than T. S. Eliot, and even those who strongly disagree with him seemed content with his selection for the Nobel Prize in 1948. *The Complete Poems and Plays* (1952) is a relatively small volume, but it represents an artist whose ideas are large, whose craftsmanship is the expression of artistic responsibility, and whose poems represent the progressive refinement and illustration of his aesthetics.

The Love Song of J. Alfred Prufrock[1]

> *S'io credessi che mia risposta fosse*
> *a persona che mai tornasse al mondo,*
> *questa fiamma staria senza più scosse.*
> *Ma per ciò che giammai di questo fondo*
> *non tornò vivo alcun, s'i'odo il vero,*
> *senza tema d'infamia ti rispondo.*[2]

Let us go then, you and I,
When the evening is spread out against the sky
Like a patient etherised upon a table;
Let us go, through certain half-deserted streets,
The muttering retreats   5
Of restless nights in one-night cheap hotels
And sawdust restaurants with oyster-shells:
Streets that follow like a tedious argument

Of insidious intent
To lead you to an overwhelming question…
Oh, do not ask, "What is it?"
Let us go and make our visit.

In the room the women come and go
Talking of Michelangelo.

The yellow fog that rubs its back upon the window-panes,
The yellow smoke that rubs its muzzle on the window-panes,
Licked its tongue into the corners of the evening,
Lingered upon the pools that stand in drains,
Let fall upon its back the soot that falls from chimneys,
Slipped by the terrace, made a sudden leap,
And seeing that it was a soft October night,
Curled once about the house, and fell asleep.

And indeed there will be time[3]
For the yellow smoke that slides along the street
Rubbing its back upon the window-panes;
There will be time, there will be time
To prepare a face to meet the faces that you meet;
There will be time to murder and create,
And time for all the works and days[4] of hands
That lift and drop a question on your plate;
Time for you and time for me,
And time yet for a hundred indecisions,
And for a hundred visions and revisions,
Before the taking of a toast and tea.

In the room the women come and go
Talking of Michelangelo.

And indeed there will be time
To wonder, "Do I dare?" and, "Do I dare?"
Time to turn back and descend the stair,
With a bald spot in the middle of my hair—   40
(They will say: "How his hair is growing thin!")
My morning coat, my collar mounting firmly to the chin,
My necktie rich and modest, but asserted by a simple pin—
(They will say: "But how his arms and legs are thin!")
Do I dare   45
Disturb the universe?
In a minute there is time
For decisions and revisions which a minute will reverse.

For I have known them all already, known them all—
Have known the evenings, mornings, afternoons,   50
I have measured out my life with coffee spoons;
I know the voices dying with a dying fall[5]
Beneath the music from a farther room.
    So how should I presume?

And I have known the eyes already, known them all—   55
The eyes that fix you in a formulated phrase,
And when I am formulated, sprawling on a pin,
When I am pinned and wriggling on the wall,
Then how should I begin
To spit out all the butt-ends of my days and ways?   60
    And how should I presume?

And I have known the arms already, known them all—
Arms that are braceleted and white and bare
(But in the lamplight, downed with light brown hair!)
Is it perfume from a dress   65
That makes me so digress?

Arms that lie along a table, or wrap about a shawl.
    And should I then presume?
    And how should I begin?

          *   *   *

Shall I say, I have gone at dusk through narrow streets   70
And watched the smoke that rises from the pipes
Of lonely men in shirt-sleeves, leaning out of windows?...

I should have been a pair of ragged claws
Scuttling across the floors of silent seas.[6]

          *   *   *

And the afternoon, the evening, sleeps so peacefully!   75
Smoothed by long fingers,
Asleep...tired...or it malingers,
Stretched on the floor, here beside you and me.
Should I, after tea and cakes and ices,
Have the strength to force the moment to its crisis?   80
But though I have wept and fasted, wept and prayed,
Though I have seen my head (grown slightly bald) brought in upon a platter,[7]
I am no prophet—and here's no great matter;
I have seen the moment of my greatness flicker,
And I have seen the eternal Footman hold my coat, and snicker,   85
And in short, I was afraid.

And would it have been worth it, after all,
After the cups, the marmalade, the tea,
Among the porcelain, among some talk of you and me,
Would it have been worth while,   90
To have bitten off the matter with a smile,

To have squeezed the universe into a ball
To roll it towards some overwhelming question,
To say: "I am Lazarus, come from the dead,[8]
Come back to tell you all, I shall tell you all"— 95
If one, settling a pillow by her head,
    Should say: "That is not what I meant at all.
    That is not it, at all."

And would it have been worth it, after all,
Would it have been worth while, 100
After the sunsets and the dooryards and the sprinkled streets,
After the novels, after the teacups, after the skirts that trail along the floor—
And this, and so much more?—
It is impossible to say just what I mean!
But as if a magic lantern threw the nerves in patterns on a screen: 105
Would it have been worth while
If one, settling a pillow or throwing off a shawl,
And turning toward the window, should say:
    "That is not it at all,
    That is not what I meant, at all." 110

        *   *   *

No! I am not Prince Hamlet, nor was meant to be;
Am an attendant lord, one that will do
To swell a progress[9], start a scene or two,
Advise the prince; no doubt, an easy tool,
Deferential, glad to be of use, 115
Politic, cautious, and meticulous;
Full of high sentence[10], but a bit obtuse;
At times, indeed, almost ridiculous—
Almost, at times, the Fool.

Chapter 31   T. S. Eliot

I grow old...I grow old...   120
I shall wear the bottoms of my trousers rolled.

Shall I part my hair behind? Do I dare to eat a peach?
I shall wear white flannel trousers, and walk upon the beach.
I have heard the mermaids singing, each to each.

I do not think that they will sing to me.   125

I have seen them riding seaward on the waves
Combing the white hair of the waves blown back
When the wind blows the water white and black.

We have lingered in the chambers of the sea
By sea-girls wreathed with seaweed red and brown   130
Till human voices wake us, and we drown.

Notes

1. Composed at Harvard, this dramatic monologue is a symbolist poem written in intermittently rhymed free verse. The title suggests an ironic contrast between a "love song" and a poem that proves to be about the absence of love, while the speaker's name suggests an ironic contrast between his ordinary surname (that of a St. Louis furniture dealer) and the elegant convention of using the first initial and middle name as a form of address, in a world which includes Prufrock but renders him profoundly alien in it.

2. "If I thought that my reply would be to one who would ever return to the world, this flame would stay without further movement; but since none has ever returned alive from this depth, if what I hear is true, I answer you without fear of infamy" (Dante's *Inferno*, Canto XXVII. 61–66). The speaker, Guido da Montefeltro, consumed in flame as punishment for

giving false counsel, confesses his shame without fear of its being reported since he believes Dante cannot return to earth.
3. an echo of Andrew Marvell's seductive plea in *To His Coy Mistress* (1681): "Had we but world enough and time…"
4. works and days: *Works and Days* is a didactic poem about farming by the Greek poet Hesiod (eighth century B.C.)
5. echo of Duke Orsino's self-indulgent invocation of music in Shakespeare's *Twelfth Night*, Act I, Scene I. 1, 4: "If music be the food of love, play on… That strain again! It had a dying fall."
6. *Cf.* Hamlet's mocking of Polonius in Shakespeare's *Hamlet* (1602), Act II, Scene II. 205–206: "for you yourself, sir, should be old as I am, if, like a crab, you could go backward."
7. as did John the Baptist, beheaded by the temptress Salome, who presented his head to Queen Herodias, in the story recounted in Matthew 14: 3–11, Mark 6: 17–20, and Oscar Wilde's play *Salome* (1894)
8. The resurrection of Lazarus is recounted in Luke 16: 19–31 and John 11: 1–44.
9. progress: a journey or procession made by royal courts and often portrayed on Elizabethan stages
10. high sentence: opinions, sententiousness

Preludes

I

The winter evening settles down
With smell of steaks in passageways.
Six o'clock.
The burnt-out ends of smoky days.
And now a gusty shower wraps   5
The grimy scraps
Of withered leaves about your feet
And newspapers from vacant lots;
The showers beat
On broken blinds and chimney-pots,   10

And at the corner of the street
A lonely cab-horse steams and stamps.
And then the lighting of the lamps.

II

The morning comes to consciousness
Of faint stale smells of beer   15
From the sawdust-trampled street
With all its muddy feet that press
To early coffee-stands.
With the other masquerades
That times resumes,   20
One thinks of all the hands
That are raising dingy shades
In a thousand furnished rooms.

III

You tossed a blanket from the bed,
You lay upon your back, and waited;   25
You dozed, and watched the night revealing
The thousand sordid images
Of which your soul was constituted;
They flickered against the ceiling.
And when all the world came back   30
And the light crept up between the shutters
And you heard the sparrows in the gutters,
You had such a vision of the street
As the street hardly understands;
Sitting along the bed's edge, where   35
You curled the papers from your hair,
Or clasped the yellow soles of feet
In the palms of both soiled hands.

IV

His soul stretched tight across the skies
That fade behind a city block,   40
Or trampled by insistent feet
At four and five and six o'clock;
And short square fingers stuffing pipes,
And evening newspapers, and eyes
Assured of certain certainties,   45
The conscience of a blackened street
Impatient to assume the world.

I am moved by fancies that are curled
Around these images, and cling:
The notion of some infinitely gentle   50
Infinitely suffering thing.

Wipe your hand across your mouth, and laugh;
The worlds revolve like ancient women
Gathering fuel in vacant lots.

Journey of the Magi[1]

"A cold coming we had of it,
Just the worst time of the year
For a journey, and such a long journey:
The ways deep and the weather sharp,
The very dead of winter."[2]   5
And the camels galled, sore-footed, refractory,
Lying down in the melting snow.
There were times we regretted
The summer palaces on slopes, the terraces,
And the silken girls bringing sherbet.   10
Then the camel men cursing and grumbling

And running away, and wanting their liquor and women,
And the night-fires going out, and the lack of shelters,
And the cities hostile and the towns unfriendly
And the villages dirty and charging high prices: 15
A hard time we had of it.
At the end we preferred to travel all night,
Sleeping in snatches,
With the voices singing in our ears, saying
That this was all folly.   20

Then at dawn we came down to a temperate valley,
Wet, below the snow line, smelling of vegetation,
With a running stream and a water-mill beating the darkness,
And three trees on the low sky[3].
And an old white horse[4] galloped away in the meadow.   25
Then we came to a tavern with vine-leaves over the lintel[5],
Six hands at an open door dicing for pieces of silver[6],
And feet kicking the empty wine-skins.
But there was no information, and so we continued
And arrived at evening, not a moment too soon   30
Finding the place; it was (you may say) satisfactory.

All this was a long time ago, I remember,
And I would do it again, but set down
This set down
This: were we led all that way for   35
Birth or Death? There was a Birth, certainly,
We had evidence and no doubt. I had seen birth and death,
But had thought they were different; this Birth was
Hard and bitter agony for us, like Death, our death.
We returned to our places, these Kingdoms,   40
But no longer at ease here, in the old dispensation,

> With an alien people clutching their gods.
> I should be glad of another death.

Notes

1. It is one of a series of lyrics, the "Ariel poems," on the theme of death and rebirth. The speaker is one of the three wise men whose journey to Bethlehem, the birthplace of Christ, is described in Matthew 2: 1-11.
2. The first five lines are taken from a nativity sermon by Lancelot Andrewes (1555-1626), bishop of Winchester.
3. the darkness...sky: a suggestion of the three crosses on Calvary and the "darkness over all the land" (Matthew 27: 38, 45)
4. an old white horse: "...behold a white horse; and he that sat upon him was called Faithful and True..." (Revelation 19: 11)
5. a tavern with vine-leaves over the lintel: The Israelites marked their door lintels with sacrificial blood so that the Lord would pass over them when he smote the Egyptians (Exodus 12: 7-13). Here, the vine leaves on the tavern door suggest instead the vegetation sacred to such pagan fertility gods as Dionysus, god of wine.
6. pieces of silver: a suggestion of the silver paid Judas for the betrayal of Christ

The Hollow Men

> *Mistah Kurtz—he dead.*
> *A Penny for the Old Guy*

I

We are the hollow men
We are the stuffed men
Leaning together
Headpiece filled with straw. Alas!
Our dried voices, when   5

We whisper together
Are quiet and meaningless
As wind in dry grass
Or rats' feet over broken glass
In our dry cellar   10

Shape without form, shade without colour,
Paralysed force, gesture without motion;

Those who have crossed
With direct eyes, to death's other Kingdom
Remember us—if at all—not as lost   15
Violent souls, but only
As the hollow men
The stuffed men.

II

Eyes I dare not meet in dreams
In death's dream kingdom   20
These do not appear:
There, the eyes are
Sunlight on a broken column
There, is a tree swinging
And voices are   25
In the wind's singing
More distant and more solemn
Than a fading star.

Let me be no nearer
In death's dream kingdom   30
Let me also wear
Such deliberate disguises
Rat's coat, crowskin, crossed staves

In a field
Behaving as the wind behaves   35
No nearer—

Not that final meeting
In the twilight kingdom

III

This is the dead land
This is cactus land   40
Here the stone images
Are raised, here they receive
The supplication of a dead man's hand
Under the twinkle of a fading star.

Is it like this   45
In death's other kingdom
Waking alone
At the hour when we are
Trembling with tenderness
Lips that would kiss   50
Form prayers to broken stone.

IV

The eyes are not here
There are no eyes here
In this valley of dying stars
In this hollow valley   55
This broken jaw of our lost kingdoms

In this last of meeting places
We grope together
And avoid speech

Chapter 31 T. S. Eliot

Gathered on this beach of the tumid river   60

Sightless, unless
The eyes reappear
As the perpetual star
Multifoliate rose
Of death's twilight kingdom   65
The hope only
Of empty men.

V

Here we go round the prickly pear
Prickly pear prickly pear
Here we go round the prickly pear   70
At five o'lock in the morning.

Between the idea
And the reality
Between the motion
And the act   75
Falls the Shadow
    For Thine is the Kingdom

Between the conception
And the creation
Between the emotion   80
And the response
Falls the Shadow
    Life is very long

Between the desire
And the spasm   85
Between the potency

And the existence
Between the essence
And the descent
Falls the Shadow 90
    For Thine is the Kingdom

For Thine is
Life is
For Thine is the

This is the way the world ends 95
This is the way the world ends
This is the way the world ends
Not with a bang but a whimper.

Chapter 32

F. Scott Fitzgerald (1896–1940)

F. Scott Fitzgerald was born in St. Paul, Minnesota. His family was considered socially prominent and genteelly poor. With the financial aid of relatives he was sent to prep school and to Princeton. In 1917, his senior year, he left Princeton to serve in World War I. In Alabama, where he was sent for military training, he fell hopelessly in love with Zelda Sayre, an embodiment of his romantic notions of a Southern belle. Discharged from the army in 1919, Fitzgerald was determined to win success, fame, and Zelda. He took a job with an advertising agency and worked on short stories and a novel at night. Eventually his first novel, *This Side of Paradise*, was accepted for publication. The book appeared in March 1920. A week later Fitzgerald and Zelda were married.

This Side of Paradise, with its portrayal of the casual dissipations of "flaming youth," was an immediate commercial success, and Zelda and Scott Fitzgerald attempted to live up to—or even beyond—his fictional portraits of scandalous young men and women. They swam in public fountains in New York, rode to parties on the hoods of taxis, fought with waiters, and danced on dining tables. Life had become a long cocktail party, yet Fitzgerald managed somehow to continue writing. In 1922 he published his second novel, *The Beautiful and Damned*, and a collection of short stories, *Tales of the Jazz Age*. In 1923 he wrote a satirical play, *The Vegetable, Or from President to Postman*. It was a critical and financial failure, and to maintain his extravagant lifestyle, Fitzgerald was forced to grind out short stories rapidly for money, which he squandered just as rapidly. In 1925 Fitzgerald managed to complete *The Great Gatsby*. It was a critical success but a commercial disappointment; it sold only about half as many copies as either of his first two novels, and it earned little more than enough to repay his debts to his publishers.

Over the next two years Fitzgerald wrote little. In desperation he went to Hollywood, in 1927, for his first period of screenwriting, an occupation that was to sustain him for much of his remaining life. In 1934 *Tender Is the Night* was published. The year of its publication, it sold only 13,000 copies, and although it is a precise indictment of irresponsible social values of the 1930s, the critics harshly accused Fitzgerald of ignoring the Depression while writing a frivolous novel about neurotic Americans who preferred Europe over their native land.

Battered by the illness of his wife (in the 1930s Zelda began to suffer a series of mental breakdowns), by his own alcoholism, and by the failures of his writing, Fitzgerald now worked mainly in Hollywood. He continued to engage in periodic drinking bouts and grew seriously ill. In November 1940 he suffered a heart attack and a second one a month later. On December 21, 1940 he died. He was forty-four. His last novel, *The Last Tycoon*, remained unfinished.

At the time of his death Fitzgerald was considered as a failed literary hope, a writer victimized by his own indulgences. But since the 1940s his literary reputation has steadily risen. Today he is judged to be one of the major American prose writers of twentieth century. In a number of his short stories, and in his finest novels, *The Great Gatsby* and *Tender Is the Night*, Fitzgerald had revealed the stridency of an age of glittering innocence. In vivid and graceful prose he had, at the same time, portrayed the hollowness of the American worship of riches and the unending American dream of love, splendor, and fulfilled desires.

The Great Gatsby

The Story

Young Nick Carraway decided to forsake the hardware business of his family in the Middle West in order to sell bonds in New York City. He took a small house in West Egg on Long Island and there became involved in the lives of his neighbors. At a dinner party at the home of Tom Buchanan he renewed his acquaintance with Tom and Tom's wife, Daisy, a distant cousin, and he met an attractive young woman, Jordan Baker. Almost at once he learned that Tom and Daisy were not happily married. It appeared that Daisy knew her husband was deliberately unfaithful.

Nick soon learned to despise the drive to the city through unkempt slums; particularly, he hated the ash heaps and the huge commercial signs. He was far more interested in the activities of his wealthy neighbors. Near his house lived Jay Gatsby, a mysterious man of great wealth. Gatsby entertained lavishly, but his past was unknown to his neighbors.

One day Tom Buchanan took Nick to call on his mistress, a dowdy, over-plump, married woman named Myrtle Wilson, whose husband, George Wilson, operated a second-rate auto repair shop. Myrtle, Tom, and Nick went to the apartment Tom kept and there the three were joined by Myrtle's sister Catherine and Mr. and Mrs. McKee. The party settled down to an afternoon of drinking, Nick unsuccessfully doing his best to get away.

A few days later Nick attended another party, one given by Gatsby for a large number of people famous in speak-easy society. Food and liquor were dispensed lavishly. Most of the guests had never seen their host before.

At the party Nick met Gatsby for the first time. Gatsby, in his early thirties, looked like a healthy young roughneck. He was offhand, casual, eager to entertain his guests as extravagantly as possible. Frequently he was called away by long-distance telephone calls. Some of the guests laughed and said that he was trying to impress them with his importance.

That summer Gatsby gave many parties. Nick went to all of them, enjoying each time the society of people from all walks of life who appeared to take advantage of Gatsby's bounty. From time to time Nick met Jordan Baker there, but he began to lose interest in her after he heard that she had cheated in an amateur golf match.

Gatsby took Nick to lunch one day and introduced him to a man named Wolfshiem, who seemed to be Gatsby's business partner. Wolfshiem hinted at some dubious business deals that betrayed Gatsby's racketeering activities and Nick began to identify the sources of some of Gatsby's wealth.

Jordan Baker told Nick the strange story of Daisy's wedding. Before the bridal dinner Daisy, who seldom drank, became wildly intoxicated and announced there would be no wedding, that she had changed her mind and intended to go back to an old flame, Jay Gatsby. Her friends and family, however, had argued with her until she finally married Tom Buchanan. At the time Gatsby was poor and unknown; Tom was rich and influential.

But Gatsby was still in love with Daisy, and he wanted Jordan and Nick to bring Daisy and him together again. It was arranged that Nick should invite Daisy to tea the same day he invited Gatsby. Gatsby awaited the invitation nervously.

On the eventful day it rained. Determined that Nick's house should be presentable, Gatsby sent a man to mow the wet grass; he also sent over flowers for decoration. The tea was a strained affair at first, both Gatsby and Daisy shy and awkward in their reunion. Afterward they went over to Gatsby's mansion, where he showed them his furniture, clothes, swimming pool, and gardens. Daisy promised to attend his next party.

When Daisy disapproved of his guests, Gatsby stopped entertaining. The house was shut up and the bar-crowd turned away.

Gatsby informed Nick of his origin. His true name was Gatz, and he had been born in the Middle West. His parents were poor. But when he was a boy he had become the protégé of a wealthy old gold miner and had accompanied him on his travels until the old man died. Then he changed his name to Gatsby and began to dream of acquiring wealth and position. In the war he had distinguished himself. After the war he had returned penniless to the States, too poor to marry Daisy, whom he had met during the war. Later he became a partner in a drug business. He had been lucky and had accumulated money rapidly. He told Nick that he had acquired the money for his Long Island residence after three years of hard work.

Gatsby gave a quiet party for Jordan, the Buchanans, and Nick. The group drove into the city and took a room in a hotel. The day was hot and the guests uncomfortable. On the way, Tom driving Gatsby's new yellow car, stopped at Wilson's garage. Wilson complained because Tom had not helped him in a projected car deal. He said he needed money because he was selling out and taking his wife, whom he knew to be unfaithful, away from the city.

At the hotel Tom accused Gatsby of trying to steal his wife and also of being dishonest. He seemed to regard Gatsby's low origin with more disfavor than his interest in Daisy. During the argument, Daisy sided with both men by turns.

On the ride back to the suburbs Gatsby drove his own car, accompanied by Daisy, who temporarily would not speak to her husband.

Following them, Nick and Jordan and Tom stopped to investigate an accident in front of Wilson's garage. They discovered an ambulance picking up the dead body of Myrtle Wilson, struck by a hit-and-run driver in a yellow car. They tried in vain to help Wilson and then went to Tom's house, convinced that Gatsby had struck Myrtle Wilson.

Nick learned the next day from Gatsby that Daisy had been driving when the woman was hit. However, Gatsby was willing to take the blame if the death should be traced to his car. He explained that Myrtle, thinking that Tom was in the yellow car, had run out of the house, and Daisy, an inexpert driver, had run her down and then collapsed. Gatsby had driven on.

In the meantime George Wilson, having traced the yellow car to Gatsby, appeared on the Gatsby estate. A few hours later both he and Gatsby were discovered dead. He had shot Gatsby and then killed himself.

Nick tried to make Gatsby's funeral respectable, but no one attended except Gatsby's father, who thought his son had been a great man. None of Gatsby's racketeering associates appeared. His bar-friends had also deserted him.

Shortly afterward Nick learned of Tom's part in Gatsby's death. Tom had visited Wilson and had let Wilson believe that Gatsby had been Myrtle's lover. Nick vowed that his friendship with Tom and Daisy was at an end. He decided to return to his people in the Middle West.

Chapter III

(excerpt)

There was music from my neighbor's house through the summer nights. In his blue gardens men and girls came and went like moths among the whisperings and the champagne and the stars. At high tide in the afternoon I watched his guests diving from the tower of his raft, or taking the sun on the hot sand of his beach while his two motor-boats slit the waters of the Sound[1], drawing aquaplanes over cataracts of foam. On week-ends his Rolls-Royce[2] became an omnibus, bearing parties to and from the city between nine in the morning and long past midnight, while his station wagon scampered like a brisk yellow bug to meet all trains. And on Mondays eight servants, including an extra gardener, toiled all day with mops and scrubbing-brushes and hammers and garden-shears, repairing the ravages of the night before.

Every Friday five crates of oranges and lemons arrived from a fruiterer in New York—every Monday these same oranges and lemons left his back door in a pyramid of pulpless halves. There was a machine in the kitchen which could extract the juice of two hundred oranges in half an hour if a little button was pressed two hundred times by a butler's thumb.

At least once a fortnight a corps of caterers came down with several hundred feet of canvas and enough colored lights to make a Christmas tree of Gatsby's enormous garden. On buffet tables, garnished with glistening hors-d'œuvre, spiced baked hams crowded against salads of harlequin designs and pastry pigs and turkeys bewitched to a dark gold. In the main hall a bar with a real brass rail was set up, and stocked with gins and liquors and with cordials so long forgotten that most of his female guests were too young to know one from another.

By seven o'clock the orchestra has arrived, no thin five-piece affair, but a whole pitful of oboes and trombones and saxophones and viols and cornets and piccolos, and low and high drums. The last swimmers have come in from the beach now and are dressing up-stairs; the cars from New York are parked five deep in the drive, and already the halls and salons and verandas are gaudy with primary colors, and hair shorn in strange new ways, and shawls beyond the dreams of Castile[3]. The bar is in full swing, and floating rounds of cocktails permeate the garden outside, until the air is alive with chatter and laughter, and casual innuendo and introductions forgotten on the spot, and enthusiastic meetings between women who never knew each other's names.

The lights grow brighter as the earth lurches away from the sun, and now the orchestra is playing yellow cocktail music, and the opera of voices pitches a key higher. Laughter is easier minute by minute, spilled with prodigality, tipped out at a cheerful word. The groups change more swiftly, swell with new arrivals, dissolve and form in the same breath; already there are wanderers, confident girls who weave here and there among the stouter and more stable, become for a sharp, joyous moment the center of a group, and then, excited with triumph, glide on through the sea-change of faces and voices and color under the constantly changing light.

Suddenly one of these gypsies, in trembling opal, seizes a cocktail out of the air, dumps it down for courage and, moving her hands like Frisco[4], dances out alone on the canvas platform. A momentary hush; the orchestra leader varies his rhythm obligingly for her, and there is a burst of chatter as the erroneous news goes around that she is Gilda Gray's understudy from the *Follies*[5]. The party has begun.

I believe that on the first night I went to Gatsby's house I was one of the few guests who had actually been invited. People were not invited—they went there. They got into automobiles which bore them out to Long Island, and somehow they ended up at Gatsby's door. Once there they were introduced by somebody who knew Gatsby, and after that they conducted themselves according to the rules of behavior associated with amusement parks. Sometimes they came and went without having met Gatsby at all, came for the party with a simplicity of heart that was its own ticket of admission.

I had been actually invited. A chauffeur in a uniform of robin's-egg blue crossed my lawn early that Saturday morning with a surprisingly formal note from his employer: the honor would be entirely Gatsby's, it said, if I would attend his "little party" that night. He had seen me several times, and had intended to call on me long before, but a peculiar combination of circumstances had prevented it—signed Jay Gatsby, in a majestic hand.

Dressed up in white flannels[6] I went over to his lawn a little after seven, and wandered around rather ill at ease among swirls and eddies of people I didn't know—though here and there was a face I had noticed on the commuting train. I was immediately struck by the number of young Englishmen dotted about; all well dressed, all looking a little hungry, and all talking in low, earnest voices to solid and prosperous Americans. I was sure that they were selling something: bonds or insurance or automobiles. They were at least agonizingly aware of the easy money in the vicinity and convinced that it was theirs for a few words in the right key.

As soon as I arrived I made an attempt to find my host, but the two or three people of whom I asked his whereabouts stared at me in such an amazed way, and denied so vehemently any knowledge of his movements, that I slunk off in the direction of the cocktail table—the only place in the garden where a single man could linger without looking purposeless and alone.

I was on my way to get roaring drunk from sheer embarrassment when Jordan Baker came out of the house and stood at the head of the marble steps, leaning a little backward and looking with contemptuous interest down into the garden.

Welcome or not, I found it necessary to attach myself to someone before I should begin to address cordial remarks to the passers-by.

"Hello!" I roared, advancing toward her. My voice seemed unnaturally loud across the garden.

"I thought you might be here," she responded absently as I came up. "I remembered you lived next door to—"

She held my hand impersonally, as a promise that she'd take care of me in a minute, and gave ear to two girls in twin yellow dresses, who stopped at the foot of the steps.

"Hello!" they cried together. "Sorry you didn't win."

That was for the golf tournament. She had lost in the finals the week before.

"You don't know who we are," said one of the girls in yellow, "but we met you here about a month ago."

"You've dyed your hair since then," remarked Jordan, and I started, but the girls had moved casually on and her remark was addressed to the premature moon, produced like the supper, no doubt, out of a caterer's basket. With Jordan's slender golden arm resting in mine, we descended the steps and sauntered about the garden. A tray of cocktails floated at us through the twilight, and we sat down at a table with the two girls in yellow and three

Chapter 32 F. Scott Fitzgerald

men, each one introduced to us as Mr. Mumble.

"Do you come to these parties often?" inquired Jordan of the girl beside her.

"The last one was the one I met you at," answered the girl, in an alert confident voice. She turned to her companion: "Wasn't it for you, Lucille?"

It was for Lucille, too.

"I like to come," Lucille said. "I never care what I do, so I always have a good time. When I was here last I tore my gown on a chair, and he asked me my name and address—inside of a week I got a package from Croirier's with a new evening gown in it."

"Did you keep it?" asked Jordan.

"Sure I did. I was going to wear it tonight, but it was too big in the bust and had to be altered. It was gas blue with lavender beads. Two hundred and sixty-five dollars."

"There's something funny about a fellow that'll do a thing like that," said the other girl eagerly. "He doesn't want any trouble with *any*body."

"Who doesn't?" I inquired.

"Gatsby. Somebody told me—"

The two girls and Jordan leaned together confidentially.

"Somebody told me they thought he killed a man once."

A thrill passed over all of us. The three Mr. Mumbles bent forward and listened eagerly.

"I don't think it's so much *that*," argued Lucille sceptically; "it's more that he was a German spy during the war."

One of the men nodded in confirmation.

"I heard that from a man who knew all about him, grew up with him in Germany," he assured us positively.

"Oh, no," said the first girl, "it couldn't be that, because he was in the American army during the war." As our credulity switched back to her she leaned forward with enthusiasm. "You look at him sometimes when he thinks nobody's looking at him. I'll bet he killed a man."

She narrowed her eyes and shivered. Lucille shivered. We all turned and looked around for Gatsby. It was testimony to the romantic speculation he inspired that there were whispers about him from those who had found little that it was necessary to whisper about in this world.

The first supper—there would be another one after midnight—was now being served, and Jordan invited me to join her own party, who were spread around a table on the other side of the garden. There were three married couples and Jordan's escort, a persistent undergraduate given to violent innuendo, and obviously under the impression that sooner or later Jordan was going to yield him up her person to a greater or lesser degree. Instead of rambling, this party had preserved a dignified homogeneity, and assumed to itself the function of representing the staid nobility of the country-side— East Egg condescending to West Egg, and carefully on guard against its spectroscopic gayety.

"Let's get out," whispered Jordan, after a somehow wasteful and inappropriate half-hour; "this is much too polite for me."

We got up, and she explained that we were going to find the host: I had never met him, she said, and it was making me uneasy. The undergraduate nodded in a cynical, melancholy way.

The bar, where we glanced first, was crowded, but Gatsby was not there. She couldn't find him from the top of the steps, and he wasn't on the veranda. On a chance we tried an important-looking door, and walked into a high Gothic[7] library, panelled with carved English oak, and probably transported complete from some ruin overseas.

A stout, middle-aged man, with enormous owl-eyed spectacles, was sitting somewhat drunk on the edge of a great table, staring with unsteady concentration at the shelves of books. As we entered he wheeled excitedly around and examined Jordan from head to foot.

"What do you think?" he demanded impetuously.

"About what?"

He waved his hand toward the book-shelves.

"About that. As a matter of fact you needn't bother to ascertain. I ascertained. They're real."

"The books?"

He nodded.

"Absolutely real—have pages and everything. I thought they'd be a nice durable cardboard. Matter of fact, they're absolutely real. Pages and—Here! Lemme show you."

Taking our scepticism for granted, he rushed to the bookcases and returned with Volume One of the "Stoddard Lectures."

"See!" he cried triumphantly. "It's a bona-fide piece of printed matter. It fooled me. This fella's a regular Belasco[8]. It's a triumph. What thoroughness! What realism! Knew when to stop too—didn't cut the pages. But what do you want? What do you expect?"

He snatched the book from me and replaced it hastily on its shelf, muttering that if one brick was removed the whole library was liable to collapse.

"Who brought you?" he demanded. "Or did you just come? I was brought. Most people were brought."

Jordan looked at him alertly, cheerfully, without answering.

"I was brought by a woman named Roosevelt," he continued. "Mrs. Claude Roosevelt. Do you know her? I met her somewhere last night. I've been drunk for about a week now, and I thought it might sober me up to sit in a library."

"Has it?"

"A little bit, I think. I can't tell yet. I've only been here an hour. Did I tell you about the books? They're real. They're—"

"You told us."

We shook hands with him gravely and went back outdoors.

There was dancing now on the canvas in the garden; old men pushing young girls backward in eternal graceless circles, superior couples holding each other tortuously, fashionably, and keeping in the corners—and a great number of single girls dancing individualistically or relieving the orchestra for a moment of the burden of the banjo or the traps[9]. By midnight the hilarity had increased. A celebrated tenor had sung in Italian, and a notorious contralto had sung in jazz, and between the numbers people were doing "stunts" all over the garden, while happy, vacuous bursts of laughter rose toward the summer sky. A pair of stage twins, who turned out to be the girls in yellow, did a baby act in costume, and champagne was served in glasses bigger than finger-bowls. The moon had risen higher, and floating in the Sound was a triangle of silver scales, trembling a little to the stiff, tinny drip of the banjoes on the lawn.

I was still with Jordan Baker. We were sitting at a table with a man of about my age and a rowdy little girl, who gave way upon the slightest provocation to uncontrollable laughter. I was enjoying myself now. I had taken two finger-bowls of champagne, and the scene had changed before my eyes into something significant, elemental, and profound.

At a lull in the entertainment the man looked at me and smiled.

"Your face is familiar," he said, politely. "Weren't you in the Third Division during the war?"

"Why, yes. I was in the Ninth Machine-Gun Battalion."

"I was in the Seventh Infantry until June nineteen-eighteen. I knew I'd seen you somewhere before."

We talked for a moment about some wet, gray little villages in France. Evidently he lived in this vicinity, for he told me that he had just bought a hydroplane, and was going to try it out in the morning.

"Want to go with me, old sport? Just near the shore along the Sound."

"What time?"

"Any time that suits you best."

It was on the tip of my tongue to ask his name when Jordan looked around and smiled.

"Having a gay time now?" she inquired.

"Much better." I turned again to my new acquaintance. "This is an unusual party for me. I haven't even seen the host. I live over there—" I waved my hand at the invisible hedge in the distance, "and this man Gatsby sent over his chauffeur with an invitation."

For a moment he looked at me as if he failed to understand.

"I'm Gatsby," he said suddenly.

"What!" I exclaimed. "Oh, I beg your pardon."

"I thought you knew, old sport. I'm afraid I'm not a very good host."

He smiled understandingly—much more than understandingly. It was one of those rare smiles with a quality of eternal reassurance in it, that you may come across four or five times in life. It faced—or seemed to face—the whole external world for an instant, and then concentrated on *you* with an irresistible prejudice in your favor. It understood you just so far as you wanted to be understood, believed in you as you would like to believe in yourself, and assured you that it had precisely the impression of you that, at your best, you hoped to convey. Precisely at that point it vanished—and I was looking at an elegant young roughneck, a year or two over thirty, whose elaborate formality of speech just missed being absurd. Some time before he introduced himself I'd got a strong impression that he was picking his words with care.

Almost at the moment when Mr. Gatsby identified himself, a butler hurried toward him with the information that Chicago was calling him on the wire. He excused himself with a small bow that included each of us in turn.

"If you want anything just ask for it, old sport," he urged me. "Excuse me. I will rejoin you later."

Notes
1. the Sound: the Long Island Sound, a narrow finger of the Atlantic Ocean between Long Island and the state of Connecticut on the mainland, just east of New York City
2. Rolls-Royce: a very expensive and luxurious British automobile
3. Castile: a region of Spain, once an independent kingdom renowned for its lace and embroidered shawls
4. Frisco: short for San Francisco; here, a slang term meaning rapidly, vigorously
5. the *Follies*: It refers to the *Ziegfeld Follies*, a musical theatrical revue produced by Florenz Ziegfeld, very popular in the 1920s. Gilda Gray was one of its famous stars.
6. white flannels: casual men's trousers of the 1920s made of wool flannel
7. Gothic: of or relating to a style of architecture which originated in France in the twelfth century, characterized by great height in the buildings, pointed arches, rib vaulting and large window spaces
8. Belasco: David Belasco (1853–1931), American theatrical producer, manager and writer, known for his minutely detailed and spectacular stage settings
9. traps: percussion instruments

Chapter 33

Ernest Hemingway (1899–1961)

Ernest Hemingway was born in Oak Park, near Chicago, on July 21, 1899. His father, a well-to-do physician, bequeathed his son a way of life, and of death, initiated him into the rituals of hunting and fishing in the upper Peninsula of Michigan. In 1917, after graduation from high school, Ernest Hemingway went to work as a reporter for *The Kansas City Star*. Rejected for army service in World War I because of poor vision, he volunteered to serve as a driver for an American ambulance unit in France. Hemingway then transferred to duty on the Italian front, where he was seriously wounded in the explosion of a mortar shell. He was the first American to be wounded in Italy during World War I. After his recovery, and with decorations for valor which he believed he did not deserve, Hemingway returned home. He worked for the *Toronto Star*, covered the Greco-Turkish war as a foreign correspondent, and then returned to Paris, which after the war, was a city full of intellectual life, creativity and genius.

In Paris, Hemingway—along with Gertrude Stein, Ezra Pound, T. S. Eliot, and James Joyce—accomplished a revolution in literary style and language. He developed a spare, tight, reportorial prose based on simple sentence structure and using a restricted vocabulary, precise imagery, and an impersonal, dramatic tone. His first book, *Three Stories and Ten Poems*, appeared in 1923. With the publication of *The Sun Also Rises*, three years later, Hemingway became the spokesman for what Gertrude Stein had called "a lost generation."

His works have sometimes been read as an essentially negative commentary on a modern world filled with sterility, failure, and death. Yet such a nihilistic vision is repeatedly modified by Hemingway's affirmative assertion of the possibility of living with style and courage. His primary concern was an individual's "moment of truth," and his fascination with the threat of physical, emotional, or psychic death was reflected in his lifelong preoccupation with stories of war (*A Farewell to Arms*, 1929, and *For Whom the Bell Tolls*, 1940), the bullfight (*Death in the Afternoon*, 1932), and the hunt (*The Green Hills of Africa*, 1935). To Hemingway, man's greatest achievement is to show grace under pressure, or what he described in *The Sun Also Rises* as holding the "purity of line through the maximum of exposure."

Hemingway's stature as a writer was confirmed with the publication of *A Farewell to Arms* in 1929. The novel portrayed a farewell both to war and to love. Hemingway had rejected the romantic ideal of the ultimate unity of lovers, suggesting instead that all relationships must end in death. In 1937 he became a foreign correspondent covering the Spanish Civil War. Three years later he published *For Whom the Bell Tolls*. Set in Spain during the Civil War, the novel restated his view of love found and lost and described the indomitable spirit of the common people. In 1952 the same judgment was reflected in his portrayal of the old fisherman, Santiago, triumphant even in defeat, in *The Old Man and the Sea*.

For his novels and for his short stories, which include some of the finest in the English language, Hemingway received wide acclaim. In 1954 he was awarded a Nobel Prize for his "mastery of the art of modern narration." He became a public figure whose pronouncements and adventures were publicized and scrutinized throughout the world. Numerous parallels exist between the events of Hemingway's life and those of his characters, but few were closer than those of Richard Cantwell, the hero of *Across the River and into the Trees* (1950), whose attempts at stoic control of physical and mental illness and whose eventual suicide foreshadow the struggles and defeats of Hemingway's final years. In the early morning of July 2, 1961, standing beside his beloved gunrack in his home, he died of head wounds resulting from the discharge of his favorite shot-gun, in his own hand.

🌿 A Farewell to Arms

The Story

Lieutenant Frederic Henry was a young American attached to an Italian ambulance unit on the Italian front. An offensive was soon to begin, and when Henry returned to the front from leave he learned from his friend, Lieutenant Rinaldi, that a group of British nurses had arrived in his absence to set up a British hospital unit. Rinaldi introduced him to nurse Catherine Barkley.

Between ambulance trips to evacuation posts at the front, Henry called on Miss Barkley. He liked the frank young English girl in a casual sort of way, but he was not in love with her. Before he left for the front to stand by for an attack, she gave him a St. Anthony medal.

At the front, as Henry and some Italian ambulance drivers were eating in a dugout, an Austrian projectile exploded over them. Henry, badly wounded in the legs, was taken to a field hospital. Later he was moved to a hospital in Milan.

Before the doctor was able to see Henry in Milan, the nurses prohibited his drinking wine, but he bribed a porter to bring him a supply which he kept hidden behind his bed. Catherine Barkley came to the hospital and Henry knew that he was in love with her. The doctors told Henry that he would have to lie in bed six months before they could operate on his knee. Henry insisted on seeing another doctor, who said that the operation could be performed the next day. Meanwhile, Catherine managed to be with Henry constantly.

After his operation, Henry convalesced in Milan with Catherine Barkley as his attendant. Together they dined in out-of-the-way restaurants, and together they rode about the countryside in a carriage. Henry was restless and lonely at nights and Catherine often came to his hospital room.

Summer passed into autumn. Henry's wound had healed and he was due to take convalescent leave in October. He and Catherine planned to spend the leave together, but he came down with jaundice before he could leave the hospital. The head nurse accused him of bringing on the jaundice by drink, in order to avoid being sent back to the front. Before he left for the front, Henry

Chapter 33 Ernest Hemingway

and Catherine stayed together in a hotel room; already she had disclosed to him that she was pregnant.

Henry returned to the front with orders to load his three ambulances with hospital equipment and go south into the Po valley. Morale was at low ebb. Rinaldi admired the job which had been done on the knee and observed that Henry acted like a married man. War weariness was all-pervasive. At the front, the Italians, having learned that German divisions had reinforced the Austrians, began their terrible retreat from Caporetto. Henry drove one of the ambulances loaded with hospital supplies. During the retreat south, the ambulance was held up several times by wagons, guns, and trucks which extended in stalled lines for miles. Henry picked up two straggling Italian sergeants. During the night the retreat was halted in the rain for hours.

At daybreak Henry cut out of the long line and drove across country in an attempt to reach Udine by side roads. The ambulance got stuck in a muddy side road. The sergeants decided to leave, but Henry asked them to help dislodge the car from the mud. They refused and ran. Henry shot and wounded one; the other escaped across the fields. An Italian ambulance corpsman with Henry shot the wounded sergeant through the back of the head. Henry and his three comrades struck out on foot for Udine. On a bridge, Henry saw a German staff car and German bicycle troops crossing another bridge over the same stream. Within sight of Udine, one of Henry's group was killed by an Italian sniper. The others hid in a barn until it seemed safe to circle around Udine and join the main stream of the retreat toward the Tagliamento River.

By that time the Italian army was nothing but a frantic mob. Soldiers were throwing down their arms and officers were cutting insignia of rank from their sleeves. At the end of a long wooden bridge across the Tagliamento military carabiniers were seizing all officers, giving them drumhead trials, and executing them by the river bank. Henry was detained, but in the dark of night he broke free, plunged into the river, and escaped on a log. He crossed the Venetian plain on foot. Then he jumped aboard a freight train and rode to Milan, where he went to the hospital in which he had been a patient. There he learned that the English nurses had gone to Stresa.

During the retreat from Caporetto Henry had made his farewell to arms. He borrowed civilian clothes from an American friend in Milan and went by train to Stresa, where he met Catherine, who was on leave. The bartender of the hotel in which Henry was staying warned Henry that authorities were planning to arrest him for desertion the next morning; he offered his boat by means of which Henry and Catherine could escape to Switzerland. Henry rowed all night. By morning his hands were so raw that he could barely stand to touch the oars. Over his protests, Catherine took a turn at the rowing. They reached Switzerland safely and were arrested. Henry told the police that he was a sportsman who enjoyed rowing and that he had come to Switzerland for the winter sports. The valid passports and the ample funds that Henry and Catherine possessed saved them from serious trouble with the authorities.

During the rest of the fall and the winter the couple stayed at an inn outside Montreux. They discussed marriage, but Catherine would not be married while she was with child. They hiked, read, and talked about what they would do together after the war.

When the time for Catherine's confinement approached, she and Henry went to Lausanne to be near a hospital. They planned to return to Montreux in the spring. At the hospital Catherine's pains caused the doctor to use an anaesthetic on her. After hours of suffering she was delivered of a dead baby. The nurse sent Henry out to get something to eat. When he went back to the hospital, he learned that Catherine had had a hemorrhage. He went into the room and stayed with her until she died. There was nothing he could do, no one he could talk to, no place he could go. Catherine was dead. He left the hospital and walked back to his hotel in the dark. It was raining.

Chapter XLI

One morning I awoke about three o'clock hearing Catherine stirring in the bed.

"Are you all right, Cat?"

"I've been having some pains[1], darling."

"Regularly?"

"No, not very."

Chapter 33 Ernest Hemingway

"If you have them at all regularly we'll go to the hospital."

I was very sleepy and went back to sleep. A little while later I woke again.

"Maybe you'd better call up the doctor," Catherine said. "I think maybe this is it."

I went to the phone and called the doctor. "How often are the pains coming?" he asked.

"How often are they coming, Cat?"

"I should think every quarter of an hour."

"You should go to the hospital, then," the doctor said. "I will dress and go there right away myself."

I hung up and called the garage near the station to send up a taxi. No one answered the phone for a long time. Then I finally got a man who promised to send up a taxi at once. Catherine was dressing. Her bag was all packed with the things she would need at the hospital and the baby things. Outside in the hall I rang for the elevator. There was no answer. I went downstairs. There was no one downstairs except the night-watchman. I brought the elevator up myself, put Catherine's bag in it, she stepped in and we went down. The night-watchman opened the door for us and we sat outside on the stone slabs beside the stairs down to the driveway and waited for the taxi. The night was clear and the stars were out. Catherine was very excited.

"I'm so glad it's started," she said. "Now in a little while it will be all over."

"You're a good brave girl."

"I'm not afraid. I wish the taxi would come, though."

We heard it coming up the street and saw its headlights. It turned into the driveway and I helped Catherine in and the driver put the bag up in front.

"Drive to the hospital," I said.

We went out of the driveway and started up the hill.

At the hospital we went in and I carried the bag. There was a woman at the desk who wrote down Catherine's name, age, address, relatives and religion, in a book. She said she had no religion and the woman drew a line in the space after that word. She gave her name as Catherine Henry.

"I will take you up to your room," she said. We went up in an elevator. The woman stopped it and we stepped out and followed her down a hall.

Catherine held tight to my arm.

"This is the room," the woman said. "Will you please undress and get into bed? Here is a night-gown for you to wear."

"I have a night-gown," Catherine said.

"It is better for you to wear this night-gown," the woman said.

I went outside and sat on a chair in the hallway.

"You can come in now," the woman said from the doorway. Catherine was lying in the narrow bed wearing a plain, square-cut night-gown that looked as though it were made of rough sheeting. She smiled at me.

"I'm having fine pains now," she said. The woman was holding her wrist and timing the pains with a watch.

"That was a big one," Catherine said. I saw it on her face.

"Where's the doctor?" I asked the woman.

"He's lying down sleeping. He will be here when he is needed."

"I must do something for Madame, now," the nurse said. "Would you please step out again?"

I went out into the hall. It was a bare hall with two windows and closed doors all down the corridor. It smelled of hospital. I sat on the chair and looked at the floor and prayed for Catherine.

"You can come in," the nurse said. I went in.

"Hello, darling," Catherine said.

"How is it?"

"They are coming quite often now." Her face drew up. Then she smiled.

"That was a real one. Do you want to put your hand on my back again, nurse?"

"If it helps you," the nurse said.

"You go away, darling," Catherine said. "Go out and get something to eat. I may do this for a long time the nurse says."

"The first labor[2] is usually protracted," the nurse said.

"Please go out and get something to eat," Catherine said. "I'm fine, really."

"I'll stay awhile," I said.

The pains came quite regularly, then slackened off. Catherine was very excited. When the pains were bad she called them good ones. When they

Chapter 33 Ernest Hemingway

started to fall off she was disappointed and ashamed.

"You go out, darling," she said. "I think you are just making me self-conscious." Her face tied up. "There. That was better. I so want to be a good wife and have this child without any foolishness. Please go and get some breakfast, darling, and then come back. I won't miss you. Nurse is splendid to me."

"You have plenty of time for breakfast," the nurse said.

"I'll go then. Good-by, sweet."

"Good-by," Catherine said, "and have a fine breakfast for me too."

"Where can I get breakfast?" I asked the nurse.

"There's a café down the street at the square," she said. "It should be open now."

Outside it was getting light. I walked down the empty street to the café. There was a light in the window. I went in and stood at the zinc bar and an old man served me a glass of white wine and a brioche. The brioche was yesterday's. I dipped it in the wine and then drank a glass of coffee.

"What do you do at this hour?" the old man asked.

"My wife is in labor at the hospital."

"So. I wish you good luck."

"Give me another glass of wine."

He poured it from the bottle slopping it over a little so some ran down on the zinc. I drank this glass, paid and went out. Outside along the street were the refuse cans from the houses waiting for the collector. A dog was nosing at one of the cans.

"What do you want?" I asked and looked in the can to see if there was anything I could pull out for him; there was nothing on top but coffee-grounds, dust and some dead flowers.

"There isn't anything, dog," I said. The dog crossed the street. I went up the stairs in the hospital to the floor Catherine was on and down the hall to her room. I knocked on the door. There was no answer. I opened the door; the room was empty, except for Catherine's bag on a chair and her dressing-gown hanging on a hook on the wall. I went out and down the hall, looking for somebody. I found a nurse.

"Where is Madame Henry?"

"A lady has just gone to the delivery room."

"Where is it?"

"I will show you."

She took me down to the end of the hall. The door of the room was partly open. I could see Catherine lying on a table, covered by a sheet. The nurse was on one side and the doctor stood on the other side of the table beside some cylinders. The doctor held a rubber mask attached to a tube in one hand.

"I will give you a gown and you can go in," the nurse said. "Come in here, please."

She put a white gown on me and pinned it at the neck in back with a safety pin.

"Now you can go in," she said. I went into the room.

"Hello, darling," Catherine said in a strained voice. "I'm not doing much."

"You are Mr. Henry?" the doctor asked.

"Yes. How is everything going, doctor?"

"Things are going very well," the doctor said. "We came in here where it is easy to give gas[3] for the pains."

"I want it now," Catherine said. The doctor placed the rubber mask over her face and turned a dial and I watched Catherine breathing deeply and rapidly. Then she pushed the mask away. The doctor shut off the petcock.

"That wasn't a very big one. I had a very big one a while ago. The doctor made me go clear out[4], didn't you, doctor?" Her voice was strange. It rose on the word doctor.

The doctor smiled.

"I want it again," Catherine said. She held the rubber tight to her face and breathed fast. I heard her moaning a little. Then she pulled the mask away and smiled.

"That was a big one," she said. "That was a very big one. Don't you worry, darling. You go away. Go have another breakfast."

"I'll stay," I said.

We had gone to the hospital about three o'clock in the morning. At noon

Chapter 33 Ernest Hemingway

Catherine was still in the delivery room. The pains had slackened again. She looked very tired and worn now but she was still cheerful.

"I'm not any good, darling," she said. "I'm so sorry. I thought I would do it very easily. Now—there's one—" she reached out her hand for the mask and held it over her face. The doctor moved the dial and watched her. In a little while it was over.

"It wasn't much," Catherine said. She smiled. "I'm a fool about the gas. It's wonderful."

"We'll get some for the home," I said.

"*There one comes*," Catherine said quickly. The doctor turned the dial and looked at his watch.

"What is the interval now?" I asked.

"About a minute."

"Don't you want lunch?"

"I will have something pretty soon," he said.

"You must have something to eat, doctor," Catherine said. "I'm so sorry I go on so long. Couldn't my husband give me the gas?"

"If you wish," the doctor said. "You turn it to the numeral two."

"I see," I said. There was a marker on a dial that turned with a handle.

"*I want it now*," Catherine said. She held the mask tight to her face. I turned the dial to number two and when Catherine put down the mask I turned it off. It was very good of the doctor to let me do something.

"Did you do it, darling?" Catherine asked. She stroked my wrist.

"Sure."

"You're so lovely." She was a little drunk from the gas.

"I will eat from a tray in the next room," the doctor said. "You can call me any moment." While the time passed I watched him eat, then, after a while, I saw that he was lying down and smoking a cigarette. Catherine was getting very tired.

"Do you think I'll ever have this baby?" she asked.

"Yes, of course you will."

"I try as hard as I can. I push down but it goes away. *There it comes. Give it to me.*"

At two o'clock I went out and had lunch. There were a few men in the café sitting with coffee and glasses of kirsch or marc on the tables. I sat down at a table. "Can I eat?" I asked the waiter.

"It is past time for lunch."

"Isn't there anything for all hours?"

"You can have *choucroute*."

"Give me *choucroute* and beer."

"A demi[5] or a bock?"

"A light demi."

The waiter brought a dish of sauerkraut with a slice of ham over the top and a sausage buried in the hot wine-soaked cabbage. I ate it and drank the beer. I was very hungry. I watched the people at the tables in the café. At one table they were playing cards. Two men at the table next me were talking and smoking. The café was full of smoke. The zinc bar, where I had breakfasted, had three people behind it now; the old man, a plump woman in a black dress who sat behind a counter and kept track of everything served to the tables, and a boy in an apron. I wondered how many children the woman had and what it had been like.

When I was through with the *choucroute* I went back to the hospital. The street was all clean now. There were no refuse cans out. The day was cloudy but the sun was trying to come through. I rode upstairs in the elevator, stepped out and went down the hall to Catherine's room, where I had left my white gown. I put it on and pinned it in back at the neck. I looked in the glass and saw myself looking like a fake doctor with a beard. I went down the hall to the delivery room. The door was closed and I knocked. No one answered so I turned the handle and went in. The doctor sat by Catherine. The nurse was doing something at the other end of the room.

"Here is your husband," the doctor said.

"Oh, darling, I have the most wonderful doctor," Catherine said in a very strange voice. "He's been telling me the most wonderful story and when the pain came too badly he put me all the way out[6]. He's wonderful. You're wonderful, doctor."

"You're drunk," I said.

Chapter 33 Ernest Hemingway

"I know it," Catherine said. "But you shouldn't say it." Then "*Give it to me. Give it to me.*" She clutched hold of the mask and breathed short and deep, pantingly, making the respirator click. Then she gave a long sigh and the doctor reached with his left hand and lifted away the mask.

"That was a very big one," Catherine said. Her voice was very strange. "I'm not going to die now, darling. I'm past where I was going to die. Aren't you glad?"

"Don't you get in that place again."

"I won't. I'm not afraid of it though. I won't die, darling."

"You will not do any such foolishness," the doctor said. "You would not die and leave your husband."

"Oh, no. I won't die. I wouldn't die. It's silly to die. There it comes. *Give it to me.*"

After a while the doctor said, "You will go out, Mr. Henry, for a few moments and I will make an examination."

"He wants to see how I am doing," Catherine said. "You can come back afterward, darling, can't he, doctor?"

"Yes," said the doctor. "I will send word when he can come back."

I went out the door and down the hall to the room where Catherine was to be after the baby came. I sat in a chair there and looked at the room. I had the paper in my coat that I had bought when I went out for lunch and I read it. It was beginning to be dark outside and I turned the light on to read. After a while I stopped reading and turned off the light and watched it get dark outside. I wondered why the doctor did not send for me. Maybe it was better I was away. He probably wanted me away for a while. I looked at my watch. If he did not send for me in ten minutes I would go down anyway.

Poor, poor dear Cat. And this was the price you paid for sleeping together. This was the end of the trap. This was what people got for loving each other. Thank God for gas, anyway. What must it have been like before there were anaesthetics? Once it started, they were in the mill-race. Catherine had a good time in the time of pregnancy. It wasn't bad. She was hardly ever sick. She was not awfully uncomfortable until toward the last. So now they got her in the end. You never got away with anything. Get away hell! It would have been the same if we had been married fifty times. And what if she should die? She won't die. People don't die in childbirth nowadays. That was what all husbands thought. Yes, but what if she should die? She won't die. She's just having a bad time. The initial labor is usually protracted. She's only having a bad time. Afterward we'd say what a bad time and Catherine would say it wasn't really so bad. But what if she should die? She can't die. Yes, but what if she should die? She can't, I tell you. Don't be a fool. It's just a bad time. It's just nature giving her hell. It's only the first labor, which is almost always protracted. Yes, but what if she should die? She can't die. Why would she die? What reason is there for her to die? There's just a child that has to be born, the by-product of good nights in Milan. It makes trouble and is born and then you look after it and get fond of it maybe. But what if she should die? She won't die. But what if she should die? She won't. She's all right. But what if she should die? She can't die. But what if she should die? Hey, what about that? What if she should die?

The doctor came into the room.

"How does it go, doctor?"

"It doesn't go," he said.

"What do you mean?"

"Just that. I made an examination—" He detailed the result of the examination. "Since then I've waited to see. But it doesn't go."

"What do you advise?"

"There are two things. Either a high forceps delivery which can tear and be quite dangerous besides being possibly bad for the child, and a Caesarean[7]."

"What is the danger of a Caesarean?" What if she should die!

"It should be no greater than the danger of an ordinary delivery."

"Would you do it yourself?"

"Yes. I would need possibly an hour to get things ready and to get the people I would need. Perhaps a little less."

"What do you think?"

"I would advise a Caesarean operation. If it were my wife I would do a Caesarean."

"What are the after effects?"

"There are none. There is only the scar."

"What about infection?"

"The danger is not so great as in a high forceps delivery."

"What if you just went on and did nothing?"

"You would have to do something eventually. Mrs. Henry is already losing much of her strength. The sooner we operate now the safer."

"Operate as soon as you can," I said.

"I will go and give the instructions."

I went into the delivery room. The nurse was with Catherine who lay on the table, big under the sheet, looking very pale and tired.

"Did you tell him he could do it?" she asked.

"Yes."

"Isn't that grand. Now it will be all over in an hour. I'm almost done, darling. I'm going all to pieces. *Please give me that.* It doesn't work. *Oh, it doesn't work!*"

"Breathe deeply."

"I am. Oh, it doesn't work any more. It doesn't work!"

"Get another cylinder," I said to the nurse.

"That is a new cylinder."

"I'm just a fool, darling," Catherine said. "But it doesn't work any more." She began to cry. "Oh, I wanted so to have this baby and not make trouble, and now I'm all done and all gone to pieces and it doesn't work. Oh, darling, it doesn't work at all. I don't care if I die if it will only stop. Oh, please, darling, please make it stop. *There it comes. Oh Oh Oh!*" She breathed sobbingly in the mask. "It doesn't work. It doesn't work. It doesn't work. Don't mind me, darling. Please don't cry. Don't mind me. I'm just gone all to pieces. You poor sweet. I love you so and I'll be good again. I'll be good this time. *Can't they give me something?* If they could only give me something."

"I'll make it work. I'll turn it all the way."

"Give it to me now."

I turned the dial all the way and as she breathed hard and deep her hand relaxed on the mask. I shut off the gas and lifted the mask. She came back from a long way away.

"That was lovely, darling. Oh, you're so good to me."

"You be brave, because I can't do that all the time. It might kill you."

"I'm not brave any more, darling. I'm all broken. They've broken me. I know it now."

"Everybody is that way."

"But it's awful. They just keep it up till they break you."

"In an hour it will be over."

"Isn't that lovely? Darling, I won't die, will I?"

"No. I promise you won't."

"Because I don't want to die and leave you, but I get so tired of it and I feel I'm going to die."

"Nonsense. Everybody feels that."

"Sometimes I know I'm going to die."

"You won't. You can't."

"But what if I should?"

"I won't let you."

"Give it to me quick. *Give it to me!*"

Then afterward, "I won't die. I won't let myself die."

"Of course you won't."

"You'll stay with me?"

"Not to watch it."

"No, just to be there."

"Sure. I'll be there all the time."

"You're so good to me. There, give it to me. Give me some more. *It's not working!*"

I turned the dial to three and then four. I wished the doctor would come back. I was afraid of the numbers above two.

Finally a new doctor came in with two nurses and they lifted Catherine onto a wheeled stretcher and we started down the hall. The stretcher went rapidly down the hall and into the elevator where every one had to crowd against the wall to make room; then up, then an open door and out of the elevator and down the hall on rubber wheels to the operating room. I did not recognize the doctor with his cap and mask on. There was another doctor and

Chapter 33   Ernest Hemingway

more nurses.

"*They've got to give me something,*" Catherine said. "*They've got to give me something.* Oh please, doctor, give me enough to do some good!"

One of the doctors put a mask over her face and I looked through the door and saw the bright small amphitheatre of the operating room.

"You can go in the other door and sit up there," a nurse said to me. There were benches behind a rail that looked down on the white table and the lights. I looked at Catherine. The mask was over her face and she was quiet now. They wheeled the stretcher forward. I turned away and walked down the hall. Two nurses were hurrying toward the entrance to the gallery.

"It's a Caesarean," one said. "They're going to do a Caesarean."

The other one laughed, "We're just in time. Aren't we lucky?" They went in the door that led to the gallery.

Another nurse came along. She was hurrying too.

"You go right in there. Go right in," she said.

"I'm staying outside."

She hurried in. I walked up and down the hall. I was afraid to go in. I looked out the window. It was dark but in the light from the window I could see it was raining. I went into a room at the far end of the hall and looked at the labels on bottles in a glass case. Then I came out and stood in the empty hall and watched the door of the operating room.

A doctor came out followed by a nurse. He held something in his two hands that looked like a freshly skinned rabbit and hurried across the corridor with it and in through another door. I went down to the door he had gone into and found them in the room doing things to a new-born child. The doctor held him up for me to see. He held him by the heels and slapped him.

"Is he all right?"

"He's magnificent. He'll weigh five kilos."

I had no feeling for him. He did not seem to have anything to do with me. I felt no feeling of fatherhood.

"Aren't you proud of your son?" the nurse asked. They were washing him and wrapping him in something. I saw the little dark face and dark hand, but I did not see him move or hear him cry. The doctor was doing something to him again. He looked upset.

"No," I said. "He nearly killed his mother."

"It isn't the little darling's fault. Didn't you want a boy?"

"No," I said. The doctor was busy with him. He held him up by the feet and slapped him. I did not wait to see it. I went out in the hall. I could go in now and see. I went in the door and a little way down the gallery. The nurses who were sitting at the rail motioned for me to come down where they were. I shook my head. I could see enough where I was.

I thought Catherine was dead. She looked dead. Her face was gray, the part of it that I could see. Down below, under the light, the doctor was sewing up the great long, forceps-spread, thick-edged, wound. Another doctor in a mask gave the anaesthetic. Two nurses in masks handed things. It looked like a drawing of the Inquisition[8]. I knew as I watched I could have watched it all, but I was glad I hadn't. I do not think I could have watched them cut, but I watched the wound closed into a high welted ridge with quick skilful-looking stitches like a cobbler's, and was glad. When the wound was closed I went out into the hall and walked up and down again. After a while the doctor came out.

"How is she?"

"She is all right. Did you watch?"

He looked tired.

"I saw you sew up. The incision looked very long."

"You thought so?"

"Yes. Will that scar flatten out?"

"Oh, yes."

After a while they brought out the wheeled stretcher and took it very rapidly down the hallway to the elevator. I went along beside it. Catherine was moaning. Downstairs they put her in the bed in her room. I sat in a chair at the foot of the bed. There was a nurse in the room. I got up and stood by the bed. It was dark in the room. Catherine put out her hand. "Hello, darling," she said. Her voice was very weak and tired.

"Hello, you sweet."

"What sort of baby was it?"

"Sh—don't talk," the nurse said.

Chapter 33 Ernest Hemingway

"A boy. He's long and wide and dark."

"Is he all right?"

"Yes," I said. "He's fine."

I saw the nurse look at me strangely.

"I'm awfully tired," Catherine said. "And I hurt like hell. Are you all right, darling?"

"I'm fine. Don't talk."

"You were lovely to me. Oh, darling, I hurt dreadfully. What does he look like?"

"He looks like a skinned rabbit with a puckered-up old-man's face."

"You must go out," the nurse said. "Madame Henry must not talk."

"I'll be outside."

"Go and get something to eat."

"No. I'll be outside." I kissed Catherine. She was very gray and weak and tired.

"May I speak to you?" I said to the nurse. She came out in the hall with me. I walked a little way down the hall.

"What's the matter with the baby?" I asked.

"Didn't you know?"

"No."

"He wasn't alive."

"He was dead?"

"They couldn't start him breathing. The cord was caught around his neck or something."

"So he's dead."

"Yes. It's such a shame. He was such a fine big boy. I thought you knew."

"No," I said. "You better go back in with Madame."

I sat down on the chair in front of a table where there were nurses' reports hung on clips at the side and looked out of the window. I could see nothing but the dark and the rain falling across the light from the window. So that was it. The baby was dead. That was why the doctor looked so tired. But why had they acted the way they did in the room with him? They supposed he would come around and start breathing probably. I had no religion but I knew he ought to have been baptized. But what if he never breathed at all. He hadn't. He had never been alive. Except in Catherine. I'd felt him kick there often enough. But I hadn't for a week. Maybe he was choked all the time. Poor little kid. I wished the hell I'd been choked like that. No I didn't. Still there would not be all this dying to go through. Now Catherine would die. That was what you did. You died. You did not know what it was about. You never had time to learn. They threw you in and told you the rules and the first time they caught you off base[9] they killed you. Or they killed you gratuitously like Aymo[10]. Or gave you the syphilis like Rinaldi[11]. But they killed you in the end. You could count on that. Stay around and they would kill you.

Once in camp I put a log on top of the fire and it was full of ants. As it commenced to burn, the ants swarmed out and went first toward the centre where the fire was; then turned back and ran toward the end. When there were enough on the end they fell off into the fire. Some got out, their bodies burnt and flattened, and went off not knowing where they were going. But most of them went toward the fire and then back toward the end and swarmed on the cool end and finally fell off into the fire. I remember thinking at the time that it was the end of the world and a splendid chance to be a messiah and lift the log off the fire and throw it out where the ants could get off onto the ground. But I did not do anything but throw a tin cup of water on the log, so that I would have the cup empty to put whiskey in before I added water to it. I think the cup of water on the burning log only steamed the ants.

So now I sat out in the hall and waited to hear how Catherine was. The nurse did not come out, so after a while I went to the door and opened it very softly and looked in. I could not see at first because there was a bright light in the hall and it was dark in the room. Then I saw the nurse sitting by the bed and Catherine's head on a pillow, and she was all flat under the sheet. The nurse put her finger to her lips, then stood up and came to the door.

"How is she?" I asked.

"She's all right," the nurse said. "You should go and have your supper and then come back if you wish."

I went down the hall and then down the stairs and out the door of the hospital and down the dark street in the rain to the café. It was brightly lighted inside and there were many people at the tables. I did not see a place to sit, and a waiter came up to me and took my wet coat and hat and showed me a place at a table across from an elderly man who was drinking beer and reading the evening paper. I sat down and asked the waiter what the *plat du jour*[12] was.

"Veal stew—but it is finished."

"What can I have to eat?"

"Ham and eggs, eggs with cheese, or *choucroute*."

"I had *choucroute* this noon," I said.

"That's true," he said. "That's true. You ate *choucroute* this noon." He was a middle-aged man with a bald top to his head and his hair slicked over it. He had a kind face.

"What do you want? Ham and eggs or eggs with cheese?"

"Ham and eggs," I said, "and beer."

"A demi-blonde?"

"Yes," I said.

"I remembered," he said. "You took a demi-blonde this noon."

I ate the ham and eggs and drank the beer. The ham and eggs were in a round dish—the ham underneath and the eggs on top. It was very hot and at the first mouthful I had to take a drink of beer to cool my mouth. I was hungry and I asked the waiter for another order. I drank several glasses of beer. I was not thinking at all but read the paper of the man opposite me. It was about the break through on the British front. When he realized I was reading the back of his paper he folded it over. I thought of asking the waiter for a paper, but I could not concentrate. It was hot in the café and the air was bad. Many of the people at the tables knew one another. There were several card games going on. The waiters were busy bringing drinks from the bar to the tables. Two men came in and could find no place to sit. They stood opposite the table where I was. I ordered another beer. I was not ready to leave yet. It was too soon to go back to the hospital. I tried not to think and to be perfectly calm. The men stood around but no one was leaving, so they went out. I drank another beer. There was quite a pile of saucers now on the table in front of me. The man opposite me had taken off his spectacles, put them away in a case, folded his paper and put it in his pocket and now sat holding his liqueur glass and looking out at the room. Suddenly I knew I had to get back. I called the waiter, paid the reckoning, got into my coat, put on my hat and started out the door. I walked through the rain up to the hospital.

Upstairs I met the nurse coming down the hall.

"I just called you at the hotel," she said. Something dropped inside me.

"What is wrong?"

"Mrs. Henry has had a hemorrhage."

"Can I go in?"

"No, not yet. The doctor is with her."

"Is it dangerous?"

"It is very dangerous." The nurse went into the room and shut the door. I sat outside in the hall. Everything was gone inside of me. I did not think. I could not think. I knew she was going to die and I prayed that she would not. Don't let her die. Oh, God, please don't let her die. I'll do anything for you if you won't let her die. Please, please, please, dear God, don't let her die. Dear God, don't let her die. Please, please, please don't let her die. God please make her not die. I'll do anything you say if you don't let her die. You took the baby but don't let her die. That was all right but don't let her die. Please, please, dear God, don't let her die.

The nurse opened the door and motioned with her finger for me to come. I followed her into her room. Catherine did not look up when I came in. I went over to the side of the bed. The doctor was standing by the bed on the opposite side. Catherine looked at me and smiled. I bent down over the bed and started to cry.

"Poor darling," Catherine said very softly. She looked gray.

"You're all right, Cat," I said. "You're going to be all right."

"I'm going to die," she said; then waited and said, "I hate it."

I took her hand.

"Don't touch me," she said. I let go of her hand. She smiled. "Poor darling. You touch me all you want."

"You'll be all right, Cat. I know you'll be all right."

"I meant to write you a letter to have if anything happened, but I didn't do it."

Chapter 33   Ernest Hemingway

"Do you want me to get a priest or any one to come and see you?"

"Just you," she said. Then a little later, "I'm not afraid. I just hate it."

"You must not talk so much," the doctor said.

"All right," Catherine said.

"Do you want me to do anything, Cat? Can I get you anything?"

Catherine smiled, "No." Then a little later, "You won't do our things with another girl, or say the same things, will you?"

"Never."

"I want you to have girls, though."

"I don't want them."

"You are talking too much," the doctor said. "Mr. Henry must go out. He can come back again later. You are not going to die. You must not be silly."

"All right," Catherine said. "I'll come and stay with you nights," she said. It was very hard for her to talk.

"Please go out of the room," the doctor said. "You cannot talk." Catherine winked at me, her face gray. "I'll be right outside," I said.

"Don't worry, darling," Catherine said. "I'm not a bit afraid. It's just a dirty trick."

"You dear, brave sweet."

I waited outside in the hall. I waited a long time. The nurse came to the door and came over to me. "I'm afraid Mrs. Henry is very ill," she said. "I'm afraid for her."

"Is she dead?"

"No, but she is unconscious."

It seems she had one hemorrhage after another. They couldn't stop it. I went into the room and stayed with Catherine until she died. She was unconscious all the time, and it did not take her very long to die.

Outside the room, in the hall, I spoke to the doctor, "Is there anything I can do to-night?"

"No. There is nothing to do. Can I take you to your hotel?"

"No, thank you. I am going to stay here a while."

"I know there is nothing to say. I cannot tell you—"

"No," I said. "There's nothing to say."
"Good-night," he said. "I cannot take you to your hotel?"
"No, thank you."
"It was the only thing to do," he said. "The operation proved—"
"I do not want to talk about it," I said.
"I would like to take you to your hotel."
"No, thank you."
He went down the hall. I went to the door of the room.
"You can't come in now," one of the nurses said.
"Yes I can," I said.
"You can't come in yet."
"You get out," I said. "The other one too."

But after I had got them out and shut the door and turned off the light it wasn't any good. It was like saying good-by to a statue. After a while I went out and left the hospital and walked back to the hotel in the rain.

Notes

1. pains: the throes immediately before and during child birth
2. the first labor: the pains of the first childbirth
3. gas: anaesthetic gas
4. made me go clear out: made me completely unconscious
5. demi: demi-blonde; weak, light-colored beer
6. put me all the way out: made me completely unconscious
7. Caesarean: operation by which a baby is removed from the uterus by cutting through the abdominal wall
8. the Inquisition: court appointed by the Roman Catholic Church to discover and suppress heresy and to punish heretics in medieval and early modern times
9. off base: a technical term in baseball; here, in an unprepared state
10. Aymo: a truck driver in the Italian army
11. Rinaldi: a doctor in the Italian army
12. *plat du jour*: (French) dish of the day

Chapter 34

John Steinbeck (1902–1968)

John Steinbeck was the foremost novelist of the American Depression of the 1930s. He was born in Salinas, California, the locale of much of his finest fiction. His sympathy for the migrant workers and the downtrodden, so evident in his writing, was the result of firsthand knowledge of their struggles. From his boyhood he was self-supporting; he worked as a laborer, a seaman on a cattle-boat, newspaper reporter, bricklayer, chemist's assistant, surveyor, and migratory fruit-picker. His writing reflected his concern with the rituals of manual labor.

The publication of *Tortilla Flat* (1935), the tender, sentimental portrait of the indestructibility of the California *paisanos* brought him sudden fame. In the following year *In Dubious Battle* appeared. It was Steinbeck's most clearly "proletarian" novel of class struggle, depicting the lives of migrant workers and their resistance to exploitation by the entrenched forces of society. In *Of Mice and Men* (1937) he portrayed the friendship of two itinerant workers who yearn for a permanent home they will never find. In *The Long Valley* (1938), he described the fate of the lowly whose instinctive responses to life led only to destruction. *The Grapes of Wrath* (1939), generally regarded as his masterpiece, showed the migration of the "Okies" from the "Dust Bowls" to California, a migration that ended in broken dreams and misery but at the same time affirmed the ability of the common people to endure and prevail.

Steinbeck's treatment of the social problems of his time, particularly the plight of the dispossessed farmer, earned him a Pulitzer Prize in 1940 and, in 1962, a Nobel Prize for Literature. At its best, Steinbeck's lyric prose vividly caught the qualities of speech, the character, the legends, and the humor of his native region. He was a superb storyteller whose reforming vision led him to contrast the conflicting moral codes of people in search of permanent ideals: "What we have always wanted," he wrote in *The Sea of Cortez* (1941), "is an unchangeable, and we have found that only a compass point, a thought, an individual ideal, does not change."

The Grapes of Wrath[1]

The Story

Tom Joad was released from the Oklahoma state penitentiary where he had served a sentence for killing a man in self-defense. He traveled homeward through a region made barren by drought and dust storms. On the way he met Jim Casy, an ex-preacher; the pair went together to the home of Tom's people. They found the Joad place deserted. While Tom and Casy were wondering what had happened, Muley Graves, a die-hard tenant farmer, came by and disclosed that all of the families in the neighborhood had gone to California or were going. Tom's folks, Muley said, had gone to a relative's place preparatory to going west. Muley was the only sharecropper to stay behind.

All over the southern Midwest states, farmers, no longer able to make a living because of land banks, weather, and machine farming, had sold or were forced out of the farms they had tenanted. Junk dealers and used-car salesmen profiteered on them. Thousands of families took to the roads leading to the promised land, California.

Tom and Casy found the Joads at Uncle John's place, all busy with preparations to leave for California. Assembled for the trip were Pa and Ma Joad; Noah, their mentally backward son; Al, the adolescent younger brother of Tom and Noah; Rose of Sharon, Tom's sister, and her husband, Connie; the Joad children, Ruthie and Winfield; and Grandma and Grandpa Joad. Al had bought an ancient truck to take them west. The family asked Jim Casy to go with them. The night before they started, they killed the pigs they had left and salted down the meat so that they would have food on the way.

Spurred by handbills which stated that agricultural workers were badly needed in California, the Joads, along with thousands of others, made their

Chapter 34 John Steinbeck

torturous way, in a worn-out vehicle, across the plains toward the mountains. Grandpa died of a stroke during their first overnight stop. Later there was a long delay when the truck broke down. Small business people along the way treated the migrants as enemies. And, to add to the general misery, returning migrants told the Joads that there was no work to be had in California, that conditions were even worse than they were in Oklahoma. But the dream of a beautiful West Coast urged the Joads onward.

Close to the California line, where the group stopped to bathe in a river, Noah, feeling he was a hindrance to the others, wandered away. It was there that the Joads first heard themselves addressed as "Okies," another word for tramps.

Grandma died during the night trip across the desert. After burying her, the group went into a Hooverville, as the migrants' camps were called. There they learned that work was all but impossible to find. A contractor came to the camp to sign up men to pick fruit in another county. When the "Okies" asked to see his license, the contractor turned the leaders over to a police deputy who had accompanied him to camp. Tom was involved in the fight which followed. He escaped, and Casy gave himself up in Tom's place. Connie, husband of the pregnant Rose of Sharon, suddenly disappeared from the group. The family was breaking up in the face of its hardships. Ma Joad did everything in her power to keep the group together.

Fearing recrimination after the fight, the Joads left Hooverville and went to a government camp maintained for transient agricultural workers. The camp had sanitary facilities, a local government made up of the transients themselves, and simple organized entertainment. During the Joad's stay at the camp the "Okies" successfully defeated an attempt of the local citizens to give the camp a bad name and thus to have it closed to the migrants. For the first time since they had arrived in California, the Joads found themselves treated as human beings.

Circumstances eventually forced them to leave the camp, however, for there was no work in the district. They drove to a large farm where work was being offered. There they found agitators attempting to keep the migrants from taking the work because of unfair wages offered. But the Joads, thinking only of food, were escorted by motorcycle police into the farm. The entire family picked peaches for five cents a box and earned in a day just enough money to buy food for one meal. Tom, remembering the pickets outside the camp, went out at night to investigate. He found Casy, who was the leader of the agitators. While Tom and Casy were talking, deputies, who had been searching for Casy, closed in on them. The pair fled, but were caught. Casy was killed. Tom received a cut on his head, but not before he had felled a deputy with an ax handle. The family concealed Tom in their shack. The rate for a box of peaches dropped, meanwhile, to two-and-a-half cents. Tom's danger and the futility of picking peaches drove the Joads on their way. They hid the injured Tom under the mattresses in the back of the truck and told the suspicious guard at the entrance to the farm that the extra man they had had with them when they came was a hitchhiker who had stayed on to pick.

The family found at last a migrant crowd encamped in abandoned boxcars along a stream. They joined the camp and soon found temporary jobs picking cotton. Tom, meanwhile, hid in a culvert near the camp. Ruthie innocently disclosed Tom's presence to another little girl. Ma, realizing that Tom was no longer safe, sent him away. Tom promised to carry on Casy's work in trying to improve the lot of the downtrodden everywhere.

The autumn rains began. Soon the stream which ran beside the camp overflowed and water entered the boxcars. Under these all but impossible conditions, Rose of Sharon gave birth to a dead baby. When the rising water made their position no longer bearable, the family moved from the camp on foot. The rains had made their old car useless. They came to a barn, which they shared with a boy and his starving father. Rose of Sharon, bereft of her baby, nourished the famished man with the milk from her breasts. So the poor kept each other alive in the depression years.

Chapter XXIII

The migrant people, scuttling for work, scrabbling to live, looked always for pleasure, dug for pleasure, manufactured pleasure, and they were hungry for amusement. Sometimes amusement lay in speech, and they climbed up their lives with jokes. And it came about in the camps along the roads, on the

Chapter 34   John Steinbeck

ditch banks beside the streams, under the sycamores, that the story teller grew into being, so that the people gathered in the low firelight to hear the gifted ones. And they listened while the tales were told, and their participation made the stories great.

I was a recruit against Geronimo[2]—

And the people listened, and their quiet eyes reflected the dying fire.

Them Injuns was cute—slick as snakes, an' quiet when they wanted. Could go through dry leaves, an' make no rustle. Try to do that sometime.

And the people listened and remembered the crash of dry leaves under their feet.

Come the change of season an' the clouds up. Wrong time. Ever hear of the army doing anything right? Give the army ten chances, an' they'll stumble along. Took three regiments to kill a hundred braves—always.

And the people listened, and their faces were quiet with listening. The story tellers, gathering attention into their tales, spoke in great rhythms, spoke in great words because the tales were great, and the listeners became great through them.

They was a brave on a ridge, against the sun. Knowed he stood out. Spread his arms an' stood. Naked as morning, an' against the sun. Maybe he was crazy. I don't know. Stood there, arms spread out; like a cross he looked. Four hundred yards. An' the men—well, they raised their sights an' they felt the wind with their fingers; an' then they jus' lay there an' couldn' shoot. Maybe that Injun knowed somepin. Knowed we couldn' shoot. Jes' laid there with the rifles cocked, an' didn' even put 'em to our shoulders. Lookin' at him. Head-band, one feather. Could see it, an' naked as the sun. Long time we laid there an' looked, an' he never moved. An' then the captain got mad. "Shoot, you crazy bastards, shoot!" he yells. An' we jus' laid there. "I'll give you to a five-count, an' then mark you down," the captain says. Well, sir—we put up our rifles slow, an' ever' man hoped somebody'd shoot first. I ain't never been so sad in my life. An' I laid my sights on his belly, 'cause you can't stop a Injun no other place—an'—then. Well, he jest plunked down an' rolled. An' we went up. An' he wasn' big—he'd looked so grand—up there. All tore to pieces an' little. Ever see a cock pheasant, stiff and beautiful, ever' feather drawed an' painted, an' even his eyes drawed in pretty? An' bang! You pick him up—bloody an' twisted, an' you spoiled somepin better'n you; an' eatin' him don't never make it up to you, 'cause you spoiled somepin in yaself, an' you can't never fix it up.

And the people nodded, and perhaps the fire spurted a little light and showed their eyes looking in on themselves.

Against the sun, with his arms out. An' he looked big—as God.

And perhaps a man balanced twenty cents between food and pleasure, and he went to a movie in Marysville or Tulare, in Ceres or Mountain View. And he came back to the ditch camp with his memory crowded. And he told how it was:

They was this rich fella, an' he makes like he's poor, an' they's this rich girl, an' she purtends like she's poor too, an' they meet in a hamburg' stan'.

Why?

I don't know why—that's how it was.

Why'd they purtend like they's poor?

Well, they're tired of bein' rich.

Horseshit!

You want to hear this, or not?

Well, go on then. Sure, I wanta hear it, but if I was rich, if I was rich I'd git so many pork chops—I'd cord 'em up aroun' me like wood, an' I'd eat my way out. Go on.

Well, they each think the other one's poor. An' they git arrested an' they git in jail, an' they don' git out 'cause the other one'd find out the first one is rich. An' the jail keeper, he's mean to 'em 'cause he thinks they're poor. Oughta see how he looks when he finds out. Jes' nearly faints, that's all.

What they git in jail for?

Well, they git caught at some kind a radical meetin' but they ain't radicals. They jes' happen to be there. An' they don't each one wanta marry fur money, ya see.

So the sons-of-bitches start lyin' to each other right off.

Well, in the pitcher it was like they was doin' good. They're nice to people, you see.

I was to a show oncet that was me, an' more'n me; an' my life, an' more'n my life, so ever'thing was bigger.

Well, I git enough sorrow. I like to git away from it.

Sure—if you can believe it.

So they got married, an' then they foun' out, an' all them people that's treated 'em mean. They was a fella had been uppity, an' he nearly fainted when this fella come in with a plug hat on. Jes' nearly fainted. An' they was a newsreel with them German soldiers kickin' up their feet[3]—funny as hell.

And always, if he had a little money, a man could get drunk. The hard edges gone, and the warmth. Then there was no loneliness, for a man could people his brain with friends, and he could find his enemies and destroy them. Sitting in a ditch, the earth grew soft under him. Failures dulled and the future was no threat. And hunger did not skulk about, but the world was soft and easy, and a man could reach the place he started for. The stars came down wonderfully close and the sky was soft. Death was a friend, and sleep was death's brother. The old times came back—a girl with pretty feet, who danced one time at home—a horse—a long time ago. A horse and a saddle. And the leather was carved. When was that? Ought to find a girl to talk to. That's nice. Might lay with her, too. But warm here. And the stars down so close, and sadness and pleasure so close together, really the same thing. Like to stay drunk all the time. Who says it's bad? Who dares to say it's bad? Preachers—but they got their own kinda drunkenness. Thin, barren women, but they're too miserable to know. Reformers—but they don't bite deep enough into living to know. No—the stars are close and dear and I have joined the brotherhood of the worlds. And everything's holy—everything, even me.

A harmonica is easy to carry. Take it out of your hip pocket, knock it against your palm to shake out the dirt and pocket fuzz and bits of tobacco. Now it's ready. You can do anything with a harmonica: thin reedy single tone, or chords, or melody with rhythm chords. You can mold the music with curved hands, making it wail and cry like bagpipes, making it full and round like an organ, making it as sharp and bitter as the reed pipes of the hills. And you can play and put it back in your pocket. It is always with you, always in your pocket. And as you play, you learn new tricks, new ways to mold the tone with your hands, to pinch the tone with your lips, and no one teaches you. You feel around—sometimes alone in the shade at noon, sometimes in the tent door after supper when the women are washing up. Your foot taps gently on the ground. Your eyebrows rise and fall in rhythm. And if you lose it or break it, why, it's no great loss. You can buy another for a quarter.

A guitar is more precious. Must learn this thing. Fingers of the left hand must have callus caps. Thumb of the right hand a horn of callus. Stretch the left-hand fingers, stretch them like a spider's legs to get the hard pads on the frets.

This was my father's box. Wasn't no bigger'n a bug first time he give me C chord. An' when I learned as good as him, he hardly never played no more. Used to set in the door, an' listen an' tap his foot. I'm tryin' for a break, an' he'd scowl mean till I get her, an' then he'd settle back easy, an' he'd nod. "Play," he'd say. "Play nice." It's a good box. See how the head is wore. They's many a million songs wore down that wood an' scooped her out. Some day she'll cave in like a egg. But you can't patch her nor worry her no way or she'll lose tone. Play her in the evening, an' they's a harmonica player in the nex' tent. Makes it pretty nice together.

The fiddle is rare, hard to learn. No frets, no teacher.

Jes' listen to a ol' man an' try to pick it up. Won't tell how to double[4]. Says it's a secret. But I watched. Here's how he done it.

Shrill as a wind, the fiddle, quick and nervous and shrill.

She ain't much of a fiddle. Give two dollars for her. Fella says they's fiddles four hundred years old, and they git mellow like whisky. Says they'll cost fifty-sixty thousan' dollars. I don't know. Soun's like a lie. Harsh ol' bastard, ain't she? Wanta dance? I'll rub up the bow with plenty rosin. Man! Then she'll squawk. Hear her a mile.

These three in the evening, harmonica and fiddle and guitar. Playing a reel and tapping out the tune, and the big deep strings of the guitar beating like a heart, and the harmonica's sharp chords and the skirl and squeal of the fiddle. People have to move close. They can't help it. "Chicken Reel" now, and

Chapter 34 John Steinbeck

the feet tap and a young lean buck takes three quick steps, and his arms hang limp. The square closes up and the dancing starts, feet on the bare ground, beating dull, strike with your heels. Hands 'round and swing. Hair falls down, and panting breaths. Lean to the side now.

Look at that Texas boy, long legs loose, taps four times for ever' damn step. Never seen a boy swing aroun' like that. Look at him swing that Cherokee girl, red in her cheeks an' her toe points out. Look at her pant, look at her heave. Think she's tired? Think she's winded? Well, she ain't. Texas boy got his hair in his eyes, mouth's wide open, can't get air, but he pats four times for ever' darn step, an' he'll keep a-goin' with the Cherokee girl.

The fiddle squeaks and the guitar bongs. Mouth-organ man is red in the face. Texas boy and the Cherokee girl, pantin' like dogs an' a-beatin' the groun'. Ol' folks stan' a-pattin' their han's. Smilin' a little, tappin' their feet.

Back home—in the schoolhouse, it was. The big moon sailed off to the westward. An' we walked, him an' me—a little ways. Didn' talk 'cause our throats was choked up. Didn' talk none at all. An' purty soon they was a haycock. Went right to it and laid down there. Seein' the Texas boy an' that girl a-steppin' away into the dark—think nobody seen 'em go. Oh, God! I wisht I was a-goin' with that Texas boy. Moon'll be up 'fore long. I seen that girl's ol' man move out to stop 'em, an' then he didn'. He knowed. Might as well stop the fall from comin', and might as well stop the sap from movin' in the trees. An' the moon'll be up 'fore long.

Play more—play the story songs—"As I Walked through the Streets of Laredo."

The fire's gone down. Be a shame to build her up. Little ol' moon'll be up 'fore long.

Beside an irrigation ditch a preacher labored and the people cried. And the preacher paced like a tiger, whipping the people with his voice, and they groveled and whined on the ground. He calculated them, gauged them, played on them, and when they were all squirming on the ground he stooped down and of his great strength he picked each one up in his arms and shouted, Take 'em, Christ! and threw each one in the water. And when they were all in, waist deep in the water, and looking with frightened eyes at the master, he knelt down on the bank and he prayed for them; and he prayed that all men and women might grovel and whine on the ground. Men and women, dripping, clothes sticking tight, watched; then gurgling and sloshing in their shoes they walked back to the camp, to the tents, and they talked softly in wonder:

We been saved, they said. We're washed white as snow. We won't never sin again.

And the children, frightened and wet, whispered together:

We been saved. We won't sin no more.

Wisht I knowed what all the sins was, so I could do 'em.

The migrant people looked humbly for pleasure on the roads.

Notes
1. The title is from a line in "Battle Hymn of the Republic": "He [God] is trampling out the vintage where the grapes of wrath are stored." The novel celebrates the trek to California of the Joad family: Ma and Pa, their oldest son Tom (paroled from prison where he was serving a manslaughter sentence), the younger children Al, Ruthie and Winfield, the pregnant daughter Rose of Sharon and her husband Connie, and their grandparents. The following selections discuss the people's relish of diversion and entertainment, narrate an attempt by outsiders to break up a dance at the government camp where the Joads are living, and lament an economic system that permits simultaneous human starvation and waste of the fruits of nature.
2. Geronimo: (1829–1909) Apache chief who led his tribe in the Apache wars of the 1880s, was captured in Mexico in 1886, and later became a farmer and stock raiser in Oklahoma.
3. German soldiers kickin' up their feet: referring to the "goose step" of marching German troops
4. double: play two strings simultaneously on a violin

Chapter 35

William Faulkner (1897–1962)

Since he received the 1949 Nobel Prize for Literature, William Faulkner's reputation and influence have spread to every part of the world. The Nobel Prize was awarded largely for works that had been written before 1942. The only Faulkner novel that had come close to being a best seller in its day was *Sanctuary*, a book more famous for its shock value than for its literary quality. His brilliantly inventive fiction drew admiration from a growing number of writers and critics in America and France after 1929 during decades when wider audiences distained him. Many readers were offended by his sensationalism; others were baffled by the density and intricacies of his style. In 1944, scarcely any of his works was in print. After World War II, however, larger audiences in Europe and America responded to the power of his prose. They were gripped by Faulkner's devotion to traditional values in a world of crisis which threatened them, and by the anguish and boldness with which he himself challenged those values, recognizing the need to redefine and reaffirm them.

Faulkner was born William Cuthbert Falkner (the "u" was added to his last name when he began to publish) in New Albany, Mississippi. When he was four or five years old, the family moved to Oxford, Mississippi, where he resided for the rest of his life. Oxford was, with some fictional modifications, a prototype of Jefferson, in the mythical county of Yoknapatawpha, the setting of *Sartoris* and most of his subsequent works. His central theme, however, was not Oxford, or Mississippi, or even America. It was, as he put it, the universal theme of "the problems of the human heart in conflict with itself."

Faulkner began his literary career as a poet rather than a fiction writer, but his poetry was undistinguished and commercially unsuccessful. He turned to the writing of prose in 1925. With Faulkner's third published novel, *Sartoris*, which he completed in 1927, he "discovered," as he said later, "that my own little postage stamp of native soil was worth writing about and that I would never live long enough to exhaust it, and that by sublimating the actual into the apocryphal I would have complete liberty to use whatever talent I might have to its absolute top. It opened up a gold mine of other people, so I created a cosmos of my own." Using his own cosmos to express his universal theme of "the problems of the human heart," Faulkner created the novels for which he is now best known: *The Sound and the Fury* (1929), *As I Lay Dying* (1930), *Sanctuary* (1931), *Light in August* (1932), *Absalom, Absalom!* (1936), *The Hamlet* (1940), and *Go Down, Moses* (1942).

In 1948, after six years in which he published only a few short stories, he resumed his career with *Intruder in the Dust*. Three years later *Requiem for a Nun*, a kind of sequel to *Sanctuary*, appeared. His most ambitious single effort was, perhaps, *A Fabel* (1954), an allegorical novel, which took him at least nine years to write and which has so far proved baffling to readers and critics alike. *The Town* (1957) and *The Mansion* (1959) complete the trilogy on the Snopes family which began with *The Hamlet*. Faulkner's last novel, *The Reivers*, was published on June 4, 1962. A month later, he died.

Faulkner also published about seventy short stories, some of which were later incorporated into novels, such as "Wash" in *Absalom, Absalom!*, "Spotted Horses" in *The Hamlet*, and "The Bear" (with a long section added) in *Go Down, Moses*. Collections of short stories appeared in *These 13* (1931), *Doctor Martino and Other Stories* (1934), *Knight's Gambit* (1949), *Collected Stories of William Faulkner* (1950), and *Big Woods* (1955).

Although his home was always in Mississippi, Faulkner traveled extensively. He trained as a pilot for the Royal Canadian Flying Corps during 1918, worked in New York City in 1920 and 1921, spent most of 1925 in New Orleans and Europe, and labored off and on for several years as a script writer in Hollywood. Like many other American writers, he never graduated from college, but he read omnivorously a wide variety of literature: the Bible, Greek and Roman classics, Shakespeare, the standard English and American poets

Chapter 35 William Faulkner

and novelists, and such modern writers as the French symbolist poets and Joseph Conrad, James Joyce, and T. S. Eliot. Through the late 1920s and the 1930s his bold experiments in the dislocation of narrative time and his use of stream-of-consciousness techniques placed him in the forefront of the avant-garde. His verbal innovations and the labyrinthine organization of his novels make him difficult to read, but his popularity continues to grow, and today he is considered by many to be the greatest writer of fiction that the United States has yet produced.

A Rose for Emily

I

When Miss Emily Grierson died, our whole town went to her funeral: the men through a sort of respectful affection for a fallen monument, the women mostly out of curiosity to see the inside of her house, which no one save an old manservant—a combined gardener and cook—had seen in at least ten years.

It was a big, squarish frame house that had once been white, decorated with cupolas and spires and scrolled balconies in the heavily lightsome style of the seventies, set on what had once been our most select street. But garages and cotton gins had encroached and obliterated even the august names of that neighborhood; only Miss Emily's house was left, lifting its stubborn and coquettish decay above the cotton wagons and the gasoline pumps—an eyesore among eyesores. And now Miss Emily had gone to join the representatives of those august names where they lay in the cedar-bemused cemetery among the ranked and anonymous graves of Union and Confederate soldiers who fell at the battle of Jefferson.

Alive, Miss Emily had been a tradition, a duty, and a care; a sort of hereditary obligation upon the town, dating from that day in 1894 when Colonel Sartoris, the mayor—he who fathered the edict that no Negro woman should appear on the streets without an apron—remitted her taxes, the dispensation dating from the death of her father on into perpetuity. Not that Miss Emily would have accepted charity. Colonel Sartoris invented an involved tale to the effect that Miss Emily's father had loaned money to the town, which the town, as a matter of business, preferred this way of repaying. Only a man of Colonel Sartoris' generation and thought could have invented it, and only a woman could have believed it.

When the next generation, with its more modern ideas, became mayors and aldermen, this arrangement created some little dissatisfaction. On the first of the year they mailed her a tax notice. February came, and there was no reply. They wrote her a formal letter, asking her to call at the sheriff's office at her convenience. A week later the mayor wrote her himself, offering to call or to send his car for her, and received in reply a note on paper of an archaic shape, in a thin, flowing calligraphy in faded ink, to the effect that she no longer went out at all. The tax notice was also enclosed, without comment.

They called a special meeting of the Board of Aldermen. A deputation waited upon her, knocked at the door through which no visitor had passed since she ceased giving china-painting lessons eight or ten years earlier. They were admitted by the old Negro into a dim hall from which a stairway mounted into still more shadow. It smelled of dust and disuse—a close, dank smell. The Negro led them into the parlor. It was furnished in heavy, leather-covered furniture. When the Negro opened the blinds of one window, they could see that the leather was cracked; and when they sat down, a faint dust rose sluggishly about their thighs, spinning with slow motes in the single sun-ray. On a tarnished gilt easel before the fireplace stood a crayon portrait of Miss Emily's father.

They rose when she entered—a small, fat woman in black, with a thin gold chain descending to her waist and vanishing into her belt, leaning on an ebony cane with a tarnished gold head. Her skeleton was small and spare; perhaps that was why what would have been merely plumpness in another was obesity in her. She looked bloated, like a body long submerged in motionless water, and of that pallid hue. Her eyes, lost in the fatty ridges of her face, looked like two small pieces of coal pressed into a lump of dough as they moved from one face to another while the visitors stated their errand.

She did not ask them to sit. She just stood in the door and listened quietly until the spokesman came to a stumbling halt. Then they could hear the invisible watch ticking at the end of the gold chain.

Her voice was dry and cold. "I have no taxes in Jefferson. Colonel Sartoris explained it to me. Perhaps one of you can gain access to the city records and satisfy yourselves."

"But we have. We are the city authorities, Miss Emily. Didn't you get a notice from the sheriff, signed by him?"

"I received a paper, yes," Miss Emily said. "Perhaps he considers himself the sheriff... I have no taxes in Jefferson."

"But there is nothing on the books to show that, you see. We must go by the—"

"See Colonel Sartoris. I have no taxes in Jefferson."

"But, Miss Emily—"

"See Colonel Sartoris." (Colonel Sartoris had been dead almost ten years.) "I have no taxes in Jefferson. Tobe!" The Negro appeared. "Show these gentlemen out."

II

So she vanquished them, horse and foot, just as she had vanquished their fathers thirty years before about the smell. That was two years after her father's death and a short time after her sweetheart—the one we believed would marry her—had deserted her. After her father's death she went out very little; after her sweetheart went away, people hardly saw her at all. A few of the ladies had the temerity to call, but were not received, and the only sign of life about the place was the Negro man—a young man then—going in and out with a market basket.

"Just as if a man—any man—could keep a kitchen properly," the ladies said; so they were not surprised when the smell developed. It was another link between the gross, teeming world and the high and mighty Griersons.

A neighbor, a woman, complained to the mayor, Judge Stevens, eighty years old.

"But what will you have me do about it, madam?" he said.

"Why, send her word to stop it," the woman said. "Isn't there a law?"

"I'm sure that won't be necessary," Judge Stevens said. "It's probably just a snake or a rat that nigger of hers killed in the yard. I'll speak to him about it."

The next day he received two more complaints, one from a man who came in diffident deprecation. "We really must do something about it, Judge. I'd be the last one in the world to bother Miss Emily, but we've got to do something." That night the Board of Aldermen met—three gray-beards and one younger man, a member of the rising generation.

"It's simple enough," he said. "Send her word to have her place cleaned up. Give her a certain time to do it in, and if she don't..."

"Dammit, sir," Judge Stevens said, "will you accuse a lady to her face of smelling bad?"

So the next night, after midnight, four men crossed Miss Emily's lawn and slunk about the house like burglars, sniffing along the base of the brickwork and at the cellar openings while one of them performed a regular sowing motion with his hand out of a sack slung from his shoulder. They broke open the cellar door and sprinkled lime there, and in all the outbuildings. As they recrossed the lawn, a window that had been dark was lighted and Miss Emily sat in it, the light behind her, and her upright torso motionless as that of an idol. They crept quietly across the lawn and into the shadow of the locusts that lined the street. After a week or two the smell went away.

That was when people had begun to feel really sorry for her. People in our town, remembering how old lady Wyatt, her great-aunt, had gone completely crazy at last, believed that the Griersons held themselves a little too high for what they really were. None of the young men were quite good enough for Miss Emily and such. We had long thought of them as a tableau; Miss Emily a slender figure in white in the background, her father a spraddled silhouette in the foreground, his back to her and clutching a horsewhip, the two of them framed by the back-flung front door. So when she got to be thirty and was still single, we were not pleased exactly, but vindicated; even with insanity in the family she wouldn't have turned down all of her chances if they had really materialized.

When her father died, it got about that the house was all that was left to her; and in a way, people were glad. At last they could pity Miss Emily. Being left alone, and a pauper, she had become humanized. Now she too would know the old thrill and the old despair of a penny more or less.

The day after his death all the ladies prepared to call at the house and offer condolence and aid, as is our custom. Miss Emily met them at the door, dressed as usual and with no trace of grief on her face. She told them that her father was not dead. She did that for three days, with the ministers calling on her, and the doctors, trying to persuade her to let them dispose of the body. Just as they were about to resort to law and force, she broke down, and they buried her father quickly.

We did not say she was crazy then. We believed she had to do that. We remembered all the young men her father had driven away, and we knew that with nothing left, she would have to cling to that which had robbed her, as people will.

III

She was sick for a long time. When we saw her again, her hair was cut short, making her look like a girl, with a vague resemblance to those angels in colored church windows—sort of tragic and serene.

The town had just let the contracts for paving the sidewalks, and in the summer after her father's death they began the work. The construction company came with niggers and mules and machinery, and a foreman named Homer Barron, a Yankee—a big, dark, ready man, with a big voice and eyes lighter than his face. The little boys would follow in groups to hear him cuss the niggers, and the niggers singing in time to the rise and fall of picks. Pretty soon he knew everybody in town. Whenever you heard a lot of laughing anywhere about the square, Homer Barron would be in the center of the group. Presently we began to see him and Miss Emily on Sunday afternoons driving in the yellow-wheeled buggy and the matched team of bays from the livery stable.

At first we were glad that Miss Emily would have an interest, because the ladies all said, "Of course a Grierson would not think seriously of a Northerner, a day laborer." But there were still others, older people, who said that even grief could not cause a real lady to forget *noblesse oblige*—without calling it *noblesse oblige*. They just said, "Poor Emily. Her kinsfolk should come to her." She had some kin in Alabama; but years ago her father had fallen out with them over the estate of old lady Wyatt, the crazy woman, and there was no communication between the two families. They had not even been represented at the funeral.

And as soon as the old people said, "Poor Emily," the whispering began. "Do you suppose it's really so?" they said to one another. "Of course it is. What else could…" This behind their hands; rustling of craned silk and satin behind jalousies closed upon the sun of Sunday afternoon as the thin, swift clop-clop-clop of the matched team passed: "Poor Emily."

She carried her head high enough—even when we believed that she was fallen. It was as if she demanded more than ever the recognition of her dignity as the last Grierson; as if it had wanted that touch of earthiness to reaffirm her imperviousness. Like when she bought the rat poison, the arsenic. That was over a year after they had begun to say "Poor Emily," and while the two female cousins were visiting her.

"I want some poison," she said to the druggist. She was over thirty then, still a slight woman, though thinner than usual, with cold, haughty black eyes in a face the flesh of which was strained across the temples and about the eye-sockets as you imagine a lighthouse-keeper's face ought to look. "I want some poison," she said.

"Yes, Miss Emily. What kind? For rats and such? I'd recom—"

"I want the best you have. I don't care what kind."

The druggist named several. "They'll kill anything up to an elephant. But what you want is—"

"Arsenic," Miss Emily said. "Is that a good one?"

"Is…arsenic? Yes, ma'am. But what you want—"

"I want arsenic."

The druggist looked down at her. She looked back at him, erect, her face like a strained flag. "Why, of course," the druggist said. "If that's what you want. But the law requires you to tell what you are going to use it for."

Miss Emily just stared at him, her head tilted back in order to look him eye for eye, until he looked away and went and got the arsenic and wrapped it up. The Negro delivery boy brought her the package; the druggist didn't come back. When she opened the package at home there was written on the box, under the skull and bones: "For rats."

IV

So the next day we all said, "She will kill herself"; and we said it would be the best thing. When she had first begun to be seen with Homer Barron, we had said, "She will marry him." Then we said, "She will persuade him yet," because Homer himself had remarked—he liked men, and it was known that he drank with the younger men in the Elks' Club—that he was not a marrying man. Later we said, "Poor Emily," behind the jalousies as they passed on Sunday afternoon in the glittering buggy, Miss Emily with her head high and Homer Barron with his hat cocked and a cigar in his teeth, reins and whip in a yellow glove.

Then some of the ladies began to say that it was a disgrace to the town and a bad example to the young people. The men did not want to interfere, but at last the ladies forced the Baptist minister—Miss Emily's people were Episcopal—to call upon her. He would never divulge what happened during that interview, but he refused to go back again. The next Sunday they again drove about the streets, and the following day the minister's wife wrote to Miss Emily's relations in Alabama.

So she had blood-kin under her roof again and we sat back to watch developments. At first nothing happened. Then we were sure that they were to be married. We learned that Miss Emily had been to the jeweler's and ordered a man's toilet set in silver, with the letters H. B. on each piece. Two days later we learned that she had bought a complete outfit of men's clothing, including a nightshirt, and we said, "They are married." We were really glad. We were glad because the two female cousins were even more Grierson than Miss Emily had ever been.

So we were not surprised when Homer Barron—the streets had been finished some time since—was gone. We were a little disappointed that there was not a public blowing-off, but we believed that he had gone on to prepare for Miss Emily's coming, or to give her a chance to get rid of the cousins. (By that time it was a cabal, and we were all Miss Emily's allies to help circumvent the cousins.) Sure enough, after another week they departed. And, as we had expected all along, within three days Homer Barron was back in town. A neighbor saw the Negro man admit him at the kitchen door at dusk one evening.

And that was the last we saw of Homer Barron. And of Miss Emily for some time. The Negro man went in and out with the market basket, but the front door remained closed. Now and then we would see her at a window for a moment, as the men did that night when they sprinkled the lime, but for almost six months she did not appear on the streets. Then we knew that this was to be expected too; as if that quality of her father which had thwarted her woman's life so many times had been too virulent and too furious to die.

When we next saw Miss Emily, she had grown fat and her hair was turning gray. During the next few years it grew grayer and grayer until it attained an even pepper-and-salt iron-gray, when it ceased turning. Up to the day of her death at seventy-four it was still that vigorous iron-gray, like the hair of an active man.

From that time on her front door remained closed, save for a period of six or seven years, when she was about forty, during which she gave lessons in china-painting. She fitted up a studio in one of the downstairs rooms, where the daughters and granddaughters of Colonel Sartoris' contemporaries were sent to her with the same regularity and in the same spirit that they were sent to church on Sundays with a twenty-five-cent piece for the collection plate. Meanwhile her taxes had been remitted.

Then the newer generation became the backbone and the spirit of the town, and the painting pupils grew up and fell away and did not send their children to her with boxes of color and tedious brushes and pictures cut from the ladies' magazines. The front door closed upon the last one and remained closed for good. When the town got free postal delivery, Miss Emily alone refused to let them fasten the metal numbers above her door and attach a mailbox to it. She would not listen to them.

Daily, monthly, yearly we watched the Negro grow grayer and more stooped, going in and out with the market basket. Each December we sent her a tax notice, which would be returned by the post office a week later, unclaimed. Now and then we would see her in one of the downstairs windows—she had evidently shut up the top floor of the house—like the carven torso of an idol in a niche, looking or not looking at us, we could never tell which. Thus she passed from generation to generation—dear, inescapable, impervious, tranquil, and perverse.

And so she died. Fell ill in the house filled with dust and shadows, with only a doddering Negro man to wait on her. We did not even know she was sick; we had long since given up trying to get any information from the Negro. He talked to no one, probably not even to her, for his voice had grown harsh and rusty, as if from disuse.

She died in one of the downstairs rooms, in a heavy walnut bed with a curtain, her gray head propped on a pillow yellow and moldy with age and lack of sunlight.

V

The Negro met the first of the ladies at the front door and let them in, with their hushed, sibilant voices and their quick, curious glances, and then he disappeared. He walked right through the house and out the back and was not seen again.

The two female cousins came at once. They held the funeral on the second day, with the town coming to look at Miss Emily beneath a mass of bought flowers, with the crayon face of her father musing profoundly above the bier and the ladies sibilant and macabre; and the very old men—some in their brushed Confederate uniforms—on the porch and the lawn, talking of Miss Emily as if she had been a contemporary of theirs, believing that they had danced with her and courted her perhaps, confusing time with its mathematical progression, as the old do, to whom all the past is not a diminishing road, but, instead, a huge meadow which no winter ever quite touches, divided from them now by the narrow bottle-neck of the most recent decade of years.

Already we knew that there was one room in that region above stairs which no one had seen in forty years, and which would have to be forced. They waited until Miss Emily was decently in the ground before they opened it.

The violence of breaking down the door seemed to fill this room with pervading dust. A thin, acrid pall as of the tomb seemed to lie everywhere upon this room decked and furnished as for a bridal: upon the valance curtains of faded rose color, upon the rose-shaded lights, upon the dressing table, upon the delicate array of crystal and the man's toilet things backed with tarnished silver, silver so tarnished that the monogram was obscured. Among them lay a collar and tie, as if they had just been removed, which, lifted, left upon the surface a pale crescent in the dust. Upon a chair hung the suit, carefully folded; beneath it the two mute shoes and the discarded socks.

The man himself lay in the bed.

For a long while we just stood there, looking down at the profound and fleshless grin. The body had apparently once lain in the attitude of an embrace, but now the long sleep that outlasts love, that conquers even the grimace of love, had cuckolded him. What was left of him, rotted beneath what was left of the nightshirt, had become inextricable from the bed in which he lay; and upon him and upon the pillow beside him lay that even coating of the patient and biding dust.

Then we noticed that in the second pillow was the indentation of a head. One of us lifted something from it, and leaning forward, that faint and invisible dust dry and acrid in the nostrils, we saw a long strand of iron-gray hair.

References

Baym, Nina, et al., eds. *The Norton Anthology of American Literature*. 3rd edition. New York: W. W. Norton, 1989.

Beardsley, M. C. *Theme and Form: An Introduction to Literature*. New Jersey: Prentice-Hall, Inc., 1956.

Brooks, Cleanth, et al. *American Literature: The Makers and the Making*. New York: St. Martin's Press, 1973.

Cunliffe, Marcus. *The Literature of the United States*. Baltimore: Penguin Books, 1954.

Doren, C. V., and M. V. Doren. *American and British Literature Since 1890*. New York: Century, 1925.

Fuller, E. *Adventures in American Literature*. New York: Harcourt, Brace & World, Inc., 1963.

Hart, James D. *The Oxford Companion to American Literature*. 5th edition. Oxford: Oxford University Press, 1983.

Long, E. Hudson, et al. *The American Tradition in Literature*. New York: McGraw-Hill Higher Education, 1990.

Mack, Maynard, et al., eds. *The Norton Anthology of World Masterpieces*. New York: W. W. Norton, 1986.

McMichael, George. *Anthology of American Literature*. 2nd edition. London: Macmillan Publishing Company, 1980.

Rohrberger, Mary, *et al. An Introduction to Literature*. New York: Random House, 1968.

Vinson, James, ed. *Great Writers of the English Language: Novelists and Prose Writers*. New York: St. Martin's Press, 1979.

Ward, Alfred C. *Longman Companion to Twentieth Century Literature*. 3rd edition. Harlow: Longman, 1981.